CW00537613

HISTORIC GARDENS
of CORNWALL

A charcoal drawing of 1958 by Patrick Heron of Eagles Nest. © Estate of Patrick Heron. All Rights
Reserved, DACS

HISTORIC GARDENS
of CORNWALL

Timothy Mowl

TEMPUS

For Sue and Barry Hawkes

The publication of this volume has been made possible by a grant from
THE LEVERHULME TRUST
to cover all the necessary research work

First published 2005

Tempus Publishing Limited
The Mill, Brimscombe Port,
Stroud, Gloucestershire, GL5 2QG
www.tempus-publishing.com

© Timothy Mowl, 2005

The right of Timothy Mowl to be identified as the Author
of this work has been asserted in accordance with the
Copyrights, Designs and Patents Act 1988.

All rights reserved. No part of this book may be reprinted
or reproduced or utilised in any form or by any electronic,
mechanical or other means, now known or hereafter invented,
including photocopying and recording, or in any information
storage or retrieval system, without the permission in writing
from the Publishers.

British Library Cataloguing in Publication Data.
A catalogue record for this book is available from the British Library.

ISBN 0 7524 3436 5
Typesetting and origination by Tempus Publishing Limited
Printed in Great Britain

Contents

Acknowledgements

My first thanks go to Professor Sir Richard Brook and his Trustees at the Leverhulme Trust whose generous funding of the research for this study and for the next two books in the series has made the present Cornish travelling and garden visiting a positive delight rather than a financially painful pleasure. I am indebted to Trish Gibson for going through my text to ensure that I have taken down all the Latin plant names of the great plant-spotter gardens correctly. Angela Broome at the Courtney Library of the Royal Institution of Cornwall in Truro has been a mine of useful information and always ready to help with my enquiries. I must acknowledge my debt to Douglas Ellory Pett's *Parks and Gardens of Cornwall*, without which I would have missed so many important historic sites. His all-inclusive, encyclopaedic and my more selective, chronological approaches to the gardens of the county will, I hope, be seen as mutually complementary. May I thank Peter Fairbank and the Cornwall Gardens Trust for supporting this venture and for allowing me access to their often inspired and always thorough series of garden surveys.

Other owners, friends, colleagues and Bristol University MA Garden History students who have been particularly helpful include: Earl St Germans, Elisabeth and Peter Prideaux-Brune, The Hon Evelyn Boscawen, Lord Falmouth, Lady St Aubyn, Lord Boyd, Sir Ferrers Vyvyan, Anthony Fortescue, Martin Wood, Katharine and Susanna Heron, Chunky and Catherine Penhaul, Jonathan and Sarah Treffry, Graham Reid, Jeremy Pearson, Howard and Jay Milton, Rosemary Lauder, Clare Hickman, Shirley Evans, Cynthia Troup, Kate Felus, James Reynolds, Richard Rashleigh, Michael Williams, John Schofield, Josie Linton, Mike O'Mahony, Anthea Paice, Claudia Bittencourt, Penny Scott-Barrett, Pamela Chope, James and Fiona Colville, Richard Oldaker, Angela and Les Ockwell, Susan Kellerman, Stephen Parker, David Cottington, Philip White, Angela and Jack Ross, John Harris, Tom Hudson, Dave Bishop, Dr Mark Sullivan, Alison Clough, Hazel and Bryn Danson, Claude Farmer, Sue Nathan, Vicki Reader, Robin Fletcher, Peter Copeland, Chris and Lisa Rowe, Bill Ward, Martin Mattock, Mr F.J. Williams, Charles Williams, Rob Wilson-North, Jeff Cherrington, Molly and Barry Rose, Julian Gibbs, Sue Goodsir, Kate Johnson,

Ian Berry, Cynthia Gaskell Brown, Pat Hughes, Stephen Daniels, John Phibbs, André Rogger, Barry Litton, Andrew Bayliss, Vanessa and Andrew Leslie, Bob and Linda Johns.

Although this is the first book in the series to be illustrated with my own digital photographs, Ann Pethers has once again photographed and developed the archival images from my own university's Special Collections. I must thank Michael Richardson for bringing many important texts to my notice. Peter Kemmis Betty and Fran Gannon at Tempus have been as encouraging and efficient as ever as publisher and editor, Douglas Matthews has compiled a thorough index, and my agent, Sara Menguc, has been a constant source of encouragement for this and for all my other literary projects.

As with all the books in the series, *Historic Gardens of Cornwall* has been researched alongside my teaching of Bristol University's MA in Garden History, so I must thank my Co-Director, Michael Liversidge, for his advice on matters art historical and my students for their lively debate on matters related to garden history. My friend and collaborator on architectural studies, Brian Earnshaw, has accompanied me on almost all the garden visits, undertaken several areas of the research and done his usual intellectually combative job of editing the text at manuscript stage. My wife, Sara, and daughter, Olivia, have joined me on many of the garden visits in our holiday county making academic work into a happy excursion. Finally I must thank Sue and Barry Hawkes, my father and mother-in-law, to whom this book is dedicated, for making it all possible through their lifelong family connection with the Camel estuary.

Timothy Mowl
Bristol, Winter 2004

Introduction –
to an off-beat Duchy

Honest confession is as good for the brain as for the soul. Everyone comes to gardens from a personal viewpoint and a set of favourites in flowers, bushes and trees, and with prejudices towards one gardening style or another. My preference is towards hard landscape and that has left me with reservations about Cornwall's gardens. By hard landscape I mean gardens where the actual plants, though not the trees and hedges, are secondary and what makes the garden is the spatial arrangement of permanent features: terraces, steps, garden buildings, lakes, canals, fountains and, of course, trees and hedges. What I enjoy and value are the vistas, the compositions and the surprises that a 'hard' garden or landscape offers, not merely in snowdrop time, lilac time, rose time or autumn leaf time, but in its abiding character, whether visited in December or in August. If that seems to be asking a lot then it is no more than one expects from a house, and to me gardens are a gentle extension of architecture. That is my point of approach, and it explains my reservations about Cornish gardens, even at times a certain impatience with their general character, which is predominantly 'soft'.

Part of the problem came from beginning with such high expectations. Not many would argue with the claim that Cornwall is England's premier garden county. With a fertile, acid soil, a reliable rainfall pattern that makes trees grow almost as fast on the peninsula as they do in New Zealand, a mild, generally frost-free climate in many areas and a tourist industry to satisfy, Cornish gardens have been driven to high standards of excellence by an economic and geographical inevitability. The northern half of the county is windswept and austere, often treeless, often savage, but the southern half is a potential Arcadia of long sea inlets and lush valleys with sub-tropical microclimates where tender alien plants can be persuaded to flourish as nowhere else in the country.

Initially, walking Carclew, Glendurgan, Trebah and Carwinion on a first day I was bowled over by the place. Here, uniquely in England, one finds major gardens, every one a firestorm of exotic colour, lying within a mile of each other. They offer mazes of camellias, magnolias, azaleas and rhododendrons so overwhelmingly bright and profuse with bloom that not only are they un-paintable, but they edge beyond the reach of even good photography. A century of dextrous hybridization has resulted in flowering bushes whose colour combinations, shades, flushes and tints are virtually nameless because they have outrun our vocabulary. Carclew, my first Cornish garden, made an unforgettable impression. It lies in a deep hollow, decadent with colour, with the great ruined portico of the house, gutted by fire in 1934 and more beautiful in ruin than it ever was when whole.

They can grow gardens in Cornwall, but they cannot often build a beautiful house. Granite is the one natural curse of the county. Igneous intrusions have ensured an acid soil where Himalayan flowering bushes can riot, and tin and copper from the metamorphic aureole of granitic decay can enrich the gentry. But try turning granite on a lathe to make balusters for a garden terrace or try to carve granite into Corinthian capitals and acanthus scrolls for some garden temple and the lack of hard landscaping in the county is soon understood. Despairing in his Red Book for Catchfrench, Humphry Repton had to suggest that balusters of a proposed Gothic parapet be carved from wood 'painted and sanded in imitation of stone, or rather in the artificial stone of "Code's manufactory"'.[1] Limestone makes great garden temples, but its soil is a death sentence for rhododendrons. In Cornwall, however, the lollipop pink blooms of *Rhododendron ponticum*, can safely stalk the roadsides of the county like a Triffid army, a giant, invasive, granite-loving weed.

Mention of the metal-bearing lodes of the metamorphic aureole raises the problem of Cornwall's gentry and their historic failure to give their county an imaginative lead in garden fashions. I am normally a shameless defender of county aristocracies. In the usual English county, however eccentric and extravagant the upper classes may be, they do tend to make great gardens. For some obscure, possibly Celtic reason (Wales has the same problem) Cornwall's gentry have only cultivated gardens of character when they lived near Plymouth and the border with Devon. Mount Edgcumbe, Antony and Port Eliot are in the first rank, but when Mount Edgcumbe's grounds were first laid out they were actually, before boundary changes in 1844, a part of Devon. Penheale Manor, which has one of the most impressive garden complexes in Cornwall, looks across to Devon five miles away, and it was remodelled by a retiree Scot, Colonel Norman Colville. There is a Brenta-like scatter of fine houses and gardens on the west bank of the Tamar, but that river again is the county boundary; they are all a mere stone's throw from un-Celtic England.

There is also a curious predilection in Cornish estates towards linear garden drives rather than to parks as spatial landscapes. Time and again one finds the long arms of drives reaching out to quite remote and usually rather dull lodges, but running, not through graciously landscaped and tree-clumped parkland, but commonplace farmland fields. When, as at Tregothnan, the drives run scenically for miles beside picturesque tidal inlets, this is good planning. At the vast estate, ducal in scale, of Boconnoc, however, the multiple drives run like ordinary country lanes through an unkempt, but potentially impressive, valley terrain which has received little or no cosmetic landscaping. It was at Boconnoc that I was obliged to rethink my longstanding prejudice against Lancelot Brown. With his big teams of ditch diggers, turf layers and tree planters he destroyed so many existing templed Arcadian landscapes of charm that I had seen him as a destructive force, a malign influence in eighteenth-century park design; the creator of soulless simplified elegance in parkscapes. But looking down from the church terrace at Boconnoc at the Lerryn, an ordinary country brook snaking close to the house between rough untrimmed banks, I could see the real need for a Brown, or one of Brown's followers, in Cornwall.

Money could hardly have been the problem. Sidney Godolphin grew so wealthy from the tin mining around Godolphin house that he could afford, in his long years as Queen Anne's favourite chancellor, to be that rarest of all creatures, a chancellor who was incorruptible. Yet he put none of his wealth into his sixteenth- and seventeenth-century house, and his garden remained an untouched relic of nine ill-presented Jacobean squares divided by walls of stone and earth. It may be a pleasure for modern garden historians to wrangle over, but it was no kind of example in formal garden design for his native county. If we remember what the Cavendish Bentincks did at Chatsworth for their county, Derbyshire, with the mineral wealth which they drew from Derbyshire's rocks, it puts the Cornish gentry into a feeble perspective. At Lanhydrock and Trewarthenick the drives did expand into superb linear gardens, but there again there was little feeling for parkscapes. Humphry Repton, being always short of money, made more of a mark on the county than Brown, but even his Red Books are obsessed with the courses which drives should follow.

My immediate personal problem with Cornwall has been the difficulty of arranging its gardens into the usual chronological sequence of chapters. This is important because the whole point of this book is that it is not yet another glossy guide to the 'glorious flowering gardens' of the county, but a sequential and selective historical survey of Cornwall's gardens. There, I have to admit in retrospect, the county has nevertheless been an unpredictable purveyor of dazzling 'firsts' and unexpected episodes. There may have been precious few Elizabethan gardens, meagre examples of seventeenth-century formal layouts, pitifully few Arcadian Picturesque gardens of the mid eighteenth century and, of course, not even a footprint of Capability Brown. To compensate there have been a number of gardens, so unexpected and so beautiful that I hesitate to list them as they will read like my inventions and wish dreams, and what else but a wish dream realised is the Eden Project? Why travel the world when you can walk those amazing galleries every day of a Cornish holiday?

Prehistoric and Plantagenet gardens at Chysauster and Tintagel go a long way to compensate for a dearth of Tudor and Carolean examples. There are, in addition, a wealth of odd, loveably strange and essentially Cornish gardens, hidden away around creeks and remote peninsulas to reward persistent garden hunters. They will find an absolute contrast in styling and professionalism between the gardens of the south coast and those of the north. Not that there are many gardens at all along that hyperactively savage cliff-bound north coast. Lord Bath, of the first creation, tried to make a formal garden at Stowe, just south of Bude; the weather and the terrain defeated him, as they seem to have defeated the National Trust, which owns the interesting earthworks. I was made to feel anything but welcome on my exploration of that atmospheric site.

Such north coast gardens as exist make up in quirky individuality and imaginative flair for what they lack in restaurants, shops and banks of cosseted, exotic flowering bushes, compared with those smooth operations on the sea inlets of the south. Working up from west to east, Eagles Nest above Zennor, the Japanese Garden at St Mawgan, Prideaux Place in Padstow, Long Cross above Port Isaac and St Nectan's Glen, all merit, as the *Michelin Guide* puts it, a detour when they are open.[2]

St Nectan's Glen with its spectacular waterfall, the Kieve or cauldron, represents so dramatically the persistent strain of Cornish nationalism that runs through many gardens of the peninsula, that it is worth taking it here out of its chronological sequence. It emphasises that Age of Saints theme which distinguishes Cornish gardens far more strongly than prehistory influences Wiltshire gardens, or the Arts and Crafts movement those of Gloucestershire. Medieval or earlier wayside crosses are a standard feature of Cornish gardens, Trebartha has a jumble of them and fogous are treasured features. But no garden in Cornwall is as wrapped up in Christian and pre-Christian mysticism as the Kieve. It is a numinous chasm, a fertility symbol so theatrical that it rivals the Rose of Fire in Rider Haggard's *She*. But that was a volcanic flame in darkest Africa. St Nectan's Kieve lies less than a mile off the B3262 at Trevethey, and a Victorian tea garden sits daintily on the brink of the gulf within the sound of the tumbling waters. That linking of the very old and very tourist is pure Cornwall.

St Nectan was a sixth-century hermit, one of the twenty-four children of St Brechan, a defender of Celtic Christianity against the alien Roman form. When he died his sisters buried him in an oak chest deep under the bed of the Trevillet River and there, apparently, he still lies. His cell became a chapel on one side of the river where it plunges down into the Kieve. Then, in the eighteenth century, according to C S Gilbert, who included a sensational illustration of the Waterfall in his survey of the county,[3] the Wood family of Trevillet Hall built a 'small temple or summer-house' poised on the very brink of the cliff, so that they could relish the picturesque chaos of rock and wild water below them as they ate their picnics. Sadly both Temple and Hall have gone, but the hermit's cell became a cottage and, as Romanticism became a popular movement, Arthurian legends were woven around the Kieve, one stating that Arthur's knights were baptised below the Kieve before setting out on their quest for the Holy Grail. A tea garden was laid out on the little rock platform outside the Hermitage with a gate commanding access down to the Kieve. Charles Dickens and the artist,

Daniel Maclise, were visitors, and all the time the feeling endured that this was a place where God or the gods answered prayers. On the morning of my visit a group of pilgrims had arrived at 6 am, woken the guardian, and spent an hour down in the chasm.[4] They were long gone when I made my way down the grey rock-stairs, half overgrown with trees and bushes, but their prayers, in the form of ribbons, some with words and pictures attached, dangled on the branches down there by the thundering waters.

No illustration quite prepares one for the strangeness of the Waterfall (*1*). It topples down out of sight into a rock cauldron, the Kieve, twenty feet deep, that it has shaped for itself over centuries from the shale, then the water bursts out through a great round hole in the rock wall, to tumble finally into St Nectan's

1 *Above this natural prodigy with its potent symbolism of natural fertility, the Cornish have established a holy Hermitage, a Meditation Room and a demure tea garden*

baptismal pool and burial place, before hurrying off down the narrow wooded valley. It is not a cheerful place, but it is the very essence of Edmund Burke's 'Sublime' and most memorable. Back up at the Hermitage the Meditation Room has shelves which are alive with candles and New Age spiritual images, bare rock glistens below modern walls. Certain natural sites, places like this, bring out an awed human response that never varies through Celtic, Catholic, Anglican, Nonconformist or agnostic periods. Some kind of spiritual force seems near and people try to tap into it. At the same time and in the same place they order pots of tea, eat scones and ice cream in a garden.

On the far side of the peninsula, Menacuddle, near St Austell, offers the same numinous mix of falling water, chapel, rocks and a dark, wooded valley; and again there is a designed garden. Enys, near Falmouth, has something of the same dim, watery magic, but both Enys and Menacuddle must wait for their proper chronological places, as the county made, over the centuries, its token and half-convincing response to the garden fashions of what one is tempted to call the English mainland, for Cornwall is a spiritual island.

The county's great breakaway from English garden patterns came with its quite sudden renaissance of planting around 1830. The gardens, laid out between then and the Great War of 1914-18, brilliantly commercialised and projected in the last twenty years or so, are the gardens that bring the tourists flocking to the county, second only as an attraction to the beaches and the surf. And these gardens are almost all 'soft', hence my uneasy reservations. While the nineteenth-century gentry of the county sat tight on their drives and their mining investments, a group of Quaker merchant and banking families took the horticultural lead from them and a movement of friendly rivalry, similar to the Dutch tulip mania of the early seventeenth century, set in. Geography again was partly responsible. Cornwall has splendid harbours; merchants and investment bankers tend to have maritime connections.

The collecting mania began. This was the one corner of England where sub-tropical plants could be coaxed into flower in sheltered microclimates. Intrepid young men were sent out to the wilder regions of India, China, Indonesia and South America, sometimes by the merchant families themselves, more often by the Veitch nurseries in Exeter which found an eager Cornish market for their findings. Three Cornish families were dominant in this movement. Between them, by one marital connection or another, the Bolitho bankers directed the garden developments of fourteen properties around Penzance, the Foxes from their Falmouth trading base shaped fifteen gardens, the most celebrated being those in narrow valleys leading down to the Helston River, and the Williamses of Caerhays Castle and Werrington gardened another eleven: forty gardens from three families, there is no other national precedent.

Their grounds created an etymological imprecision which can be ignored, but which is real. 'Garden' as used in a phrase like 'garden history', or in the title of this series 'Historic Gardens of', usually includes 'parks' as well as any designed area of pleasure grounds close to a parent house. But a park and a garden are usually quite separate concepts. Now here in Cornwall the two were being fused together, with an entire valley or park area being turned into an intensively planted composition of flowering bushes and the composing silhouettes of specimen trees. In some of the greater mid eighteenth-century gardens, like Stourhead in Wiltshire or Stowe in Buckinghamshire, a generous scatter of garden buildings achieved the same effect, making park and garden one. Here in Cornwall it was the exotic plant imports that effected the union, creating a gardened park.

2 *When in doubt the standard Cornish response to a garden over the last 150 years has been to plant exotic flowering bushes, as here in a corner of Heligan, and to rely on a predictable barrage of bloom*

My problem is one with which Cornwall's garden lovers are unlikely to sympathise. All these 'gardens' are 'soft'. They are admittedly wonderful shows of colour, but they treat their flowering bushes much as specimens are displayed in a museum, or rare animals in a zoo. Steep paths make a circuit down a valley and back up again passing ravishingly beautiful bursts of colour from bush after bush, plant after plant (*2*). It is all incredibly exotic, un-English and remarkable, that plants from the Himalayas and the Andes have been coaxed into English flowering. My criticism is not just that their colours from subtle hybridization are often brash, chemical and alien, but that spatial compositions are relatively rare and that, after June, the gardeners have to fall back on banks of sky blue, mauve and purple hydrangeas.

In recent years there have been welcome moves to infiltrate features into these shows of colour. Much as in the so-called 'Rococo' gardens of the mid-eighteenth century, when eclectic garden buildings – Gothick, classical, Chinese, or whatever foreign reference took the owner's fancy – were used to pilot visitors from one garden prospect to another, so today the directors of these hugely successful tourist traps are giving form to their garden maps by whimsical points of interest. It would, however, be foolish and imperceptive not to notice that, as in French Impressionist paintings, most Cornish gardens have achieved subtle colour compositions that would leave Monet gasping.

I promised honest confession at the outset and have made my bias and my personal standpoint clear. Cornwall is a great garden county. For those aficionados who can bandy double-barrelled Latin names and visualise what they are talking about, Cornwall is probably the greatest. We live and we learn; 2004 has been my year of a sharp learning curve, one that has left me at least a little more open-minded to the possibilities of flowers and the gardens of the Sunday supplements and garden magazines. With gardens you never stop learning and there are only another thirty-two counties to go! By the time I reach Northumberland and the Scottish border I may well have begun to plant mixed grasses by my back door and come to salivate at the mere mention of a new hybrid rhododendron.

My last practical advice is that if you wish to experience Cornwall's gardens at their most awesome, make your visit between February and June. Now, off to Worcestershire, where the seasons are still in their right places on the calendar.

1

Chysauster and Tintagel – early gardens of utility and Romantic gesture

By happy accident these two extraordinarily early gardens not only strike an intensely individual and distinctive Cornish note, one that sets the county as a place apart from the rest of England in its garden history, but they catch the county in two very different moods. While both are treeless and open to the winds, Chysauster is peaceful, inland and mild, a place of wide views, wild flowers and bird song. Tintagel, in alarming contrast, has a garden exposed to Nature at its most aggressive, where harsh and undeniably ugly black cliffs have been battered into an angular wreck by the remorseless pounding of seas that can break in foam fountains 100 feet high, taller than most Cornish church towers.

A helpful notice at the entrance to the Tintagel garden claims that this was where, in the Middle Ages, ladies of the castle came to hear music and enjoy poetry. Visitors reading it, with a west wind pummelling them and the waves booming against concave cliffs, will have their doubts. Another and more helpful English Heritage notice among the courtyard houses of Chysauster draws attention to the banked and levelled 'garden' areas that lie around at least six of the, so far excavated, nine houses, and suggests in addition that their wide walls of stones and turf could have served as viewing terrace walls from which Romano-British Cornish men and women could have observed the growth and health of whatever they were planting.[1] Again some visitors will have their doubts. But in both sites the garden questions are most stimulating, ones that Cornwall poses uniquely as a county whose garden history begins a staggering 1,500 years before the Tudor enclosures of more parvenu and commonplace English counties.

All intelligent and open-minded visitors to Cornwall should, at some time, preferably in late August on a sunny day, make the long, easy climb up from the lane and the custodian's kiosk to the nine houses and their more-or-less six garden areas (*colour plate 1*). The experience is not so much mind-bending as mind-expanding. Roman villas are a concept easily taken on board, but to absorb the fact that even earlier, and without foreign intervention, our ancestors were living in a roughly standardised housing type with front and sometimes back gardens, brings the past almost too close to assimilate. There is something so suburban and absurdly familiar about the way most of the houses seem to be set in pairs, as if on a housing estate, with two apparently semi-detached pairs to make them even more modern in their anticipations.

In the otherwise admirable English Heritage guidebook to the 'village', by Patricia Christie, the artist Judith Dobie has painted a convincing recreation of two of the houses – numbers 4 and 6 – in their prehistoric prime, showing the wide, terrace-like walls, open courtyards and the trulli-type rooms opening off them in picturesquely varied profiles of conical thatched roofs.[2] But she has baulked at presenting those raised and levelled 'garden' areas that the excavators discovered as actual cultivated plots. That apparently was too modern for her to accept. Instead she has littered the grass with big granite stones which the lazy Cornish Celts were too dim or too idle to pick up and pile onto their house walls. In the distance there is a field with stooks of corn, but the herbs and vegetables which common sense suggests were grown on these raised plots are not shown. Influenced perhaps by the *Flintstones* cartoon strip, Dobie implies that those early Cornish villagers only grew stones.

It is the rude, but clearly shared and evolved order of design in the houses that suggests there must have been an equally evolved horticulture at Chysauster. Each of the well-preserved and, it has to be assumed, carefully excavated and restored houses – numbers 3,4,5,6 and 7 – is a rough and irregular circle of very wide stone walls (3). The garden or raised areas lie usually to the south and more sheltered east of the houses except for number 4 and number 6 which have had to be banked up on their south sides to create level platforms against the slope. Their entrances funnel in between walls four to five feet high into a courtyard. On the left is a recessed bay, possibly for birds or animals, straight ahead is a large round room, usually retaining the hollowed stone that once held the central post to support a conical thatched roof.[3] To the right of this round room is a long narrow room, purpose unknown and sometimes subdivided. According to individual builder's tastes there are one or two smaller round rooms, which were probably stone roofed. Some floors are paved and every house has a covered water channel leading across their courtyards to what seem to have been rainwater sumps.[4]

House 3 and House 5 are semi-detached pairs; each of the smaller houses in these pairs has its own 'garden' area, raised about a foot and levelled. To have some idea as to what would have been grown in them it is useful to remember John Harris's beds of 'primitive' white carrots which he cultivates at Tresillian, near Newquay, and which will be discussed in a later chapter. With potatoes still undiscovered in America these gardeners would have relied upon early and undeveloped vegetables like carrots, peas, beans, charlock, fat hen and parsnips.

3 *Around each of the six excavated houses at Chysauster is a raised garden area which would have been planted with kitchen herbs and vegetables*

What, however, is most likely to have been grown so close to kitchen hearths are herbs, for flavouring and for health. This raises an interesting possibility. Herbs flower in a pleasant mauve, blue, pink, purple spectrum. Were they then also valued for their looks and is that how flower gardens evolved? It seems plausible, as any civilisation which has evolved jewellery must have aesthetic yearnings. Dobie might, therefore, have been reconstructing the Chysauster settlement within arguable scholarly limits if she had illustrated her houses numbers 4 and 6 surrounded by a subdued show of colour rather than by those tumbled stones.

Whatever the reconstructed uncertainties of past gardens at Chysauster, there can be no doubt about the subtle and textured beauty of the wild gardens that have taken over the roofless walls of the houses themselves. Delicate grey, green and golden lichens pattern the silvery granite of the gate-stones. Heather, ling, harebells, devilsbit, scabious, birdsfoot trefoil and sheepsbit have invested the turf with effects that cultivated rock gardeners would be hard put to rival. Because the site is so open up there at the edge of the moors above Penzance, the eye moves immediately from this rich patterning of the low houses out to the matching blue vistas of the distances and the sea.

Where the precise dating of this most fortunately preserved complex is concerned, the acid soils of Cornwall, which are so kind and welcoming to rhododendrons and azaleas, have destroyed most of the evidence. Not a scrap of bone has survived, but some cordoned (string impressed) pottery, a few shards of Roman Samian ware, some Roman beads and rust-rotted iron indicate dates in the century before and the century after the first Roman occupation of Britain (AD 50). Apart from one fort at Wadebridge the Romans seem never to have needed to lay heavy military hands on the south-western peninsula; which is surprising considering its known mineral wealth. Chysauster has a broken fogou, but whether for storage, worship or concealment is not known. Only the village's remote and lofty siting indicates some nervous awareness of the need for defence.

One possibility about these particular surviving houses is that they belonged to tribal leaders living on high ground at the top of the village and were, therefore, of superior quality. The fields on the way up to Chysauster from the lane were once scattered with dwellings, which have been destroyed to build walls for the fields themselves, after clearance. Early in the nineteenth century the Chysauster walls were the scene of Methodist revival meetings and it was not until 1849 that an antiquary and writer named Crozier realised their historic importance. Excavations and repair work followed in 1873 when William Copeland Borlase cleared house number 6. Unfortunately at that time no techniques of soil analysis existed for checks to be made on the gardens. Further campaigns of excavation followed in 1928, a major effort, then in 1931 and between 1937 and 1939; but there are still houses to be examined so more information on their gardens could yet emerge.

There is no mystery about the Chysauster gardens, despite their age. They are simply functional responses to normal human routines, areas designed to provide herbs and carrots at the front door. It is the garden up on Tintagel rock that is mysterious. Tintagel has to be climbed to be believed, and even then it is difficult. Everyone has heard of the place and knows the Arthurian associations: the unwanted, dangerous baby handed over to Merlin to be brought up, and the parallel legend of adulterous love of Tristan and Yseult, the wrath of Yseult's wronged husband, King Mark of Cornwall. What people only realise when they have actually climbed up to the inner castle is that Tintagel is still as dangerous as its legends. I met a stout American woman half way up the cliff as I was coming down and she was resting. There was an October gale blowing, the fag-end of a hurricane that had been making headlines across the Atlantic. We were on slippery steps of beautiful, colour-streaked stone with just a firm handrail between us, and the sea a hundred feet below. That sea was not simply raging. It had gone mad, a boiling brown and white chaos with two or three seals apparently enjoying the ride. If it were not for the angle of the headland the breakers would quite easily have been reaching us up there on the stairs, yet the American was thrilled by the situation. And it was thrilling. Richard Carew had a similar response in 1602, describing the path 'as everywhere narrow, so in many places through his stickleness occasioning, and through his steepeness threatening, the ruin of your life with the failing of your foot'.[5] Cornwall is a much more exotic and exciting place than most expect.

Tintagel is not really one castle, but two. One commands a headland with cliffs on three sides, the other stands on a semi-island rock and this is where the garden has been built. At one time a drawbridge linked the two castles, but cliff falls destroyed this and now a permanent wooden bridge crosses the gulf. 'Under the island', Carew recorded with a shiver, 'runs a cave through which you may row at full sea, but not without a kind of horror at the uncouthness of the place',[6] which sounds as if he had made the trip in person. All in all it is the most improbable site for a garden in the entire county, which is what makes the garden such a puzzle.

The reign of Henry III (1216-72) was a relatively quiet interlude in medieval English history, something of a break for culture and European art between King John sealing Magna Carta and King Edward Longshanks invading Scotland. Henry III did not merely build the choir and crossing of Westminster Abbey as a theatre for future coronations; he brought in Italian experts in mosaic work to decorate the interior, a very unusual, un-English action. His brother, Richard, Earl of Cornwall, on the evidence of Tintagel, was either a genuine romantic enthusiast for the Arthurian legends or a gesture politician. Either way he built Tintagel Castle after 1233 on a splendidly defensive, but strategically quite useless position, protecting neither rich farmland nor a commercially important port. Then he constructed Tintagel's garden (*colour plate 2*), a rectangle of walls of mortared slates about a metre high and roughly twenty metres by fourteen metres in extent with, if modern excavations are to be believed, a path all round it and a path across its middle section, those paths all demarcated by angular slates. It may be relevant to the purposes of this strange enclosure that Earl Richard was an enthusiastic lover. He had three wives, all beauties; Isabella of Gloucester, Sanchia of Provence and Beatrice of Falkenberg. His third wife was German, and, in Gottfried von Stassburg's *Tristan* of about 1210, the lovers are discovered by King Mark asleep under an olive tree in the orchard at Tintagel.[7] By his Cornish mistress, Joan, he had two children, Walter and Joan; but how much time he ever spent in Tintagel is not recorded.

The puzzle is why the 'garden' should have been sited where it is.[8] Carew does not mention it in his *Survey*, only 'a decayed chapel, a fair spring of water'.[9] But John Leland, the Tudor antiquary, writing in 1540, describes 'a ground quadrant wall as yt were a garden plot'. This 'as yt were' is not definitive,[10] but Sir Richard Grenville's plan of 1583 labels the enclosure 'a garden walled'.[11] Earl Richard's inner castle with its Great Hall for entertaining guests was built, very sensibly, in the lee of the western heights of the island peninsula. It cowers there, out of those dreadful winds and was the perfect place for a garden, where flowers might just possibly have been persuaded to climb walls, and where an arbour might not have been blown over by every second storm. It would have been between these ambitious walls of a Great Hall, Kitchen, Buttery and Earl's Privy Chamber

4 *Could this be a planting bed for creepers to climb the little wall of the garden at Tintagel, or merely what the 1930s' archaeologists expected to find?*

and the steep, sheltering slope of the hill. Earl Richard's men had levelled a considerable area, burying the Dark Age ruins already on the site; so a garden could have been planted there in the obvious place.

Instead the garden rectangle has been built well away from this inner courtyard, a steep climb up onto the totally exposed top of Tintagel rock, even further away than the existing eleventh-century Chapel. The official English Heritage guidebook writes lyrically of how the women of Earl Richard's court would come up here on his apparently rare visits to this most dysfunctional and unnecessary stronghold to a green retreat 'where tales could be told of King Arthur and Queen Guinevere, or the ill-fated lovers Tristan and Yseult'.[12] Excavations of the garden have revealed a long narrow bed, about half a metre wide, between the paths that runs right round the rectangle and the walls (*4*). This, it is assumed, is where creepers could have been grown to climb the walls. More plausibly the guidebook suggests that for any further floral furnishing prefabricated wooden arbours and tubs of soil would be brought in for temporary adornment.

In garden history terms this is an important issue as the Tintagel Garden would have been an anticipation of the 'fret' enclosures popular in the late seventeenth century, so often illustrated in the Kip and Knyff bird's-eye views of them, published in the first twenty years of the eighteenth century, and described in John Rea's *Flora*.[13] Tentatively, however, and after personal experience of the site in adverse conditions, I would suggest that, while a few brave roses might have been coaxed to climb those low walls, and while the rectangle does seem to have been for recreation, it is most likely to have been laid out there on the only level ground on the main Tintagel rock as a bowling green or a hurling court to keep the garrison amused. No one can be sure what the rules and requirements of thirteenth-century bowls were, and boules today can be played in France on virtually any level ground. In his account of Hall Walk, near Polruan, Carew makes it clear that bowls could be played on any level, linear strip.[14] Hurling, a favourite Cornish game, could, in one of its two forms, be played on a court with a goal at each end made of two bushes: 'some eight or ten feet assunder'. Fifteen, twenty or thirty players, 'more or less, chosen out on each side, who strip themselves into their slightest apparel, and then join hands in rank, one against another. Out of these ranks they match themselves by pairs, one embracing another, and so pass away, every of which couple are specially to watch one another during the play.' To retain the ball a player had to sustain being punched by an opponent in the 'breast with his closed fist to keep him off, which they call butting, and place in well doing the same no small point of manhood'.[15]

In his article on the medieval garden at Tintagel, Peter Rose fails, as his title suggests, even to consider the possibility of a games area. Yet he points out that the enclosure is not an exact rectangle because its builders avoided a section of gently rising ground, which would have spoilt a level playing area. The ground in the rectangle has been worked to a spade's depth, but that might only mean for the preparation of a lawn. That path crossing the centre of the rectangle could well have divided two fairly small courts and there, far from listening to poetry and song, the ladies of the castle may have sat on the flat and turfed wall tops to cheer on their hurling husbands and handle refreshment breaks. On the other, floral, side of the argument the Garden is sited close to Tintagel's only well, but it is difficult to believe that on such a rain-blasted site a well for water was ever a prime necessity.

Earl Richard died in 1272. Subsequently the history of his symbolic and imaginatively conceived castle was one of gradual dismantling and decay.

2

'A place of diversified pleasings' – Tudor and Elizabethan gardens

In the larger houses of the county where the owners grew rich on industry or trade their gardens have been altered so often over the subsequent four centuries that it is hard to recreate the original sixteenth-century ambience, or indeed to define just how long the stylistic period normally described as 'Tudor' or 'Elizabethan' actually lasted in this remote and conservative county. Lanhydrock should be a warning. It has an apparently typical gatehouse of about 1570, ornate with obelisks and housing a banqueting chamber on its upper floor. Between the Gatehouse and the front court of the main house extend wide open lawns set with yews, flower beds and metal urns. The chronological reality is that this 'Elizabethan' Gatehouse was completed in 1651, during the Commonwealth, so it is not even Jacobean or Caroline in date. Furthermore, a careful drawing by Edmund Prideaux, made in 1727, shows a narrow high-walled forecourt between the Gatehouse and the house, claustrophobic in its effect and quite unlike the present garden scene. [1]

The best way to take in an accurate profile of the county's Tudor and Elizabethan gardens is to look at the grounds of minor manor houses, those just above the status of large farmhouses. [2] There the original garden enclosures are often intact, a movement from functional medieval chaos to genteel symmetry can be traced and the extreme conservatism of Cornish architectural preferences will become apparent.

Trecarrell Manor, a few miles south of Launceston, is of the middle years of Henry VIII's reign; Trenethick, on the outskirts of Helston, is Elizabethan. Trewane Manor, near St Kew, is, in its garden front at least, of Charles I's reign, though the date of 1640, which has become attached to it with no firm scholarly backing, is perhaps too late. In all three houses the garden dispositions, or lack of them, have been preserved in enduring granite.

Trecarrell must have been begun after 1524, by which time its owner, Sir Henry Trecarrell, had completed his ambitious rebuilding of Launceston's St

Mary Magdalene, one of only two Cornish churches where the masons managed to enrich the carving of the granite as if they were working in limestone. Sir Henry obviously had high standards and Trecarrell shows this as clearly as does his church, but those standards were entirely Gothic and medieval, classical symmetries do not feature at all. The complex of the house lies tucked away in a sheltered dip below a narrow lane between Trebullet and Larrick. Its individual features are quite miniature in scale, but still astonishingly rich in detail, far more moving than Cotehele because they are so bucolic. A duck pond and a barn stand right in front of the entrance door to the domestic range and neither gunnera nor pampas grass can conceal the incongruity. The Great Hall, which could easily pass for 1370 in date by its committed Perpendicular tracery, stands roughly at right-angles to that domestic range and a Privy Garden is enclosed in that angle. Lawned now and planted with flowering bushes, it would originally have been more utilitarian with herbs and vegetables. Up on a slope, and reached by a path of slates, is the Chapel, quite unrelated to the house it serves or to the conventional east–west orientation. Each unit – house, hall, barn, chapel – has been dropped down, handsomely detailed but casually sited. The garden alone would have been conveniently placed near to the kitchens and there is no sign of fortified enclosure, even though the Wars of the Roses would still have been a living memory in 1524. Sir Henry's only son, a baby, drowned in a bowl of water in 1540 and that personal tragedy may have left Trecarrell incomplete.

Trenethick, though built in a time of Elizabethan peace, is quite different. Its front garden, if it was originally a garden space as it is now and not a cobbled courtyard, is strongly fortified and enclosed, with none of Trecarrell's open slopes and duck pond. A little Gatehouse guards the entrance and the house itself has not a single arched Gothic window, all the fenestration is rectangular under dripstones, conventionally Tudor. Two plain lawns lie between the Gatehouse and the front door and at some antiquarian stage a medieval roadside cross has been brought in for sanctuary on the right-hand lawn. The wall on which the Gatehouse stands has been massively extended downhill to protect a large garden area that would have been utilitarian, not formal.

This pattern of fortified front garden with a gatehouse has endured, though with additional garden subtleties, at Trewane, a Caroline house, and because of its siting on a steep hill this much later garden looks even more defensible. The back of Trewane is much older than its garden and formal entrance front. It came into the possession of the Nicholls in 1525, but the front, which John Nicholls, a Royalist, constructed just before the Civil War, is strictly symmetrical though vernacular and mullioned in its fenestration and central doorway. It has lost its original gabled second storey and so looks even more classical than it once was. Here again the centrally sited Gatehouse leads to twin lawns (5), their geometry emphasised by a heavily pollarded Irish yew in each square of grass. Twin five-centred Tudor arches in the flanking walls lead into this front garden on each side, suggesting that the Gatehouse with its supposed 'dungeon chamber' was

5 *Just before the Civil War broke out in 1642 the Nicholls of Trewane were still defending their symmetrical front garden with a fortified gatehouse*

little used. C.S. Gilbert, writing in 1820, records that 'near the house are the remains of good gardens and fishponds';[3] the same could be said today. A chapel originally stood on the right-hand side of the front, gatehouse court, related to the house and not set airily away on a hillside as at Trecarrell. Where it once stood is now a series of little gardens at slightly varying levels. In the first, set back behind a lawn, is a stone garden seat in a recess. Then comes the Ladies' Walk paved with suspiciously smooth stone slabs that may have once floored the chapel. At the top of this Walk is an extraordinary aspen tree. Normally the word 'aspen' evokes Tennyson's 'Lady of Shalott': 'Willows whiten, aspens quiver, / Little breezes dusk and shiver', but this aspen is a massive mature tree, thirty to forty feet high, prevented from any quivering by the thick shroud of ivy climbing up it. The Ladies' Walk ends in steep steps down to what was a fishpond, but is now an ornamental water with azaleas. On the further side of the Walk is another lawned area with a 'holy' well and a number of carved stones, relics again of the chapel. The prevailing geometry of this section has been wisely emphasised by a long, straight hedge of hebe running immediately below the Gatehouse and the retaining wall. Hedges of camellia and a presiding *Magnolia grandiflora* can be taken for granted in Cornwall, but it is the fortified symmetry of Trewane and its late date of about 1640 that are so remarkable and which set contemporary work at Lanhydrock into context. Formal gardening was being practised, but only on a very homely and domestic scale.

While Cornish gentry of the sixteenth century were limited in their garden layouts they were not slow to create deer parks both for sport and as living larders of roe deer to feed them over the lean winter months. Whether they were as anxious as the gentry of other counties to create deer parks as a mark of their social distinction and local power is doubtful. Elsewhere in England deer parks tended to expand over the centuries into ornamental parks surrounding their parent houses. But on his tour of the county Defoe noted a marked lack of such conventional parks, and it will be remarked frequently over subsequent chapters that the Cornish upper classes were inclined to think linear rather than spatially in the surroundings of their houses. They often laid out a network of long drives, but through ordinary farmland or alongside rivers and estuaries to command picturesque scenery rather than through the Arcadian eclectic, or later Brownian, manicured and tree-clumped landscapes general on the other side of the Tamar.

Before 1550 there were forty-nine deer parks in Cornwall firmly recorded, with a possible twenty-six less certain. Later another forty-eight were enclosed, but not many of them seem to have been licensed.[4] The Duchy, as opposed to the earlier Earldom of Cornwall, came into existence in 1337, in Edward III's reign, so this failure to license is surprising and suggests that the royal hand did not lie very firmly on this distant possession. Almost all the parks were for fallow, not roe or red deer. Stags were killed in the summer and the does in winter between Martinmas (11 November) and Candlemas (2 February), when plump, tender venison would have been most appreciated. Some parks, Godolphin is an example, were dotted with pillow mounds to encourage rabbits as an extra source of meat.

The deer could either be chased on horseback, shot from butts or coursed past a stand, where visitors could lay bets on which hound would be the first to catch the deer, which had been released with a head start. Those three methods demanded different layouts to the deer park. That at Godolphin was large enough for a hunt on horseback, but Peter Herring notes in addition: 'curious side walls at the lower edges of the park, near the house, may have served both as walks and butts for 'stables'; and a course complete with a possible stand has been identified alongside the medieval garden'.[5] Local topography dictated whether these deer parks were secluded and private, set down in a valley, like those at Restormel, Penhallam and Cardinham, or proudly flaunted on a hill like that at Godolphin and an almost exactly oval park at Carn Brea. A few like that at Launceston Castle were wrapped closely around the parent town, controlling it and confining townfolk, as St Germans does today on its narrow peninsula.

It is something of a social and economic puzzle that Cornwall should have so few palatially grand Tudor and Elizabethan houses with lavish attendant gardens. In his definitive *Tudor Cornwall*, A.L. Rowse quotes a comment from the *Topographer and Genealogist* written in Queen Mary's reign (1553-8):

> In those days men of worship sought no curious buildings, nor had any great regard to their estimation or calling or to seek to place themselves according to their estate … I see no great excess in the building of the country at this day, unless a few in number that swim in wealth; but I am sure the great number of gentlemen in the country be contented with their father's old house for want of new.[6]

Yet Richard Carew, writing in 1602, speaks of 'the golden shower of rain'[7] that had fallen on the gentry after the Dissolution of the monasteries, while mineral wealth should have begun to make a difference. Godolphin, Lanhydrock and Penheale all have, nevertheless, gardens of the first thirty years of the seventeenth, not the sixteenth century.

Generalisations on national or racial characteristics are unsafe, but it does appear that the Celts of both Wales and Cornwall had less feeling for the distinction and apartness of their aristocracy than Saxons had in England. Cornish interests seem to have been predominantly maritime and mercantile. In a reversal of usual patterns of development the town and port of Falmouth were built around John Killigrew's fine 1567 house and garden at Arwenack (*6*), immediately below Pendennis Castle.[8] As at Trewane a fortified wall with a gatehouse lay in front of the house, then, enclosed by a second fortified wall, was a large area of fields, a fishpond and a little parterre. Within a much wider paled deer park was a windmill, a stone cross and a long grove of trees. In 1646 the mansion was burnt by the garrison at Pendennis Castle to prevent its occupation by Sir Thomas Fairfax and his army. A contemporary account records that 'the besiegers ravaged the gardens, house, and park in constructing lines of trenches and batteries….In the garden between the banqueting hall and the ancient stables, the surface has been raised, 4ft 6in above the original level of a paved court-yard and gutter'.[9] The Killigrews lived on at Arwenack after the Civil War until 1745, Martin Killigrew erecting the great granite Pyramid in Arwenack Grove between 1737 and 1738,[10] but the Tudor banqueting hall was never rebuilt. Further along the harbour was Trefusis, described by Leland as 'extremely pleasant by its situation … to the south of the house is a fine grove, and a walk, at the end of which is a pleasure house'.[11]

Place, home to the Treffrys of Fowey, who had loyally supported Henry Tudor long before Bosworth, stood then, as now, in the very middle of a lively port town. The Mohuns' Hall at Polruan matched it across the estuary. Both houses had significant gardens of the sixteenth century that have survived, the Treffrys' under a theatrical Regency overlay of machicolated fortifications in the manner of work recorded on a map of Henry VIII's reign.[12] But Godolphin has the most controversial 'Tudor' garden in the county, so controversial that it may not even be sixteenth-century in date, and the Hall at Polruan has the most innovative

Elizabethan garden. Neither is walled, except for the King's or Privy Garden at Godolphin, and neither has the usual sixteenth-century moat or water garden with an island pavilion. There is, however, a mundane practical Cornish version of such water gardens at Antony on the shore of a tidal inlet. Richard Carew had personally created an artificially contrived 'fishful pond' by throwing a dyke across a small creek.[13] Sir Arthur Champernowne, 'that perfectly accomplished gentleman',[14] designed a wooden pavilion for Carew to build on an island in this pond. It was to have been a two-storey affair with a round tower at each corner and balustraded balconies on each floor. Sadly, Carew never got down to constructing this pleasant folly, but he still spent thoughtful hours brooding on the banks of the lake.

It is also possible to see behind the National Trust's carefully tended flower beds at Cotehele the bones of the garden laid out by Sir Richard and Piers Edgcumbe after they, like the Treffrys of Fowey, backed Henry Tudor against Richard III. The terracing in front of the house is dated in the Trust's guidebook to a Victorian reshaping of 1862,[15] but the four terraces, with their central path down to the perfectly framed views of the valley, were only tidied up versions of earlier terracing clearly shown on a pre-1862 photograph in the Trust's first, 1989,

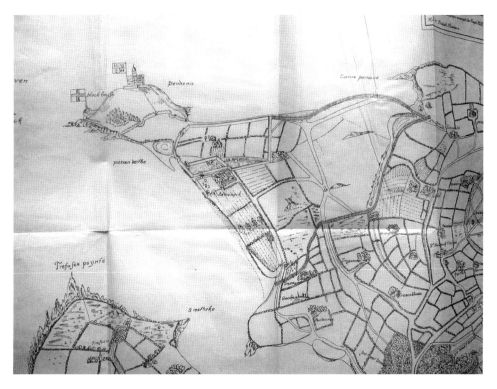

6 *A map of about 1580 of the grounds, which the Killigrews had laid out after 1567 around Arwenack, shows a fortified wall, groves of trees, a parterre, a fishpond and a deer park with a windmill, all lying just west of Pendennis Castle in what is now Falmouth.* Royal Institute of Cornwall, Courtney Library

guidebook.[16] If it is possible today to ignore the gloriously lush flowering bushes down in this sheltered valley, then hidden among them is the domed fifteenth-century dovecote, a stew pond, now lilied over, a holy well and, further down near the river, a chapel in the wood built by Sir Richard in gratitude for his escape in 1468 from the pursuing soldiery of King Richard's supporters. These are all genuine Tudor survivals of Cotehele's lower grounds.

Back in the Hall Court of the main house there is less floral distraction, with only chaste white hydrangeas to distract from the cobbles, the grass and the quite remarkable anticipation of an Oxford college quadrangle: all staircases, no corridors. No fewer than ten doors open onto this one quite small courtyard which was, functionally, itself the main connecting 'corridor' of the house. Up through the Retainers' Court, with the pink and white cyclamen that are omnipresent in Cotehele's grounds, there is, in the North Garden, a possible Tudor or Jacobean layout that no one seems to have noticed, even though the prospect tower (7), heightened in 1627, was obviously raised for the pleasure of commanding it. Under the rough grass of the steeply sloping ground are the shadows of a terraced pleasaunce with a big medlar and a copper beech, rising up to the pampas grass markers of a top terrace walk backed by a battlemented wall. This was the prospect which King Charles I could have enjoyed when he was given the top room of that brand new tower apartment. The rest of the admirable, but much later, gardens belong to another chapter, but the terraces, walks, stew pond, Dovecote and Chapel at Cotehele still present a satisfying Tudor whole better than any other house in the county. The entrance front of Trerice is elegantly gabled, but its three terraces to the side and its Bowling Green are all it has to show for the sixteenth century, and even these are supposed to be Victorian re-workings of what was obviously in place before.[17]

The gardens, or what remains of them, at Godolphin House, have to be approached with caution because so many earnestly proposed theories as to their nature and original extent are set out in the literature available to visitors and scholars. Douglas Pett, in his encyclopaedic and most valuable *The Parks and Gardens of Cornwall*, gives Godolphin an unusually brief entry, as if nervous of offending so many vocal experts.[18] These include the present owner, John Schofield, with his *Godolphin, The Side Garden: A Brief Guide*,[19] a landscape report by the consultant John Phibbs,[20] a 1995 Royal Commission on Historical Monuments report entitled: *Godolphin and its Gardens*, and two substantial archaeological reports, one carried out by the Cornwall Archaeological Unit.[21]

Before becoming too involved in problems of interpretation, it needs to be stressed at the outset that the large Side Garden, presumably Tudor in its actual extent, has lost most of the interesting, probably late seventeenth-century, formal planting. This was recorded on a 1791 map (*colour plate 5*), taken from a 1786 survey,[22] drawn for the Duke of Leeds at the end of the long period of ownership by the native Cornish Godolphin family. As noted earlier in this chapter, the 'curious side walls' of the Side Garden, and their linking up with

7 *The Prospect Tower at Cotehele was raised a storey in 1627 the better to command a terraced pleasaunce on the steep slope at its foot. King Charles I occupied the new top floor apartment*

the deer coursing walls and Hunting Stand, are early, though not precisely dated. However, all the really significant garden features at Godolphin are of early seventeenth-century date and belong to the next chapter.

Several writers on Godolphin have pointed out the 'inexplicable' oddity of the layout of the Side Garden, which it is set at an angle to 'the praty house' that, so Leland reported in 1535, 'Thomas Godalcan, younger son to Sir Willyam buildeth'.[23] One explanation for this Tudor oddity in planning is that the Side Garden follows the lines of an earlier medieval garden attached to 'Godollan Castle in Lodollan town ruined', which William of Worcester described in 1478.[24] When Thomas Godollan (most chroniclers stumble over spelling the Godolphin surname) built his house around 1535 he was apparently indifferent to the niceties of its relationship with the existing garden walls. But the precise site of that older ruined house has never been satisfactorily established; and anyone looking for a grand Tudor or Elizabethan garden at Godolphin will have to be satisfied with high surrounding terrace walkways of stone-faced turf banks and two water tanks in the north-western corner. Even these last two are of doubtful date. That richly detailed map of 1786 recorded a garden that had been assiduously, but conservatively, tended for the previous fifty-four year reign of the 2nd and last Earl Godolphin, a man born back in 1678 when Franco-Dutch formal gardening was the fashion.

Much simpler, but of far more innovative significance, is the genuine Elizabethan garden feature at Sir Reginald Mohun's Hall at Polruan, overlooking Fowey town and harbour on the other side of the Fowey estuary (*colour plate 3*). The real excitement of this terrace walk is not simply that it was a formal feature anticipating those eighteenth-century gardens directed to the enjoyment of architecture and natural prospects like the Rievaulx Terrace in Yorkshire, but that Richard Carew in his *Survey* of 1602, and presumably Sir Reginald Mohun who had the terrace dug out, were both conscious, delightedly conscious in Carew's case, of the aesthetic advance which was being made. 'A place of diversified pleasings', Carew hailed the garden and promised, 'I will therefore do my best to trace you a shadow thereof, by which you shall (in part) give a guess at the substance'.

There is, happily, still no need for guesswork because the Hall Walk, as it is called, survives today in the care of the National Trust, with much of its original planting of whitethorn and hawthorn (*8*). Furthermore, virtually every feature of the complex views which it commands, human and natural, survive just as Carew described them. The Hall Walk is a rare opportunity to re-examine the seventeenth-century visuals of a dramatically lovely coastline which, by their sheer quality, propelled Elizabethan Cornish gentry into the kind of pleasures more common to Romantic poets like Wordsworth almost two centuries later. While wary of extreme claims, I would suggest that this single terrace garden is the most important in the county and important in English garden history. Carew goes in detail into the construction of the terrace:

> It is cut out in the side of a steep hill whose foot the salt water washeth, evenly levelled to serve for bowling, floored with sand for soaking up the rain, closed with two shorn hedges, and banked with sweet scenting flowers. It wideneth to a sufficient breadth for the march of five or six in front, and extendeth to not much less than half a London mile; neither doth it lead wearisomely forthright, but yieldeth varied and yet not over-busy turnings as the ground's opportunity affordeth, which advantage increaseth the prospect, and is converted on the foreside into platforms for the planting of ordnance and the walkers' sitting, and on the back part into summer-houses for their more private retreat and recreation.[25]

This means that, like the garden at Tintagel, it was a place for playing bowls, or more exactly 'boules' in the French sense of the term. It was also dry ground where ladies could walk safely in their shoes. Today it is still 'closed with two shorn hedges' for much of its 'half a London mile'; still broad enough 'for the march of five or six in front' and with 'platforms for the planting of ordnance' on the foreside. One summerhouse, a rough affair of rubble stone, survives 'on the back part' for 'more private retreat and recreation'.

What a modern visitor needs, in order to appreciate the extreme perfection of Hall Walk's visual survival, is to have Carew's description in hand as the half mile is paced out. Everything remains, as beautiful and as humanly diversified as when Carew wrote:

> the vast ocean sparkled with ships that continually this way trade forth and back to most quarters of the world. Nearer home, they take view of all sized cocks, barges, and fisherboats, hovering on the coast. Again, contracting your sight to a narrower scope, it lighteth on the fair and commodious haven, where the tide daily presenteth his double service of flowing and ebbing, to carry and recarry whatsoever the inhabitants shall be pleased to charge him withal, and his creeks (like a young wanton lover) fold about the land with many embracing arms… before, the town of Fowey subjecteth his whole length and breadth to your overlooking; and directly under you ride the home and foreign shipping.[26]

8 *The rare charm of the late sixteenth-century Hall Walk overlooking Fowey is that it is still 'closed with two shorn hedges, and banked with sweet scenting flowers' as when Richard Carew described it admiringly in 1602, an unchanged Elizabethan prospect walk*

It is not pressing the parallel too far to mention in the same breath Wordsworth's sonnet on Westminster Bridge. In both writings there is that feeling for the vital beauty of human creation and activity, of man responding successfully to God's natural setting.

As for the date of the Hall Walk, Sir Reginald Mohun was already, when Carew wrote in 1602, 'a widower of two wives', a seasoned actor on the stage of Cornish county administration, the officer commanding in any muster of Cornish forces 'six companies, 600 men, 200 pikes, 210 Muskets, 190 Calivers'.[27] So 1580-90 seems a reasonable timeframe for a garden feature mature by 1602.

Mohun Hall is now a small bed and breakfast establishment, but with the ruins of the chapel in which Sir Reginald worshipped and the service buildings of his manor house. The complex lies quite separate, several hundred yards away up the hill from Hall Walk, and it is unlikely that house and garden were ever connected except by a field path. A visit either in February for the whitethorn blossom, or in May for the hawthorn, will put to test Carew's claim that it is 'banked with sweet scenting flowers'. On my visit the hedges were thick with red haws and dark purple sloes: minor pleasures compared with Cornwall's usual garden diet of camellias and azaleas, but this is the place to experience an Elizabethan garden in its primitive but sensitive simplicity. Yet it was here, when he was walking this idyllic terrace with his entourage in August 1644, that King Charles narrowly escaped the bullet of an unknown assassin firing from the town of Fowey far below him. A firearm of that era would have been inaccurate at that distance and of low velocity, but one of the King's sailor bodyguards sustained a shallow wound. Eden gardens require their serpents.

With Carew's evocative prose account of Hall Walk we are reminded that the age of Shakespeare's natural awareness, as in Sonnet 33:

> Full many a glorious morning have I seen
> Flatter the mountain tops with sovereign eye,
> Kissing with golden face the meadows green,
> Gilding pale streams with heavenly alchemy,[28]

was not very far removed from that of Wordsworth's:

> Magnificent
> The morning was, a memorable pomp,
> More glorious than I ever had beheld.
> The sea was laughing at a distance; all
> The solid mountains were as bright as clouds.[29]

The surprising fact is that, in garden design as in so much else: poetry, architecture and art, an age of stilted formalism had to intervene and separate two such mutually sympathetic sensibilities as the Elizabethan and the Romantic.

3

The county in a cautious dalliance with formal garden design

This is the time to move, treading uneasily among rival theories, into the gardens of Godolphin House, if rough tussocky grounds, dim woodlands and some desultory modern planting can be described as gardens. The house stands low in unrewarding country, Cornwall's clapped-out, industrial west, and it will be a mistake to spend too much energy trying to determine the dating and the original layout of the grounds, because the actual north front of Godolphin, an elevation of the most engaging charm and stylistic hedging of bets, is itself a garden design marker of national distinction (*9*). The design is a deliberate and successful device to lure the outer green world of gardens through a chunky, double colonnade of Doric columns right into the interior courtyard of a rich industrialist's mansion. It is a very early and very Cornish instance of applied and functional garden classicism.

The problem here is which Godolphin, of a long and potent dynasty of mining magnates and Westminster politicians, ordered those classical columns into place, but then backtracked conservatively to top them with a trim, but anachronistic, Gothic battlement. It was F. Hitchins and S. Drew who confirmed many modern architectural historians on the chronology of Godolphin in their second volume of the *History of Cornwall*. This book was published as early as 1824, when the authors were close enough to events to have known better. Douglas Pett was also guilty of quoting them without analysis with their inaccurate: 'The elegant portico which was built by Francis Earl of Godolphin, of white moorstone, brought from Tregoning Hill had rooms over it that were never finished, and that now assist in swelling the triumphs of desolation'.[1]

Francis, 2nd and last Earl Godolphin, the son of the great 1st Earl, Sidney, Queen Anne's incorruptible Chancellor, ruled at Godolphin from 1712 to 1766,

9 *This seven-bay Loggia on the north front of Godolphin dates to the 1620s and represents one of Cornwall's most remarkable garden innovations drawing the outside spaces into the main house*

when he died aged eighty-eight after controlling the house and its estate for a quiet fifty-four years. But he could not possibly have built that naively handsome north front because of what he wrote to his godfather John Evelyn in 1690, when he was only a twelve-year-old boy and his father was in London in mid career. Francis described Godolphin as: ''Tis a large old house built of stone the front upon Pillers with flat Arches… [an] abundance of trees about it and a great deal of garden not walled but fenced with Hedges',[2] proving that the double colonnade was already old by 1690. That should have been self evident to any informed architectural historian with an eye for detail, but in an earlier 1915 *Country Life* article Lawrence Weaver had followed Hitchins and Drew and condescendingly described that wonderfully advanced and innovative granite colonnade as early eighteenth-century in date and an instance 'of the slow impact of new architectural ideas in so remote a county as Cornwall'[3], which was the exact reverse of truth. There would be no similar transparency of colonnades in any other great English country house until Robert Adam's Osterley Park, built in 1763-80. Those solid Doric colonnades were one of the rare initiatives in Cornwall's architectural history, an essentially welcoming transparency and a feature borrowed from Florence. There is a similar, though less effective, colonnade at Penheale in the north of the county with date stones of 1620 and 1636. That suggests a contemporary date, Caroline or Jacobean, for Godolphin's colonnades. Then there is the Laudian quadrangle at St John's College, Oxford with the same uncertain but attractive confusion of classical work with Gothic battlements. That was completed in 1636 and is more sophisticated though not as spatially directional as the Godolphin colonnades.

The north front of Godolphin has to be experienced. Initially it looks low and solid, but those masculine columns lead visitors into a stony hollow space with glimpses, through an unexpectedly old-style Gothic archway, probably resited, of a second colonnade on the far side. Then comes the daylight and a half-ruined and cobbled inner courtyard which has been reached without passing through any definable interior room.

This is real architecture, unfortunately the innovator who designed it is not known, nor is its projector, the reigning Godolphin who ordered it, quite certain. But it does seem likely that it was Sir Francis II who ruled his industrial kingdom of the west from 1613 to 1667. His were the golden experimental years of King Charles before the storm of Civil War, the years when Inigo Jones was designing Wilton House's south front for Isaac de Caus to construct for the Earl of Pembroke. Godolphin is Cornwall's granitic version of Wilton, less graceful, less exquisite in detail, but a far more successful handling of outer and inner space. Godolphin House lies rather subdued and self-pitying, slowly recovering under the Schofields from its long years as a farmhouse. In its prime it must have been a bustling hub of foundries and blowing houses, with smoke and metallurgical fumes thick in the air as the Godolphin labourers sweated tin and copper ore from the hill behind the house.[4] Quite how the deer of that hill's deer park co-existed with the miners is hard to determine, but they seem to have achieved a compromise. King Charles I naturally visited Godolphin and will have enjoyed the quiet of that small, walled King's or Privy Garden to the right of the north front. What other garden pleasures the King enjoyed there is less certain. In that 1690 letter young Francis Godolphin mentions 'a great deal of garden not walled but fenced in with Hedges'. The present Side Garden at Godolphin could be described as 'a great deal of a garden' with its nine subdivisions, three-by-three in apparent compliment to the Blessed Trinity, but it is more walled than hedged, walled with 'Cornish hedges', which are turf terraces faced with stone (*10*). Are these Francis's hedges? Trinitarian conceits were a favourite Elizabethan garden device; the earlier Wilton garden of the 2nd Earl of Pembroke featured Trinitarian threesomes of tree planting.[5] Lord Burghley's Theobalds also had nine knot gardens with walks, and Sir Francis was in regular correspondence with Burghley.[6] Did Sir Francis Godolphin II, who had a tremendous cash flow from his mines, try to imitate Burghley and Pembroke by stuffing nine compartments into an earlier irregular rectangle of stone-faced hedges? There must have been 'a great deal of garden' to impress the younger Francis in 1690; but were those nine enclosures a response to Franco-Dutch formal gardens, like the multiple compartments set up at Longleat in Wiltshire post-1683 by the Brompton Park Nurseries?[7] It seems unlikely that a formal garden of that date would have ventured into Metaphysical

10 *When young Francis Godolphin described in 1690 his garden as 'not walled but fenced in with Hedges',
he meant the typical Cornish 'hedges' of stone and turf like these still sturdily enduring in Godolphin's Jacobean
enclosure*

Trinitarian imagery, and Francis's letter to Evelyn does not give the impression
that the gardens at Godolphin were brand new in 1690.

Whatever the date of the nine areas they were certainly formal, though more
repetitive than inventive. Even from the careful, almost aerial photographic, detail
of the 1791 estate map for the Duke of Leeds (*colour plate 5*), taken from a 1786
survey,[8] they had been carefully tended during the 2nd Earl Godolphin's fifty-
four year rule. Godolphin's gardens were certainly not in romantic decay when
the Duke took over; it was the Duke who cast the estate into 'the triumphs
of desolation' that Hitchins and Drew describe. In 1786 each of the nine
compartments was neatly geometric. There was a four tree-by-four tree orchard,
a square of four smaller squares, each square with four bushes, and a central
square fountain pool in a privacy of square yew hedges. Only in the north-west
corner near the house was there the variation of two water tanks, probably for
fish. It was a large garden, but it was not the creation of an ambitious foreign-
trained gardener, though the sycamores surrounding its hedges would still have
been fashionable enough in the early seventeenth century.[9] If a guess had to be
made then a planting of about 1670 in a frame much older, of about 1620, might
be offered, but with no certainty.

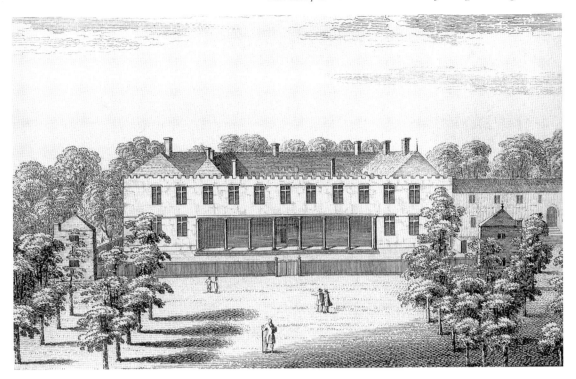

11 *Borlase's 1758 engraving of the north entrance front to Godolphin shows the lost Jacobean Lodges with a connecting fence to prevent livestock from entering into the inner court and Loggia.* Bristol University Special Collections

Nikolaus Pevsner was really to blame for setting off the whole Godolphin controversy by his unusually sly hint that the 'remains of quite an ambitious garden can still be seen in the solitude which surrounds present-day Godolphin'.[10] Unfortunately the guessing game that Pevsner set in motion has distracted attention from the very real experimental advance of that double colonnade. That, however, still leaves one last Godolphin garden problem. Borlase's view of the north front, dated 1758 (*11*), shows not only the colonnade, but twin gazebos or banqueting pavilions in front of it with a paled fence running between them to keep animals from the forecourt. Some authorities would date these pavilions to the 2nd Earl's eighteenth-century reign, but such twin garden houses are usually Jacobean in date. They have been swept away now so there can be no architectural dating of their detail. Paled forecourt fences are usually bucolic late seventeenth-century devices, and the pavilions themselves look as chunky and masculine as the Doric colonnade; the trees that Borlase drew in the avenue leading away from them look no older than forty years. The best advice is to visit Godolphin's gardens and enjoy their multiple puzzles. Unless further documentary evidence emerges those puzzles are unlikely to be solved. Was the 2nd Earl Francis so old, so conservative, that he raised Jacobean-style pavilions in the middle of the eighteenth-century? They are more likely to be of the same date as the colonnade, the time of the 2nd Sir Francis, not the 2nd Earl Francis.

Godolphin may still be something of a 'triumph of desolation', but the intact formal gardens of Bochym Manor and Rosteague will restore a sense of seventeenth-century order. They are two improbable, and in Rosteague's case, miraculous survivors of bijou formalism, genuine time-trips hidden down narrow winding lanes where one quite small car met head-on can enforce a reverse of several hundred yards, but both are most rewarding. There is a manuscript book of drawings of Cornish houses and gardens, the Spoure Book, which was drawn as a wedding present somewhere around 1690.[11] This illustrates two very similar gardens, neat, axial and strictly symmetrical. One of them, that at Trebartha Hall under the lee of Bodmin Moor, has two arches leading to a little domed pavilion at the far side of a garden square lined with neatly trimmed conifers.[12] In each quarter lawn of the square is a statue, and in the square's centre Atlas carries the world on his shoulders. It must have been a civilised delight to sit in that pavilion, but every trace of the layout was swept away in the mid eighteenth century.

It comes then, as an almost visionary surprise, to find that the other small Spoure Book garden, at Bochym Manor in a shallow valley of the Lizard, has hardly suffered a scrap of change, but remains one of the most likeable and covetable gardens in the county. There is a later nineteenth-century drive to it up the valley from a lodge on the main road, but the authentic seventeenth-century approach is down a public lane from Helston. That way the garden opens up suddenly on the left at the bottom of a steep hill, with Bochym Manor, a pleasantly amateurish, two-wing shambles of seventeenth- and nineteenth-century creation, up on the right-hand side of the lane.

The particular charm of the garden is its mystery. Laid out axially along a central path, like that lost garden at Trebartha, it still contrives to disappear down into the valley: each of its three authentically Italian modelled terraces arriving as a surprise after the rough initial punctuation of gatepiers topped with stone balls. Evergreen oaks line the upper side of the first lawn, copper beeches the lower side, but everything is on a diminutive scale. A few strides bring a visitor to Bochym's most winning feature. Where moon steps drop down to the next small terrace, twin stone benches (*12*), semi-circular, face each other companionably across the path. By their coy charm they should be Edwardian period love seats, but they are authentic seventeenth-century work from the time when Francis Billet was given the Manor, with his Mohun bride, by Reginald Mohun her generous father. The Cornwall Gardens Trust report on Bochym notes that Christopher Billet spent much money on the estate from 1666 to 1699, therefore a possible timeframe for the garden.[13]

This second terrace is, like the first, a lawn, but may originally have featured a parterre. Then, with a very slight sideways wriggle, the axial path with its steps dives down to a Bowling Green, walled on three sides, open to the valley stream on the fourth. There is an enormous mulberry tree, plausibly claimed as the oldest in the county, a holy well, which may have originally been a sheep dip,

12 *In between the top and middle terraces of Bochym's late seventeenth-century miniature formal garden are twin stone benches at the top of a flight of moon steps, perfectly placed to enjoy the parterre that once must have occupied the middle terrace*

and a gardener's bothy. And that is all. An 1890 Ordnance Survey map shows an orchard up on the hillside above the three terraces where there is still a medlar tree, but Bochym is wonderfully uncrowded in a county of gardens usually crammed with flowering bushes. Traces remain of a terraced Higher Garden behind the 1699 wing of the Manor. The ugly clock tower commemorating the 50th anniversary of Queen Victoria's coronation fits rather unhappily into an otherwise generally rough and relaxed complex of farm buildings, quite separate from the tri-partite garden.

Bochym's failure to preserve a parterre on its middle terrace is seen as an aesthetic loss after a visit to Rosteague, far out down the Roseland peninsula. For Rosteague, sheltered behind a slate-roofed wall of granite rubble and cob, has preserved that holiest of horticultural relics, one possibly unique in England, its original box parterre, arthritic with age, even senile, but still solid enough almost to be sat upon. One-and-a-half feet high and a one-and-a-half feet broad, its patterns seem just too flowing (*colour plate 4*), too Paisley-style to be Elizabethan, and Sir Roy Strong's guess of post-1660 for its planting seems just right.[14] Locals call it the 'French Garden', and that seems equally right. Rosteague has, against the odds, retained a garden planted early in the reign of Charles II when the celebrated French garden designer, André Mollet, author of the parterre-packed *Le Jardin de Plaisir*, was working for the King at St James's Palace and all things French were in favour with Royalist gentry of a notably loyal county.

As rare as the box hedging is a thatched summerhouse fitted into one corner of the cob wall. Fronted by rustic wooden columns it shelters a curved wicker seat, and the wall behind this has been crudely patterned with cockles and mussel shells in star shapes, very repetitively and unimaginatively. Black pebbles have been inlaid in zig-zags and castellated designs, all far too crude to be eighteenth-century Rococo work so it might conceivably be seventeenth-century in date. From that wicker seat the four quarters of the parterre can be observed under the low sweep of the thatched roof. A shallow terrace separates the two upper quarters from the two lower ones near the house (*13*). Roses, nerines and agapanthus were flowering in the interstices of the box hedges on my visit. One

13 *At Rosteague on the Roseland Peninsula an almost unchanged formal garden of conservative mid-seventeenth-century date survives with geometric box parterres on two levels protected from the sea breezes by a wall of cob*

or two yews have had to be cut back into ungainly shapes, but one brilliantly clipped box bush is shaped like a perfect classical urn, exactly the kind of garden topiary work that Alexander Pope and Joseph Addison mocked contemptuously in the 1720s. Yet here the urn of box is a homely wonder of scissor work and completely in place. Between 1670 and 1720 most moderately sized English gardens must have been planted like Rosteague with more or less clipped box patterning. That so few have survived is explained by one glance at those fat, exact swirls of box. Even in a garden as compact as this the labour of the upkeep must be a burden. Economic rather than purely aesthetic considerations must have dictated the subsequent development of English garden styles.

Considered together, Godolphin, Bochym and Rosteague suggest that formal gardening fashions worked better in human terms when those gardens were small. Rosteague is virtually a single cell, Bochym is three small cells. In its supposed Trinitarian prime, a large garden like the Side Garden at Godolphin consisted only of eight garden enclosures ranged around one central unit; there is unlikely to have been any sense of progression there. The vistas must have been inward-looking from those high raised terrace-hedges. There is, in fact, a faltering, as if Cornish gentry, who seem generally to have been an unassuming tribe, lacked the necessary bombast to project the great formal layouts of Wimpole in Cambridgeshire, Cassiobury in Hertfordshire and Eaton Hall in Cheshire that made the pages of Kip and Knyff's 1707 *Britannia Illustrata* such a testament to applied garden geometry.[15] A few long carriage drives seem to have satisfied most Cornish gentry aspirations.

A 1734 Buck engraving of the south-west view of St German's Priory shows formal lawns and statues up a flight of steps at the east end of the church and the gatepiers of a formal tidal garden north of the house. The upper area is also shown on a 1747 map, 'The Borough of St Germans', as a rough hexagon of formal paths with a round Bowling Green in the centre.[16] The Bowling Green was still there when Repton made his visit in November 1792. Lord Edward Eliot, the dynamic 1st Baron, who ruled there from 1748 to 1804 and anticipated Repton in his Picturesque zeal, would soon have swept away the rest of the geometrical layout.

Better recorded were Heligan's formal gardens on the Ashey, north of the house, now covered by the Flower and Vegetable Gardens. Squire John Tremayne made an agreement[17] for the construction of these with John and William White, James Tory, John Grubb and John Gavel on 9 March 1736, a very late date for such formalism and a sign of how conservative back-country squires were out there in the West.

> The partners Doe agree to Turft the Fosse & Sloop & in all things to Finish the same and also to Finish the Two Higher Terras's and Porter and after to Turft the Design'd Garden plot in the higher end of the Ashey and after to Finish the Great Gravel Walk (Gravel Excepted) & Sloopes belonging … and after to Turft and Finish the Sloope in the Ashey.[18]

14 *Edmund Prideaux's 1727 sketch of Glynn is taken from the south and shows the dull Carolean house with twin garden pavilions more appropriate to a Caroline garden.* From the collection at Prideaux Place

Work had already started with the digging of shrubbery borders and the construction of a 'Bastian' viewpoint on the Terrace in the preceding February,[19] but none of this seems to have been very ambitious, more a way of tastefully covering up an area of parterres which had proved too expensive to keep up.

The real treasury of visual records for Cornish gardens at the end of the formal period is contained at Prideaux Place in a volume of drawings made by Edmund Prideaux in his travels about the country in the 1720s.[20] He was an able amateur artist capable of catching the charm of buildings reflected in garden pools. Glynn, near Bodmin (*14*), is shown with a walled garden and twin gazebos; Bake, near Trerulefoot, with a terrace, parterre and orchard, all modest in scale; Antony (*16*) in a maze of recent avenue planting; Werrington, near Launceston, in the same avenue style of development. Trewarthenick in Cornelly is shown desperately bare of landscape features; Hexworthy in Lawhitton littered with the standard round and conical conifers; Stowe poised above walled and terraced enclosures, and Port Eliot, St Germans, most surprising of all, still a functioning port where now the lawns extend.

Inevitably the great exception to most generalisations about Cornish gardens is Mount Edgcumbe which, though now a firmly anchored part of the county, was originally not only a part of Devon, but an integral part of Plymouth's social structures. Even now surviving features of Mount Edgcumbe's formal garden link that remarkable castle-style house securely to its parent city. A grand avenue of chestnut and beech, far too steep to contain a carriage drive, points down from the entrance front to the Cremyll ferry and the boats to Stonehouse. Sir

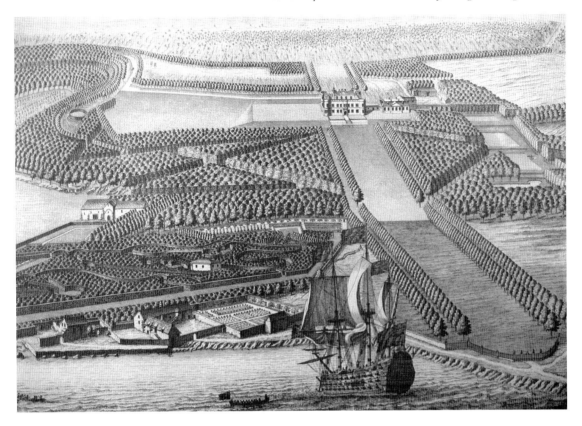

15 *High up on the right on Badeslade's 1737 view of Mount Edgcumbe are the water basins connected by cascades. The view catches the formal grounds just moving towards Arcadian sinuosities in the paths of the Lower Garden.* Mount Edgcumbe House & Country Park

Richard Edgcumbe, who planted it, and who reigned from 1667 to 1688 was a cousin of John Evelyn, the celebrated author of *Sylva*, a patriotic advocate of planting tree avenues.

On the east side of the great avenue there were three terraces, each with its water basin connected by cascades to the basin below (15). Only one of these basins still contains water, but the earthworks of the others can still be traced. Whether these were seventeenth-century work, inspired by the Evelyns of Wotton, who favoured the standard Italian three-terraced layout, is doubtful. C. Lilly's 'A General Plan of Plymouth Harbour' of 1718[21] shows the house at the heart of a radiating network of tree avenues, but no system of canals is shown in that area. The formal garden on the site of the later Amphitheatre is clearly marked in its walled enclosure with two Summerhouses facing the sea. This garden is divided into two with the geometric parterre nearest the sea and an ornamental orchard of fruit trees precisely laid out in lines to the rear. Further up the valley was a wood. That seems to have been all Sir Richard achieved before his death in 1688. The dense artificial woodland or Wilderness on the west side

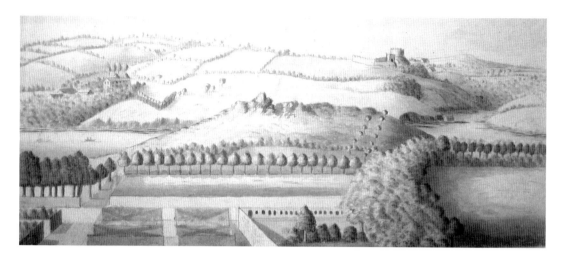

16 *When Edmund Prideaux drew Antony's grounds in 1727, they were still cluttered with immature formal avenues of trees and a large walled garden to the north. On Repton's advice the garden would be moved to the west side.* From the collection at Prideaux Place

of the avenue, with its decisive geometry of walks, as illustrated by Badeslade in 1735, post-dates Sir Richard's time. His successor, Richard, Ist Baron Edgcumbe, must have had these designed, along with the sequence of canals, more in tune with fashions introduced by John Vanbrugh and Charles Bridgeman in the early eighteenth century.[22]

Antony had a large parterre, or alternating topiary, in a big walled garden down the northern slope to the Lynher river (*16*). But it seems that the great trio of vistas down to the estuary and Saltash, that now make Antony's grounds so memorable, were at least latent in Prideaux's time, as he sketched complex avenues of trees reaching out in at least three northerly directions. There is in addition at Antony a forecourt, severely rectangular in ground plan but, for Cornwall, uniquely Baroque in visual impact (*17*). This can, by gently widening the term, be described as a garden feature and one that goes some way to relax and enliven the distinctly unyielding classicism of the small but oddly demanding house which it serves. Four cheerfully curvaceous domes dramatise the end pavilions of the brick-arched cloisters, and the open side of the forecourt is enriched with an ironwork screen which picks up the ironwork of the gate far away up the hill, but axially aligned to the forecourt.[23] Roses are trained over the wall supporting the ironwork and these, together with the magnolias on the cloisters, support the claim that this is a garden. The house is so intensely stiff and the courtyard so confidently relaxed with long, vaulted vistas along the cloisters, that it seems likely that a first ranking architect was employed here and Cornwall has, in all probability, if not in documented evidence, a garden here by James Gibbs.[24]

17   *In the design of his tentatively Baroque garden forecourt, James Gibbs, if he was the architect, was enlivening with four curvaceous domes the chilly severity of the house itself*

The irony of Antony's present-day gardens is that they include far and away the grandest and the most enjoyable of all Cornish formal gardens in the seventeenth-century French manner. But these are to the planting of William Henry Pole Carew, Cornwall's greatest native garden designer and belong in the mid nineteenth century: the opportunity was seized two centuries late. With a Baroque landscape to the south and ravishingly picturesque vistas to the north, not to mention terraced French grandiosity east and west, Antony's gardens have it all.

The stone available for garden buildings is not always a controlling factor in the ambition of the design. Croan, Edward Hoblyn's demure Queen Anne-style house on the hill overlooking Wadebridge, has brick piers and its garden walls, like the house, are built of freestone rubble.[25] Its containing walls venture to use ball finials and urns, one or two of modern concrete, but the garden architecture of the walled enclosure west of the house is limited to square pavilions with pyramid roofs in the north-east and south-east corners, one a tool shed, the other panelled with a moulded, domed ceiling.

In contrast, at Newton Ferrers, an immensely assertive, though simple, house of the 1690s, granite has been deployed with such a defiant panache of pinnacles topped with oversized balls that Gertrude Jekyll is said to have been disturbed by the masculine show.[26] Cornish masons tended to shy clear of granite, but here the march of three balustrades down from the garden front is said to have been 'done by an Italian' who was possibly more patient.[27] This granite triple diadem of garden formalism is tucked away in a valley so remote from Callington that when the house caught fire in 1940 one whole wing was gutted before the fire engine could reach it. Nothing, however, could ruin its garden except a severe earthquake. It descends axially, the first balustrading linking the two arms of the house to enclose a terrace. Then three big flights of segmental steps march down through austere lawns and two more balustrades on each terrace edge punctuated by forty squared terminals with those emphatic balls. A flower garden is way to the side so as not to compromise the masculine logic of the three terraces. If Sir William Coryton could have persuaded his Italian to add twin pavilions, Montacute-style, it would be the garden jewel of Cornwall, as it is it stamps order on a half-wild landscape of pines and rocky knolls.

It has been the fate of the county's larger seventeenth-century formal gardens to be either gloriously overlaid in a romantic riot of trees and giant bushes, or to be abandoned and left bare in a baffling but suggestive maze of grass-grown earthworks. Enys, a mile or so south of Truro, is the perfect instance of the former transformation act; Stowe, far away north on the savage north coast, is a desolate but most rewarding example of the second progression.

It is not easy to be affectionate about the lost seventeenth-century gardens at Stowe, a mile to the blustery west of Kilkhampton. Here there is no shortage of vistas, only a near absolute dearth of garden plants, bushes or trees. It is, nevertheless, a most memorable place and the hamlet in the deep valley below the site of the house will be a lure and a pleasure for any enthusiast of the Arts and Crafts movement. Stowe is more history than garden, and not, it has to be said, very sensible history; the house and its pleasure grounds, as its chroniclers record with gloomy relish, went up and came down within the lifetime of one generation.[28] It was the wrong house and the wrong garden in the wrong place: brick in a bare granite country, Franco-Dutch formalism on a very steep hill.

Even in a royalist county like Cornwall, John Grenville was exceptionally loyal. Knighted at Bristol in 1643, wounded at Newbury in 1644, he proclaimed Prince Charles king after Charles I's execution, defended the Scilly Islands until 1651, won respect from the Commonwealth and was one of the movers who persuaded General Monk to bring Charles II back in 1660. Rewards flowed in: Steward of the Duchy, Groom of the Stole, Lord Warden of the Stannaries, Lord Lieutenant, Earl of Bath, Captain and Governor of Plymouth. Naturally, with those offices, came considerable wealth. He amassed £3,000 a year from duties on the pre-emption and coinage of tin, £2,000 a year as First Gentleman Usher of the Bedchamber. Bishop Burnet described him as 'a mean minded man who thought nothing but of getting and spending money'.[29] Hence Stowe house was built on that bleak inhospitable site after 1679 purely because it was the old home of the Grenvilles. In 1701 Grenville, then Lord Bath, died and his son, Viscount Lansdowne, shot himself accidentally, while cleaning a pistol before attending his father's funeral. One wonders if it is usual for pistols to be taken to funerals. His son, William, 3rd Earl of Bath, died of smallpox aged nineteen in 1711. Lawsuits ravaged the estates, in 1736 the gardens were described as being in decay and in 1739 'the noblest house in the West of England'[30] was demolished, large sections of it ending up in South Molton Guildhall.

Fortunately we have two important views of Stowe in its brief glory, a water-colour by Adrian van Diest and a sketch by Edmund Prideaux (*18*).[31] These show the pompously bland Carolean house, eleven bays wide, five deep and cupola-crowned with a three-part walled pleasure garden, but facing east into the valley and Kilkhampton, not west out to the sea views. A carriage is rolling away from its empty walled forecourt in the van Diest painting, and on the left is a Fountain Court with plants climbing its walls and a jet playing in a round pond. Behind this is a Gazebo and a tall, domed Dovecote overlooking a double

18 *This Prideaux sketch of Stowe shows the house defending itself from the surrounding wild nature by a cluster of walled gardens with a domed Gazebo for sheltered viewing.* From the collection at Prideaux Place

parterre. A servants' wing stands on the seaward side of the house; the stables, at the time the view was painted, stood to the right. Later they were rebuilt lavishly further back on the road which that carriage appears to be avoiding as it plunges down a one-in-six slope to the valley bottom and a drive to Kilkhampton. This placing of the stables dates the van Diest painting to pre-1694, by which time the new stables had gone up: a big, new H-shaped block clearly shown on the 1690s Grenville 'Estate Atlas of Stowe Barton' (*colour plate 6*) by Joel Gascoyne.[32]

It is curious that so many Carolean houses, Belton in Lincolnshire and Ramsbury in Wiltshire for instance, were built in imitation of Lord Clarendon's London town house since Clarendon himself was unpopular and his house was pulled down long before Stowe was demolished. But dull brick façades were cheap and fashionable, though they always suggest the streets of a city rather than the control of broad country areas. The tedium of their façades was usually redeemed at this period by extensive formal gardens elaborately planted with the kind of 'greens' that delighted King William, but Stowe did not have such a garden. High walls for shelter from sea winds must have been Lord Bath's first priority. It must have been a remarkably inconvenient house to reach, to provision and to garden.

Today there is one major survival of that strange complex. A winding road through tree-less country from Kilkhampton offers wild glimpses of the sea ahead and a deep wooded valley to the north. At one point an alert traveller can look down on the shelf of land where Stowe once stood, otherwise the first signpost of the site is a large farm complex, Stowe Barton, of gloomy, dark-brown bricks laid in the old-fashioned English bond. This is that 1693 new stable block turned to farmhouse and barns. A track leads up beside it to a hummocky tract of land where a few bricks of the same kind remain from the basement of the lost house and that circular fountain pond has left a shadow of its outline. An ugly little cottage seems to have been built out of the walls of that first smaller stable block and it faces onto a cobbled yard, another authentic relic.

Most impressive of these sad remains is a long, ramped brick wall running down the steep slope (*19*). Sections of this can be traced on the Prideaux drawing. What cannot be traced is a Royal Tennis Court, but some walling on this slope is supposed to be a survivor of Stowe's Court. It is all very atmospheric, but a relief to walk back down to the lane where a length of buttressed wall down in a dip is what survives of Stowe's carriage wash. On the other side of the lane are the depressions left by three artificial ponds that were in the Orchard of the house, not a good site for an orchard with no shelter from the sea winds. To relieve any sense of morbid depression a visit to the small hamlet of Coombe down in the valley is strongly recommended. Stowe's workforce must always have lived warm and watered down here. It is as picturesque and welcoming with attractively designed woodwork as Stowe is bleak, unfriendly, unexplained and brackish; and Coombe has a good beach. If Lord Bath had had the sense to build down here his house would have survived to become a popular National

19 *This long, ramped wall in English bond survives on the impractically steep formal entrance slope to Stowe as a reminder of the house's alien brick construction after 1679*

Trust property with a restaurant on the shore. In fact, the Trust does own that bracing site of the house up on the hill, but it makes no attempt to welcome or explain its possession to visitors.

Stowe explains, better than any social history study, why formal gardens on a grand scale never took on in the Royal Duchy. It would have been widely noticed that they did not adapt well to steep sites and that they tended to be demolished before forty years were out. Here, in the blustery north at Stowe, Nature was never given time to effect a rescue and flatter formal lines into romantic profusion, but in the sheltered, near sub-tropical south at Enys sheer natural fertility and growth has both concealed and preserved the formal planning.

Enys was the seat of a family of that name for centuries and it has been so completely romanticised by benign neglect and Cornwall's natural fertility that its real place now is in the nineteenth or even the twentieth-century chapters. Nevertheless, its structure, beneath all that lushness, was probably laid down in the early eighteenth century by Samuel Enys, who was High Sheriff of the county in 1704 and had married a rich London merchant's daughter. At some point between 1695 and 1709 he and his wife laid out the formal lines around which an expensive re-grooming, in the casual semi-Arcadian style, was begun by John King in 1748.[33] King's suggestions for change in the existing formal layout include:

> The Pond to be filled in and Raisd where the Bowling Green is intended.
> The Parterre to be converted to a Lawn with a walk on each side next the wall 39ft wide

with the border to be enclosed with a thorn hedge and a theatrical Clump of evergreen at ye bottom on each side – levelling planting and bringing to a good lawn – finishing the flower garden £5-0-0.

To finishing the walk each side ye pond, one 20ft ye other 15ft wide, to replant ye trees & pull down & level the Orchard Hedge & put in ye pipe and sluice £15-0-0.[34]

This is all very interesting as an example of how to go about naturalising a formal layout, but was any of this expensive work carried out?[35] A drab illustration of Enys in its grounds, drawn from the west for Borlase's *Natural History of Cornwall* of 1758 (*20*), suggests that it was, but only in part. Borlase shows a long walled garden to the right of the house ending in two quite tall pyramidal-roofed pavilions. In front of these there appears to be a long terrace walk with a much smaller summerhouse at each end. There is, it is true, a broad lawn in front of the typically grim Cornish granite house and some suggestion of a large service building to the rear. But the general impression is one of austere formalism intact, with a little wood or wilderness to the rear.

20 *Borlase's view of Enys in 1758 is proof that under the present romantic tangle of the gardens lie the bones of Samuel Enys' formal layout. The two domed pavilions, their roofs altered and one turned into a house, still stand in the Walled Garden.* Bristol University Special Collections

Very few Cornish gardens fit neatly, like Bochym, into one stylistic chapter, and even Bochym has a Victorian drive with a Gate Lodge, sluices on its stream and a Bog Garden of the nineteenth century. A thorough tour of present day Enys gardens, a 'lost' but still preserved dreamworld, sunken into a perfection of romantic dilapidation, will indicate the complexities surrounding an analysis of such gardens. I am indebted to the Cornwall Gardens Trust for their comprehensive report on Enys,[36] and most of all to the Enys Trust which has realised that here is a truly lost garden that needs to be handled, not as a tourist attraction with boardwalks, notices and café-shop complex like Heligan, but as an infinitely poetic garden in a choice condition of overgrown loveliness, a rare pleasure to be enjoyed in as much selfish solitariness as circumstances will allow.

Before offering my own impression of Enys, I must thank Martin Mattock, the occupant of the Perranarworthal Lodge. Almost single-handed over the years he, as the Trust's officer, has kept the garden at Enys balanced exactly right, just on the edge of ruin, but not tipping over into desolation and not needing some wildly expensive, largely destructive process of restoration. Enys is sometimes open to a discerning public; let us hope that not too many of the public ever notice the open day dates. Gardens need some attention, but they wilt with too much.

Unlike most Cornish country houses Enys has a real 'English' park, spatial not linear in projection, guarding and concealing its large inner core of pleasure grounds from the villages around it. The dreadful condition of some four gravelled and pot-holed drives has been a help. From the Perranarworthal Lodge the most surfaced drive bumps down through fine, though not over-manicured, parkland clumped with mature deciduous trees and specimen conifers. A shelter belt of sweet chestnuts, densely under-planted with rhododendron, is the outer shell that helps to produce Enys' almost frost-free microclimate.

As the drive plunges into the jungle of arboretum and shrubbery, bamboo and magnolia crowd in under towering trees, but there is no sudden Brown-style vision of the house. Instead a deeply shaded cross drive comes in, stocky gatepiers show up, and without warning the service and kitchen yard at the back of the house appears, the main façade still hidden. It is all quite unlike the Borlase view of bare, open landscape. On the right is a clock tower, still keeping time, constructed like a child's toy in a series of afterthoughts with a Caernarvon Gothic arch, Romanesque windows and a slight Renaissance flourish at the top. More afterthought gatepiers stand overshadowed by trees and at last, behind bulging rhododendron clumps, battered rose trellises and well-kept lawn, there is the singularly reserved and unrewarding elevation of the empty but watchful Greek Revival house (*21*).

Rising parkland offers its windows only limited vistas. A little Summerhouse, possibly the one shown near the lawn on the Borlase view, is smothered in bushes on the right, but there is no apparent wide lawn, merely a granite wall and ha-ha ditch to separate the house environs from the park. Down to the left a mossy green track leads to the Lady's or Flower Garden of 1833. Incidents are

21 *Empty, intact, but unrewarding, Enys House fails to live up to its gardens and is an instance of the inhibiting impact of granite on Cornish classical design*

set confusingly down separate shadowed green paths in the pleasure grounds. An old Cornish Cross stands un-revered among bushes to the right. Ahead the vegetation seems impenetrable. To the left, in a clearing, an old stone Cyder Press has been set up like a font on four stone legs. Behind it in a fern and fuchsia wilderness is a large Rockery, but then a sharp downhill bend opens into the ordered vista of the Broad Walk, still with one of the summerhouses, but entirely enclosed, with overgrown bushes of the Rockery on the left and the high walled enclosure of the Kitchen Garden on the right. This is exactly the formally laid out garden of the Borlase illustration; the bones are unchanged, but Rockery, lush borders and mature trees give the impression of a late nineteenth-century garden that has grown attractively out of itself. Rhododendrons and honeysuckle are trying to pull down the little Summerhouse's roof (*22*), magnolia and azalea half hide the long wall and at the far end of the unexpectedly well mown Walk a wisteria has climbed fifty feet up an old conifer. It all survives in a kind of over-ripe, flowery discipline.

Nothing in the gardens at Enys is announced. A turn at the end of the Broad Walk breaks into the vast walled Kitchen Garden lower down the slope. The Crib Hut or Cause Break Hut (*23*) is where the gardeners used to eat their lunch and

22 *The little Summerhouse at one end of the Broad Walk in the grounds at Enys exemplifies the enchanting state of romantic maturity into which the gardens have grown*

23 *The gardeners' Crib Hut at Enys is a perfect time capsule with the Head Gardener's office still visible and many tools still lying around the bench where the gardeners ate their lunch-time 'crib'*

next to it is where the Head Gardener kept his accounts. This is the most humanly moving of Enys' treasures, still richly textured with earthenware flowerpots ranked under the benches and a desk still in the Head Gardener's Office, which is water-tight and still useable. On the back wall one vine grows in the shattered frame, but what catches the eye most are those two tall pavilions shown on the Borlase print (*colour plate 7*). They are designed in a peculiarly nonconformist, severe, early eighteenth-century classicism with cambered-headed window openings, now either blocked or with later, nineteenth-century window frames. One, the Apple Store, is quite intact; the other has been transformed, with window architraves in a polychromatic brick Bzyantine manner, into a Gardener's Cottage, empty but still a desirable residence if someone wanted to take over again. Chickens and chicks run everywhere, producing surely the most wholesome and organic eggs.

The geography of Enys is confusing to anyone expecting the bare geometry of Borlase. From these enclosed areas a track leads out to more open parkland with the extraordinary Apprentice Tree. This is a copper beech to which an ordinary beech has been grafted half way up its trunk as, apparently, a traditional test of the skill of an aspiring young gardener. One beech spreads out sideways, the other soars, beech-like upwards as if contemptuous of its parasite growth. Then, unexpected and out of sight down a hillside from the Borlase print, comes the most idyllic garden at Enys. Down a steep, densely wooded slope is a terrace of water pools, the long, rectangular formal equivalent of the Broad Walk with the 'walk each side ye pond' that John King promised in 1748, not to lay out, but to finish: proof that these pools were part of an earlier geometric layout.[37] The first is long, islanded and noisy with the sound of falling streams. Early photographs prove that it once supported a boat, and it still supports some sinister gunnera (*24*). The water is dark yet completely clear and starred with very pale green weed: a perfect setting for the Pre-Raphaelite drowning of Ophelia with water iris flowering tastefully. Halfway along the flanking walk, with brown trout leaping on one side, a vast waterwheel skulks in among the trees. It was once turned by a leat that still runs noisily and its waters were refined at a small wrecked filter-house that then pumped them up to a tank on the roof of the main house. If it worked again it would deliver mud and newts. That leat runs fast below the terrace on its way to a tidal creek; at terrace level a second pond brims chuckling water down. Beech and eucalyptus tower up; there are no vistas in Enys; the magic of the garden is its sense of wet, leafy enclosure, of rare plants proving a little too successful.

After the two long pools of the Water Garden, a timber road that runs from one end of this still living estate to the other, leads back up to the service yard with its perfectly useable granite piggery and another rare relic, a wooden horse wheel that a pony could still easily turn. It is all lyrically forlorn, but one hopes no fairy prince will ever come to wake this sleeping beauty. Let her drowse on, drip-fed.

24 *The two formal canals at Enys preserve a waterwheel, a filter house and a leat alive with the sound of falling water. Beside them run 'the walk each side ye pond' that John King contracted to lay out in 1748, late for such formal planning*

It comes as a strange compliment that the Dutch navy call their mess hall the Enys Hall. They took refuge here during the 1939-45 war, attracted perhaps by the terrace of pools, but more likely by the close proximity of Falmouth. The concrete bases of their Nissen huts still scar the service yard.

But did the early eighteenth-century formal grounds ever give way wholly to King's recommendations of 1748? On the evidence of the Pavilions, the Kitchen Garden, the Broad Walk and the Water Garden, probably not. It was during the nineteenth century, when one of the last of the Enys family, J.D. Enys, became a much travelled plant collector, that an exotic jungle of bamboos, magnolias and camellias transformed the bare reaches of the garden shown on the Borlase view. J.D. Enys made a speciality of New Zealand flora and it is appropriate that the Chatham Island forget-me-not, *Mysiotidium hortensia*, still grows in Martin Mattock's lodge-keeper's garden. Long may the grounds of Enys flourish almost untrimmed, but its lawns mown.

4

The problem of Arcadian gardens in a naturally Arcadian county

In Cornwall it may be arguable, the county being so dedicated to massed ranks of flowering shrubs, but in the rest of England and on the European continent it is widely accepted that this country's foremost contribution to garden styling was the Arcadia, the *Jardin Anglais*, which we evolved in the first half of the eighteenth century and passed on to other countries in the second half. Some fifty years after the death, in 1682, of the French, Rome-based, painter, Claude Lorraine, the English aristocracy, who had been collecting his paintings, along with those of Annibale Carracci, the two Poussins and their several followers, began to realise that a well-wooded tract of parkland, preferably including, as in a Claude, a lake and a dramatic, moderately sized hill, could be vastly enlivened and made to advertise their own cultural background by the addition of one of Claude's temples, built at a visually strategic site.

A natural advance from creating this pleasing, if manifestly false, air of the historic past was to copy Claude even further by adding a Gothic ruin to evoke England's, as opposed to Rome's, glorious history. This eclectic practice caught on, not only because the visual results were widely admired and much visited, but because these eclectic garden buildings provided picnic places, pheasantries, rooms for private trysts and general escape routes into privacy, away from the eyes and the gossip of servants. French, German, Russian and Scandinavian aristocrats followed suit and eclectic fancy soon extended to Chinese pavilions, Turkish tents and Druidic stone circles.[1]

Cornwall got off to an early start with a lively, if unusually compact Arcadia at Prideaux Place on the hill above Padstow. Edmund Prideaux, who had inherited the house from a cousin in 1728, was an amateur artist and scholar whose detailed drawings reveal a lively awareness of contemporary garden design in England and Italy. In the same year that he inherited the house Robert Castell's *Villas of the Ancients Illustrated* was published, subsidised by Lord Burlington.[2] Castell's impressive reconstructions of the younger Pliny's villa gardens at Laurentinum and Tuscum had a more immediate influence on English garden design than Claude's paintings because Castell offered detailed ground plans which included formal areas with avenues and exedrae linked to the villa, and other areas which, with carefully contrived streams and rocky hills, were exaggeratedly natural. His book served to lure landowners by easy steps from the Franco-Dutch formalism of the seventeenth century into Claudeian gardens with temples. There was thus a semi-formal interlude of gardens between the old seventeenth-century formalism and the new eighteenth-century Arcadias. Lord Burlington's gardens at Chiswick, where he was being coaxed into the emerging fashion by William Kent, fit into this interlude and so does Edmund Prideaux's new layout at Padstow. That makes it particularly interesting, not merely in Cornwall, but nationally. Burlington and Kent were experimenting with exedras, obelisks and temples in the grounds of Chiswick in the 1730s, as was Frederick, Prince of Wales at Carlton House in the same decade. So Edmund Prideaux's modest garden works (25) were surprisingly fashionable and aware for such a remote county, but he was an unusually well travelled and observant garden fancier.

25 *Edmund Prideaux's drawing of his own Prideaux Place proves that in the 1730s he was gardening with Portico, Obelisk and pyramidal evergreens on the rigid lines suggested in Robert Castell's 1728* Villas of the Ancients, *like his contemporary Lord Burlington at Chiswick.* From the collection at Prideaux Place

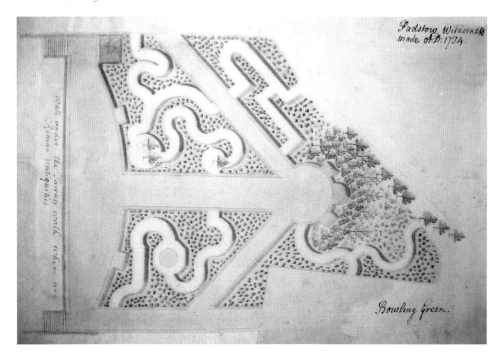

26 *For his* Wilderness *design Edmund Prideaux has followed closely the winding paths illustrated in Batty Langley's* New Principles of Gardening *of 1728.* From the collection at Prideaux Place

27 *On and around this classical Exedra of Antiquities, Prideaux displayed the Roman fragments he had acquired during his Italian travels in 1739*

His account book records, on 1 January 1739: 'To Allen for stone as by bill, 15-17-0', so he was escaping from the limitations of granite to Ralph Allen's Bath limestone; and on 17 January: 'To Mr Richard Broad freestone mason for work done in my garden…working and fitting ye Temple, Obelisk, stone seats, etc., 25.0.0.'[3] Equally interesting is Prideaux's sketch of a Wilderness (*26*) of broad, winding paths laid out next to his Exedra of Roman Antiquities: those little slabs of inscribed marble and carvings which he had collected in 1739 on an Italian tour. This Wilderness follows very closely the designs in Batty Langley's *New Principles of Gardening*, a book published by the Twickenham-based nurseryman and designer in 1728, the year of Castell's *Villas of the Ancients* and the year when Prideaux inherited the Place. It seems likely that Prideaux had read both books and been intending to copy some of their designs for ten years, but it is curious that he finally undertook the work immediately before leaving for Italy, possibly to avoid the chaos of masons working under his windows. All his additions: an Obelisk, now lost, the Temple Portico and the Exedra of Antiquities are sited within a stone's throw of each other and very near the house.

The compact nature of the Place garden is evident today. Entrance from the road is not by a lodge, but by an atmospheric scene-setter, a playfully fortified gateway of dark local stone, overshadowed by mature trees. Impressions then pile in thick and fast. On the right of the very short drive is a fortress wall, battlemented but only a few feet high, a toy which nevertheless commands the lawn. On the left is a rough, round-arched Grotto and now the Gothicised house is in full view on a broad Castell-like terrace, but with Prideaux's little Ionic Temple tucked incongruously close to it. A glance back over the shoulder will reveal the terrace's termination in a Castell-style Exedra with those dutifully collected antiquities set into its side, souvenirs of that 1739 Italian tour (*27*). It is probably no coincidence that the grounds of Stourhead and those of Prideaux Place were both laid out by men who had made their Italian Grand Tours unusually late in their lives, when they were mature and consciously absorbing visual effects which they could reproduce in Arcadias on their return. On either side of the Exedra is an urn and on the lawn a classical bust. But before all this Roman show can be digested the visitor has entered the stable yard thick with Gothick detail of quatrefoils, dripstones and arrow-slits. These are charming fakes, redolent of the 1740s, but in fact very old-fashioned work of 1818 by the Revd. Charles Prideaux-Brune and nothing to do with the classically-minded Edmund. Eclecticism can become a habit in a house.

The Batty Langley-style Wilderness and Edmund's Obelisk have gone, and my own impressions of the garden are coloured by viewing it in a fierce October gale, when I narrowly missed being crushed by a massive branch torn from one of the storm-vulnerable cedars. But for anyone wanting to understand the impact of Castell on English landscaping, Prideaux Place is a must.

In addition to the Gothick evocation of the lost St Petroc's Priory and the classical striving of Edmund's garden buildings, there is a more local Cornish echo in the fortifications. No Cornish gentleman would forget that, while the Armada may have failed, the Spaniards in 1595 still captured and burnt down Penzance. Padstow had its shore battery for protection; and gun batteries are an eclectic feature of Cornish Arcadias, ranking alongside all those Celtic crosses filched from roadsides. Port Eliot garden has its battery and a Battery Cottage, Mount Edgcumbe has two batteries and a coastal fort. St Michael's Mount has a 1940 concrete pillbox on its garden shore, in design not unlike Henry VIII's Blockhouse of 1545 on the shore garden at Mount Edgcumbe. Cornwall was and still is a frontline county.

When I was working on the gardens of Dorset I was struck by the way the county's landowners, with the honourable exception of William Benson on Brownsea Island, John Pitt of Encombe and George Burt at Durlston, had ignored the landscape possibilities of a superb coastline. Gentry of the eighteenth century would have been aware that Pliny's second villa was so close to the sea, near Ostia, that Pliny could hear the waves breaking as he lay in bed. But for a classically educated maritime nation we have rarely put the sea and classical precedent together in landscape compositions. There is, however, a multi-purpose summerhouse at Kenegie, near Penzance, now isolated absurdly in a park of holiday chalets. This originally looked out to sea on one side and commanded a Bowling Green on the other.[4]

Claude's paintings give little help in how to handle high, rocky cliffs in a view, but in the Tamar estuary, with all its winding creeks and bays, the sea in a tamed mood interpenetrates the land with bewitchingly Claudeian possibilities of trees, green slopes and shining water. Consequently most of Cornwall's eighteenth-century Arcadian parks are clustered along the Tamar, rather as Palladio's villas often fringe the banks of the Brenta. Working downstream there is Cotehele, where only a late medieval chapel relates to the river, in memory of an Edgcumbe's escape from his pursuers by pretending to have drowned. But then comes Pentillie Castle with a long, typically Cornish, landscaping drive looping downhill from the finely situated house to touch the quay on the Tamar and then curve back up again.[5]

Sometime before his death in 1712 Sir James Tillie built a Pleasure Pavilion, a viewing tower on a hill just north of the Castle. Edmund Prideaux illustrated it standing quite bare of trees, with another, larger tower next to the Castle (28). Scandalously, Sir James had a statue of himself carved sitting in a chair and arranged to be buried underneath it in the lower room of the Tower with, so the story goes, wine and food laid out before him. The Tower and the statue are still there up on Mount Ararat, though shrouded now with trees and in an inaccessible part of a very private estate. The interesting comment in Gilbert is that 'in the room above, Sir James Tillie had perhaps enjoyed the most happy hours of his life'.[6] This suggests that the Tower was, as first conceived, an Arcadian park building in no way formally related to the gardens. The house, with another of those Doric entrance loggias that Godolphin inspired, is dated

28 *Prideaux's sketch of Pentillie Castle taken from the Tamar explains why the river was the popular focus of eighteenth-century excursions. Only Sir James Tillie's pavilion and tomb, on the far right, survives, though cloaked in dense woodland.* From the collection at Prideaux Place

1698, which might offer a starting date for the Mount Ararat Tower.

Further down the widening Tamar with its own quay of granite bollards is Moditonham House. There are frail traces among its huge beech trees of an Arcadian Wilderness Walk next to its Walled Garden. When Gilbert visited there around 1815 he noted shrubberies

> occasionally intermixed with neat walls, the edges of which are embellished with innumerable flowers; and in the sudden windings, are frequently discovered small rustic buildings, incrusted with moss, lighted with stained glass, and over-hung with clustering ivy,[7]

which sounds like an archetypal Arcadia; and those moss houses were a feature of William Beckford's Fonthill gardens in Wiltshire. Little remains today of that rough Wilderness except box bushes and some stands of bamboo, with the ubiquitous montbretia and fuchsia. But twin Gothick Lodges, trim as china mantelpiece ornaments, curve their ogee windows on the drive and the 'beautiful Gothic tower, with a cupola and a clock' noted by Gilbert serves now with its arches and arrow-slits as a Pigeon House.[8] Moditonham House itself is strictly classical so it does seem that the Gothickry of stained glass and ogee curves was an escape from domestic propriety to fantasy satisfaction out in the grounds.

After Moditonham the Tamar passes under the two discordant bridges at Saltash and the Lynher estuary comes in from the west, bordered by the gardens of Antony, Trematon Castle, Ince Castle and Cornwall's most graciously perfect park and garden at Port Eliot on the St Germans peninsula. Straight ahead on yet another peninsula of this favoured tidal zone is Mount Edgcumbe. Its park was enclosed by Sir Richard Edgcumbe in 1550 when he shrewdly abandoned backwoods Cotehele to build his vast white wedding cake of a house to command Plymouth and all the maritime bustle of The Sound.

It is not possible to be as precise in the dating of Mount Edgcumbe's response to national garden trends as it is at Prideaux Place; but two 1730s' views of the grounds by Badeslade indicate that the Edgcumbes were going through much the same garden fashions as the Prideaux and at much the same time. There is, however, no comparison in national importance between the two houses. Prideaux Place was a gentry house in a small port; Mount Edgcumbe was by 1789 the seat of a prestigious earl and virtually the viceregal lodge of the West, a house and garden visited by monarchs, heroic admirals and well-known writers, an inescapable destination on any tour of the West Country. The garden and the park of Mount Edgcumbe, two quite distinct units, achieve the Arcadian ideal more completely than any others in England, with the exceptions of Stourhead and Studley Royal, and even those two grounds lack the picturesque drama of a rocky yet densely wooded coast.

To emphasise Mount Edgcumbe's unique visual impact before listing its many charms, nothing serves better than the rapturous letter which William Beckford, the richest and most unwisely romantic young man in England, the future builder of mythic Fonthill Abbey, wrote after his visit of 1781. He was travelling in the company of the celebrated Italian castrato singer, Gasparo Pacchierotti, who had been hired to sing at Beckford's expensive twenty-first birthday party. Dated 17 October, the letter needs to be quoted at length to convey quite what an intense spiritual experience an Arcadian garden in its prime could offer to someone prepared to enter into its evocations:

> Here I am breathing the soft air of Mount Edgcumbe standing upon the brink of a Cliff overlooking the Sea and singing *Notturnos* with Pacchierotti. Innumerable Insects are humming about the Myrtles and Arbutus which hang on the steeps and are covered with blossoms. I cannot help thinking myself in an Isle of the Atlantic Ocean – to which if we believe Pindar and his poetic Bretheren the Souls of Heroes are transported….I have visited all my old haunts and paid my oblations at a Spring that I am certain is the result of Sylvanus. Would that you could see me bounding along the Terrace which hangs bold and free above the Ocean. You would almost apprehend I should trust myself to the Air and leap off the edge of the precipices.
>
> We have been blessed to-day with a Sky of the purest Azure and soft breezes like those of Spring. I have been up and down and everywhere upon the Rocks. No creek, no Crevice, I believe have been left unexplored. You would delight in the picturesque fragments – the crooked pines and luxuriant shrubs amongst which I have passed my Day.

Pacchierotti, as happy and enraptured as myself, does nothing but sing and thank Heaven that he has entered a Region so like his Native Italy.[9]

Significantly, Beckford responded to the myrtles, arbutus and the 'luxuriant shrubs' of October, but makes no mention of the numerous garden buildings. He was writing in 1781 when the Arcadian mood was lapsing into that of the so-called 'American gardens', where flowering shrubs, not temples, were the attraction. Beckford would go on to plant a vast and much admired American Garden around Fonthill Abbey with wooden, not stone, garden pavilions. However, the emphasis upon Sylvanus and the classical Arcadian world, as in Milton's

In shadier bower
More sacred and sequestered, though but feigned,
Pan or *Silvanus* never slept, nor Nymph,
Nor *Faunus* haunted.[10]

still underlies the rapture over flowering bushes. This is natural because Mount Edgcumbe has a 1755 Temple actually dedicated to Milton by Richard, 1st Lord Edgcumbe with an inscription from *Paradise Lost* to evoke the Amphitheatre of trees in which it is built:

A sylvan scene, and as the ranks ascend
Shade above shade, a woody theatre
Of stateliest view.[11]

Previously that area of the grounds had been laid out, as Celia Fiennes described it in 1695: 'There is a fine terrass and a sumer house at each end'.[12] Badeslade drew the area in his 1737 bird's-eye view of the estate (*29*), which was based on an estate map of 1729, in an old-fashioned formal manner, showing it surviving exactly as Fiennes had described it. This means that, in addition to Castell's reconstructions of Roman villa gardens and Claude's paintings, Milton's description of the Garden of Eden was also influencing early eighteenth-century garden designs. Poets were beginning to count in garden directions.

Badeslade's slightly earlier, 1735, view of Lord Edgcumbe entertaining his guests in front of the Garden House (*30*) shows an amazingly primitive Doric pavilion of 1729, with a pronounced entasis, copied from a door on the Temple of Vesta at Tivoli, as illustrated by Palladio in his *Four Books of Architecture*.[13] It is set, Castell-wise, in a geometrical, revetted clearing of conifers, which indicates that Lord Edgcumbe had moved even faster than Edmund Prideaux to copy the fashion being set by Burlington and Castell at Chiswick.

Today it is essential to approach Mount Edgcumbe's gardens as victorious eighteenth-century admirals and their officers would have approached them, by

29 *A detail from Badeslade's 1737 view of Mount Edgcumbe illustrating the seventeenth-century formal garden fronting the sea shore with one of its twin Summerhouses.* Mount Edgcumbe House & Country Park

the ferry from Stonehouse to Cremyll, there to be entertained to a reception, not at the house, but at the great Orangery in the Lower Garden. After some experiences with jolly sailors rather the worse for drink, the Edgcumbes wisely decided to create a special reception area well away from the house and near enough to the ferry to enable drunken midshipmen to stagger back unsupported. This has resulted in a garden as unusual as it is beautiful, a situation described by Dr Johnson as the second noblest in Britain.

The house itself has changed far more than the gardens. Now it stands as a stumpy castle in a grim marmalade-coloured sandstone at the top of a straight, formal avenue, far too steep, like that eastern approach to Stowe, for any carriage drive. The house was originally brilliant in white stucco, with a pinnacled central hall soaring up like a keep above its side towers; but the stucco was removed in the nineteenth century and German bombs destroyed the central hall. A chain of three formal pools linked by cascades to the right-hand side of the avenue has been largely filled in. What has survived on level ground near the ferry is the deceptively entitled 'Formal' or 'Lower Garden', which is anything but solemn or orderly. Instead a deliciously confused Arcadia was developed there during the two long reigns of Richard, 1st Baron Edgcumbe (1688-1758), and George, 3rd

30 *Badeslade's 1735 drawing of the Garden House in the Lower Garden at Mount Edgcumbe with Richard Edgcumbe entertaining his guests. Wings have since been added to it, but the dense pine groves that hem it in have gone.* Mount Edgcumbe House & Country Park

Baron and 1st Earl of Edgcumbe (1761-95), with a brisk four-year interlude of Richard, the short-lived 2nd Baron.

The 1st Baron Edgcumbe allowed the outer park gardens to evolve from an area of coniferous Wilderness with formal avenues into an early Arcadia with the Gothic Ruin (1747) and Milton's Temple (1755). In the brief but hyperactive reign of the 2nd Baron, who was a friend of Horace Walpole, Thomson's Seat was built with its poetic references, and the Zig-Zag paths were laid out and planted with the arbutus, myrtles and laurustinus that so delighted William Beckford twenty years later. All these features, particularly the Zig-Zag paths, are shown in a large engraved view of the estate by Copplestone Warre Bampfylde of Hestercombe published on 5 May 1755.[14] Walpole's Strawberry Hill at Twickenham was similarly planted with scented flowering shrubs.[15]

'Admiral George', the 3rd Baron and 1st Earl, built seats and arches at commanding viewpoints, but his best achievements were the English Garden of 1770 and the great Orangery in the Italian Garden, large enough to feast a whole ship's company, designed by Thomas Pitt, Lord Camelford and constructed between 1786 and 1787.[16] Most Arcadias depend upon eclectic garden buildings for their appeal; in this formal sector at Mount Edgcumbe it is the interlocking chain of eclectic gardens that makes it such a visual adventure. Starting with Earl George's delicately pompous Italian Garden, winding paths lead through a New Zealand Garden of 1989 with a working geyser, and an American Garden of the same date, into the 1770 English Garden, the Fern Dell of 1789, the French Garden of 1803 with, as a satisfying climax, the Great Hedge of towering *Quercus ilex* sheltering the seventeenth-century Bowling Green from the one direction from which no winds are likely to blow, the south-west which is sheltered by the hill.

That is the bare list of the Lower Garden's many units, but they are full of individual garden pleasures. The English Garden is a beguiling exercise in how to handle precious specimen trees without turning an area into a dreary arboretum. Its Garden House strikes a perfect Grecian note, whilst the strangest and most venerably senile of trees, an aged cork oak, sprawls its limbs helplessly across the entry path to a lawn with a Foxglove tree, an Indian bean tree and a Japanese red cedar. A rose garden that lies to one side is predictable and the Fern Dell is a little seedy, too dry and lacking deep shade. The French Garden has a triple Pavilion with two conservatories flanking an octagon where a circular mirror repeats the geometry of box hedges outside. In the Queen's Millennium Garden the hornbeams have yet to grow into much character. Visitors will keep returning to the Italian Garden, the only truly formal area in the whole supposedly formal garden. In the centre of its four gravelled walks mermaids twist their tails in the fountain gifted by Lord Bessborough to his godson, the 2nd Earl, in 1809 (*31*). By 1819 there were statues centring each of the four flowerbeds of this area, the beds being planted out with herbaceous plants. Now only the Victorian-style bedding flowers introduced after the 1939-45 War remain.[17] Venus, Apollo and Bacchus flaunt their seductive nudities in statues on the balustraded terrace (*colour plate 8*) and a large bust of Ariosto fills the niche below them, smirking arrogantly at being placed as the centrepiece of Imperial stairways for no apparent symbolic reason. What has Ariosto's epic poem, *Orlando furioso*, to do with gardens?

This Lower Garden alone could take an hour to explore and it is only the beginning of what Mount Edgcumbe has to offer, the garden to a park that fills most of the peninsula south of Millbrook. A path along the shore leads into the Pleasure Ground past the two Batteries of 1747 and 1863 with the Henrician Blockhouse behind them.[18] A pool for many brown ducks introduces the Amphitheatre with its circular Milton Temple. Climbing steeply beside the temple the way mounts up through Spanish chestnut and oak woods to a hillside entirely open to striking views flawed only by the depressing hulks of Plymouth's post-war council housing. At one time that naval city and Mount Edgcumbe must have set each other off perfectly, with suave Regency housing on one side of The Sound and elegant garden artifice on the other; but the city has not kept its side of the visual bargain.

This is where viewing seats and vistas begin to take over the direction and where Mount Edgcumbe's present day civic guardians, who have so faithfully preserved and enriched the Lower Garden, have faltered in their duty of care.[19]

Lord Richard's Gothic Ruin works splendidly, dramatic as a Cornish tin mine in profile, yet convincing in its traceried detail. But then the woods close in and the intended vistas are missing. Lady Emma's Cottage is a feeble half-timbered affair of 1882, more suited to a Cheshire suburb. After the Cottage there should be a chain of seats: 'Red', 'White' and 'Picklecombe'. At each one a visitor was supposed to sit and admire the view, carefully composed down an open glade through the trees. They were considered the glories of this wilder park: 'by far the finest situation I ever saw, exceeding everything in the beauty of the near prospects…one of the most beautiful landscapes that can be conceived', wrote Bishop Pococke on 4 October 1750.[20]

Unfortunately ecological correctness and Gaia worship has made the cutting down of trees into a new mortal sin; even trimming them back is a wounding. As a result every vista out to sea has been lost. To make matters much worse the level terrace that used to lead in stately progress to the flowering Zig-Zag paths has been blocked by landslides. A dull detour path has been created, muddy,

31 *The Mermaid Fountain in the Italian Garden at Mount Edgcumbe was the gift of Lord Bessborough in 1809*

arduous and visually unrewarding. So a choice has to be made. The Earl's Drive leads on along the coast past Cawsand, which effectively returns visitors to the ordinary world and breaks the historic park. Further on is Queen Adelaide's uninteresting Grotto out on Penlee Point. Alternatively it is easier to wheel back across open fields to Mount Edgcumbe House.

On the Badeslade bird's-eye view of 1737 the House stood on a broad empty terrace leading eventually to a viewing circle above the Amphitheatre. Flowerbeds have been planted on the terrace since the 1790s and, on the hillside above, the 1770s Shell Seat, its shells and fossils unusually geometric and linear in their disposition, directs the eye into a thoughtful composition of specimen trees on the Cedar Lawn backed by one of the two arcaded Summerhouses of the Earl's Garden. It is not many parks that can boast of two separate Arcadias, the lower one incident-crammed, this upper one open and preciously refined. Today it is hard to recapture the wild delight that seized William Beckford on his 1781 visit. The seashore is not integrated visually with the walls and gardens now as it was then; but it is still very easy to sense how, even in this enclosure of Devon, Cornish gardeners were moving away from gardens articulated by buildings to gardens that worked around the character of the planting. If Mount Edgcumbe is kept in mind then the subtle shift of emphasis to Port Eliot, the county's second great peninsula garden discussed in the next chapter, will seem a natural step in Cornwall's unique and distinctive garden development.

First, though, must come Werrington Park, the county's tragic lost Arcadia, the garden which, had it not been dismantled by the plant-obsessed Williams family of Caerhays, who bought it in 1882, would have rivalled Wiltshire's Stourhead. Werrington lies just to the north of Launceston, in the long, open valley of the river Ottery, finely wooded, particularly on the south side facing the house. Its garden front has a big double viewing bow in the Sir Robert Taylor-style of the 1750s-60s from which the Morice family, Sir William and Nicholas his son who succeeded him, could enjoy what they had achieved in the valley below them. Sir Nicholas died in 1726. He was the son of Sir William Morice, the 1st Baronet, and he married Catherine, daughter of the Earl of Pembroke. But as the Pembrokes had little connection with the landscape designer, William Kent, and as Kent only returned to England in 1719, it is unlikely, as some have speculated, that he had anything to do with Sir Nicholas's improvements. The 3rd Baronet, the second Sir William, who rebuilt the parish church and died in 1750, is the more likely creator of the garden buildings.

The Ottery was diverted by a weir to fill a fine serpentine lake and Gilbert's plate shows the grand bridge, balustraded and topped by four urns, which carried the drive up from the South Lodge (*32*). On the southern hill a triple-pierced Triumphal Arch took the visual directions. Bishop Pococke, visiting in 1750, thought the park 'beautifully improved in wood and lawn … one of the most beautiful in England'.[21] Sir William Morice, the 3rd Baronet, had built a Temple of the Sun; below the Triumphal Arch was 'a hermitage, like that at

32 *This is Gilbert's view of the Arcadian layout at Werrington, probably Cornwall's most serious loss of a fine landscape garden. Visiting in 1750, Bishop Pococke thought it one of the most beautiful in England.* Bristol University Special Collections

Richmond',[22] which William Kent had designed for Queen Caroline, and to the side of it in the woods was the Tomb of the Horatii and Curiatii. This is known locally as the Sugar Loaves from its three odd, twenty-five foot cones, modelled on a Roman monument at Albano.[23] Stoke Park, outside Bristol, and Studley Royal in Yorkshire had other eighteenth-century copies of the Tomb.[24] Above the Temple of the Sun was 'a ruinous castle',[25] and on the northern, house side of the valley was the Warren House, which was much older. When the 1st Duke of Northumberland bought Werrington, in order to control another rotten borough in Parliament, he was impressed enough to add a second, Duchess's, Bridge and to build another temple.

Gilbert admired the 'abrupt knolls, covered with foliage, which shade the waters that are seen winding among the rocks below', but took against the new church which Sir William had built away from its old site next to the house to stand as a park marker on the skyline; he dismissed it as 'an incongruous imitation of the florid Gothic'.[26] Ironically the church is the one park building that has survived to prove the quality of what the Williams family left to decay. It is, despite Gilbert's assessment, a committed and ambitious building of the early Gothick revival, of 1742, with a trio of towers at the west end and twelve statues of the Apostles standing in Rococo-Gothick niches. Inexplicably the latest Cornwall volume of the *Buildings of England* series ignores the entire parish, church, house and park, possibly because, like Mount Edgcumbe, it was once partly in Devon.

Trelowarren's gardens are unusually inconclusive for such an old and important country house on an old site. It belonged to King Harold before Hastings and has another ecclesiastical building in an enchantingly playful Gothick style, built in the 1750s by Sir Richard Vyvyan, the 5th Baronet. A pupil of Dr William Borlase of Ludgvan Rectory,[27] he commissioned that rarest of Cornish gardens: an Arcadian wilderness with a temple laid out over an existing formal axis parallel with the Chapel. This is recorded in an estate map by Dionysius Williams.[28] The formal terrace survives today, but the twin intertwined serpentine walks through the wood and a small pond with three islands have all gone. Those woodland walks sound like features from William Mason's *The English Garden* of 1783, as in:

> then Nature glads our eye
> Sporting in all her lovely carelessness.
> There smiles in varied tufts the velvet rose,
> There flaunts the gadding woodbine, swells the ground
> In gentle hillocks, and around its sides
> Thro' blossom'd shades the secret pathway steals.[29]

Something very like the mid-eighteenth-century garden at Trelowarren still exists and has been carefully restored at Heligan. This is on the east side of the Northern Gardens, laid out for Henry Hawkins Tremayne, where paths wind through woodland leading to a modest Crystal Grotto, a Gothic Wishing Well, a viewing Mount and, ultimately, to the northern Summerhouse.[30]

There are a number of lesser Arcadias in the county. One, perhaps not the most visually ambitious, is still interesting because it was laid out in the 1740s by Charlotte, the Dowager Lady Falmouth, to celebrate King Arthur. It should be seen, therefore, as an instance of eclectic historicism, of a feeling for Cornwall's Celtic past like those roadside crosses that feature in so many Cornish gardens. Lady Falmouth's dower house was Worthyvale Manor, near Slaughterbridge, and one of several conflicting legends relates that King Arthur's last battle, the eponymous 'Slaughter', was fought on the banks of the river Camel as it flows down to Camelford, which may have been Arthur's Camelot. A little path, nicely graded, runs parallel to the drive up to Worthyvale, winding its way among the trees on the steep banks of the small stream. Recent excavations have revealed a cobbled area, of quartz stones, possibly all that is left of a Temple Seat from which modest vistas could be enjoyed. But the climax of the Arthurian path and the *raison d'être* of the complex is Arthur's Stone (*33*). This now lies atmospherically low down in the waters and mud of the Camel, a massive nine-foot block, like an outsized gatepier. It is inscribed confusingly, partly in broken Latin, partly in Ogham script. Variously interpreted the fragmentary record seems to read:

33 *Now lying forlorn in the bed of the Camel, this is the mysterious Arthurian stone around which the Dowager Lady Falmouth created in the 1740s a little Arcadia garden at Worthyvale Manor, Slaughterbridge*

LATIN HIC IACET FILIUS MAGNI ARTURI ('Here lies Latinus the son of Arthur the Great'). William Borlase, writing in 1754, the year of Lady Falmouth's death, recorded that

> A few years since, the present Lady Dowager Falmouth, shaping a rough kind of hill, about 100 yards off, into spiral walks, remov'd this Stone from the place where it serv'd as a bridge, and building a low piece of masonry for it's support, plac'd it at the foot of her improvements.[31]

The stone and its curious inscription had already been the subject of a letter in the *Gentleman's Magazine* of June 1745.[32] In Borlase's time the stone lay 'in one of the natural grotts of the hill',[33] another instance of the Cornish fondness for little cave features in gardens.

There were other such gestures in the Claudeian direction rather than full-blown schemes. Gilbert reported a shrubbery, Italian fountain, temple, canal and hot houses at Whiteford House, Stoke Climsland.[34] These are all gone, like Whiteford House itself, built on the wealth Sir John Call had earned after twenty years in the service of the East India Company.[35] But the Walled Gardens survive with a plain, pyramidal-roofed Garden House. Up the hill above them is a bold Temple with a three-arched Palladian loggia, Arcadian in function, to view and be viewed. Two exquisitely detailed

Coade stone reliefs (*colour plate 9*) set into its wings are dated 'Lambeth 1799'. These celebrate the sources of Sir John's wealth, India and America, by name. In one a now headless Ceres holds sheaves of corn and in the other an elegantly lolling nymph reclines on bales of spices while behind her a carefully composed three-masted East Indiaman sails the seas. Such is the delicacy of their detailing and precise lettering that there is a possibility that Sir John, who had gone blind in 1795, commissioned them as a triumphant Braille-like memorial to his lifetime's achievements. They are at hand-level on the façade and when he was brought up here to enjoy the air he could easily have run his hands over their inscribed surfaces. This Temple-Loggia, a rare structure in Cornwall, is not the temple mentioned by Gilbert. When Pevsner saw it in 1951 it had declined into a half-ruined cow byre up on its lonely hillside until the Landmark Trust rescued it in their usual generous and imaginative style.[36]

There was also a temple at Clowance, near Praze-an-Beeble, with an interior richly decorated with spars and mineral ores; this has been recently demolished in the Williams tradition, though its back wall survives. Given its unusual geology Cornish gardens run more to grottoes than to temples. Trebartha at Northill has a Grotto-Boathouse hollowed out of a viewing mound on the shores of its mournfully lovely Swan Pool.[37] But perhaps the most spectacular eighteenth-century grotto in the county was the Fossillary at Pendarves House, Camborne. Borlase illustrates the garden front of the house in his *Natural History* with its ha-ha and Exedra of six classical statues on plinths (*34*) and then, in discussing the local minerals and crystals of the area, continues:

> Mrs Grace Percival of Pendarves ... has offered us a fair pattern, by fixing side by side in her Fossillary an infinite number of crystals of various and the clearest waters, in all shapes, single and in clusters, mostly out of mines in her own lands, all out of her neighbourhood. So many rich subjects will well remunerate the attentive inspection of every inquisitive Fossilist.[38]

So famous was this grotto-maker that the Revd. Mr Moore published some 'Verses occasioned by seeing the fossilry at Pendarves in Cornwall' in the *Gentleman's Magazine* of 1755:

> *Stones* of all colours, and of various size,
> Diffusive shed their intermingling dies:
> Rich veins of glitt'ring *tin*, the rocks unfold,
> Or *copper* mark'd with radiant streaks of *gold*;
> In diff'rent lights, the diff'rent metals shine,
> And the *load* runs as in its <u>*native*</u> mine.[39]

Another grotto, originally one of the tourist sights of the county, was the climax to a semi-Arcadian layout at Menabilly. No garden building in Cornwall attracts a wider range of attributed dates than that Grotto: 1730s, 1750-60, 1780. Philip

34 *Pendarves House, seat of the Percivals, was best known in the mid 1750s for its rich Fossilary or Grotto, but here Borlase illustrates the formal Exedra of classical statues before its dull, granite garden front.* Bristol University Special Collections

Rashleigh, the mineralogist who built it, was born in 1729, so the first date is, to say the least, suspect. He began collecting the rare and beautiful minerals, which now glitter in Truro Museum, in 1765. Did the Grotto come before or after the collecting mania? Either way the mineralogy was, like Chinese tea houses and Cornish crosses, yet another aspect of eclecticism and a growing awareness of global riches and diversity.

When it was whole the Menabilly Grotto was constructed with the finest species of marble and serpentine, brilliant crystals, pebbles and shells, in the form of an octagon, its roof was of 'Stalactytes of singular beauty'[40] and a whale's jaw bones framed its Gothic entrance door.[41] The way down to it from Menabilly House, the Manderley of Daphne du Maurier's *Rebecca*, is overgrown and laurel-ridden today. It offers glimpses of the cove where the yacht sank in the book; in dense undergrowth is a Fernery, a stone-walled trough, dead tree ferns and a rectangular pool that once had swans. An approach via the coastal path from Fowey is more dramatic: a corner of the hill is turned and there below, backed by thick oak woods an entire creek and salt marsh has been converted into a freshwater lake by a stone dam at the beach. Beside the dam is the Grotto Cottage, built to guard those polished agates, jaspers and coraloides; beyond the woods the cliffs rise up to Gribbin Head and the lighthouse. It is one of those rare instances of coast and garden working imaginatively together. Sadly the Grotto is much decayed, roofless and brambled, though its scarred sides are still geologically various and its ruined door, minus those whale bones, opens onto a lawn with sea views.

The Rashleighs were associated with Menacuddle as well as Menabilly, but to move from the latter to the former would be to enter that subtly more natural and native Cornish evolution of the eclectic, Arcadian Picturesque into the Gardenesque; a boundary transgressed already in the Lower Garden at Mount Edgcumbe. Menacuddle is better linked in the next chapter with what, in an admittedly entirely subjective ranking, I believe to be the garden truest to Cornwall's essential topographical nature: the enchanted enclave of Lord St Germans at Port Eliot.

5

Humphry Repton in a county designed for Picturesque gardening

Humphry Repton, the self-appointed heir in landscape gardening of Lancelot 'Capability' Brown, came to Cornwall, a county which Brown never visited, in 1792 to advise on four gardens: Antony on 17 October, Catchfrench on 27 October, Trewarthenick on 30 October and Port Eliot on 2 November. He did not return until August 1809 when he advised on the grounds of Pentillie Castle and Tregothnan. While Repton shared, more or less, Brown's notions on the ideal visuals for a gentleman's 'improved' estate, he was an entirely different kind of person, functioning on his estate visits in a completely different way to Brown.

Brown had been very much a man's man, the son of a north-country farmer, a practical businessman who stood no nonsense from any of his clients, most of whom, from King George III downwards, stood in awe of his expertise. He offered not just advice on the 'capabilities' or potential of any park, but a complete package to realise that potential once a contract had been signed.[1] One of his trained teams of labourers, working under a trusted foreman, would descend on the grounds and, sometimes over a period of several years, they would drain, re-seed, plant belts and clumps of trees, engineer well-graded carriage drives and create new lakes by damming streams and stabilising the resultant banks. Garden buildings were secondary, an extra that could be provided if required. Not surprisingly Brown died a wealthy gentleman with his own country house and estate. He had worked on 170 major commissions, and if the estates are added on which his followers, landscape gardeners like William Emes and Richard Woods, had worked, then Brown can be said to have changed the country face of England and established a park aesthetic; a simplified, but not necessarily classical, Arcadia.

While Brown never actually crossed the Tamar there are at least two parks, Chyverton and Clowance, where Brownian formulas of spatial landscaping have been tried out, successfully in the one, unimaginatively in the other. Chyverton, near Zelah, is a perfect Brownian miniature. It was laid out in the 1770s for, and possibly by, a vice-Warden of the Stannaries, the Truro lawyer, John Thomas, who must have been intelligently aware of Brown's ideal English park aesthetics.

Chyverton lies at the southern base of an inland region where sudden, steep valleys are cloaked in gnarled, moist, goblin woods, mildly threatening as in some Edwardian illustrator's faery fantasy. The house itself sits in an enchanted open hollow surrounded by these dark woodlands and a twenty-foot hedge of myrtle, *Luma apiculata.*[2] It is possible to slip down into its forecourt on a mere fifty-yard turning off a public road, but its main approach drive is ingeniously long, very Brownian, and one that Repton would approve. Coming from a Tudor-style East Lodge through trees, densely under-planted in the last hundred years with camellias, it breaks out to deliver the perfect Arcadian Picturesque surprise view (*colour plate 10*). As it crosses a lily-choked serpentine lake on an elegant, single-arched stone bridge it reveals, up on the far side of a sloping lawn, Chyverton turned to the correct slight angle for drama, a silvery grey Palladian villa with Regency, but still Palladian in style, side pavilions. It is unassuming but confidently assured, absolutely right against a backdrop of mature woodland, very English, but not at all Cornish. So mature are the woods that the oaks have obscured what must originally have been a contrasting Gothic glimpse up from that bridge to a folly tower: Tinker's Castle (originally Hunter's Tower), now Chyverton Castle; it has changed its name as often as it has added to its living accommodation, but at its centre is still an original castellated octagonal tower with more than a hint of Warwick Castle (*35*).

35 *The central octagon of Chyverton Castle was originally visible as a Gothick Folly from the grounds of Chyverton House*

After Chyverton, Clowance is a disappointment. Even though a much larger park, and laid out in the 1770s by a Brown follower, John Nicholls, it has an unhelpful topography of shallow undulations. No circling carriage drive was attempted because there would have been few views to justify one. A large lake surrounded on three sides by woods and enlivened by an island lies down a long easy slope from the St Aubyns' grim, grey house. A fine plane tree on this lawn makes no kind of sense in the composition, and proves that there was a real art to Brown's tree clumping. A stable block next to the main house puts Piers St Aubyn's dismal design to shame. To an unprejudiced eye the new timeshare chalets that star the woods do more to enliven the park than anything of the preceding centuries. There was a temple by a lily pond, but that went in 1955, a bad year for park buildings. Three ancient crosses are standard Cornish park ornaments and the dates of their collecting are interesting. The cross on the lake island came from Bold Gate in 1850, one north of the house was brought from Binnerton in 1883 and the last, which was on an axis with that lost temple, came from Nine Maidens Downs, also in 1883.[3] Presumably a strongly nonconformist population was unmoved by the stripping away of Catholic symbols. Nicholls did nothing to landscape the stream that runs through the south of the park, and the cascade falling from the lake into the King's Pond is a tame affair.

Humphry Repton did more for Cornwall than any Brown disciple. But then, in contrast with Brown, he revered the aristocracy for whom he worked. For Repton happiness was spending two or three days in familiar social intercourse with gentry. He brought deference to a fine art. Seventh heaven for Humphry was sitting in the Duke of Portland's study while the Duke, at that time the Home Secretary, worked on his Cabinet papers offering the occasional wry comment.[4] Repton was an outrageous snob and he saw the landscape of a house as a precise and desirable marker to the class status of its owner. 'Rank and affluence are not crimes in England', he wrote in his Red Book for Antony, 'on the contrary we expect to see a marked difference in the stile, the Equipage, and the mansions of wealthy individuals, and this difference must also be extended to the grounds in the neighbourhood of their mansions, since congruity of stile and unity of Character are the first principles of good Taste'.[5] 'In this Country,' he added with servile relish, 'there will I hope for ever exist different orders and degrees of society.'[6]

While he was a competent surveyor, able to mark out new grounds, Repton could offer no prepared team of skilled labourers. Instead, during his two- or three-day visits there would be hours of discussion and heavy flattery to be followed a couple of months later by the celebrated and highly educational gimmick that has made Repton such a significant figure in garden history: a Red Book.[7] Handwritten in his own copperplate these clarified his spoken suggestions for improvements. Before and after watercolours illustrated key aspects of a park, first as they were when Repton was shown them, then, when a 'slide' or flap of paper was pulled back, as they would look, infinitely more attractive, once

Repton's suggestions had been carried through, with trees strategically clumped, fences and old barns removed, even earthworks carried out to expose new vistas. It would then be left to the owner to follow, reject or modify Repton's schemes. Whatever happened, the recipient would be the possessor of a delightful toy to set conversations flowing in a drawing room. A Red Book was a visual education in itself and, to compare the influence of the two landscape designers, against Capability Brown's 170 commissions, more than 300 Repton Red Books have been traced.[8] They were treasured items and both men worked for the royal family. Repton prepared a brilliant Hindu pastiche Royal Pavilion at Brighton for the Prince Regent, though John Nash's Sino-Muslim design was actually built.[9]

Because he was so quaintly oleaginous it is easy to dwell on Repton's sometimes silly snobbish proposals, like building lodges on a public road to Antony to pretend that it was really a private drive, and then to forget that where his Red Books had fallen on Antony and Port Eliot, two of the most exquisitely refined and memorable garden landscapes were eventually realised largely by following his directions. Of his other Cornish visitations Catchfrench achieved, by massive earth movements, an attractive new view to the west and an atmospheric Quarry Garden; at Trewarthenick a subtle middle ground of trees improved the house's vast view out to the east and at Tregothnan a wonderful web of panoramic drives, perhaps more Cornwall than Repton but very fine, followed his visit. Only Pentillie was a disappointment.

Pentillie Castle once rose like Windsor Castle with a tremendous profile of towers on a steep hill above the Tamar, a favourite spectacle for visitors on boat trips up and down the river. What Repton advised for this sensational site is not yet known, as the Red Book is held at the house and inaccessible. But the current planting on the hill is unremarkable and successive owners have demolished, first the towers that the sketch by Prideaux and Peacock's *Polite Repository* recorded, and then the dazzling Gothic extravaganza (*36*) that William Wilkins raised in 1810 above terraces on that dramatic hill.[10] Repton was obsessed with the problem of absorbing a steep hill landscape visually, and his Red Book on Pentillie will be of great interest if and when it is ever seen.[11] What would be most interesting to know is whether Repton was responsible for the rare picturesque feature at the entrance to the main drive. On the right, set back against a framing line of woods, is a prim Palladian miniature, the Steward's House, a small classical villa between quadrant arms with end pavilions. In striking contrast, clustered by the drive gates where normally a gate lodge could be expected, there is a pretty, picturesque hamlet of very rough, rock-faced cottages, three in all, placed in a casual disposition to each other to suggest a natural feudal appendage to the Castle. While the Wilkins range of the main house survived, the feudal association would have been apparent, but now the drive leads, with sensational views down to the right, into a forecourt fronted with Doric columns in that Cornish classical loggia manner of Godolphin and

36 *William Wilkins' exciting Gothic additions of 1810 once topped a Repton landscape at Pentillie Castle. Only the much earlier loggia range to the left survives and Repton's Red Book is currently inaccessible to scholars.* Bristol University Special Collections

Penheale. The loggia is in no way feudal, but predates the Wilkins work by almost two centuries and may originally have faced a formal garden court. It is difficult to imagine what Repton, so alert to Grecian and Gothic contrasts, would make of the surroundings of Pentillie in his proposed improvements.

His initial introduction into the charmed circle of Cornish gentry was a typical social triumph. In 1791 he had been working for the Prime Minister, the younger Pitt, on his estate at Holwood in Kent, and Pitt had recommended him to his own political agent, Reginald Pole Carew of Antony House. Pole Carew was an enthusiastic amateur landscape designer. In 1792 Repton was at the peak of his career immediately before the slump in business caused by the long wars with France, and he intended to use his prestigious commissions in Cornwall as material for the projected *Observations on the Theory and Practice of Landscape Gardening*, which would be published in 1803. Always at the back of his mind was the possibility of persuading a landowner to give his eldest son, John Adey Repton, the task of designing an ambitious garden building as proposed in a Red Book. At Antony, Repton proposed a lodge with carriage shelters at the public ferry, with a servant guard for 'fear of its becoming the rendezvous of improper people',[12] and two pavilions for the Terrace (*37 & 38*):

37 *The North Terrace at Antony in one of Repton's before and after views of how improvements could be made. A scruffy hedge confuses the lawn.* Bristol University Special Collections

38 *The central portion of the triple seat, which Repton was hoping his son could build, was erected much further back up the hillside as an eyecatcher to a revised design by Ptolemy Dean in 2003.* Bristol University Special Collections

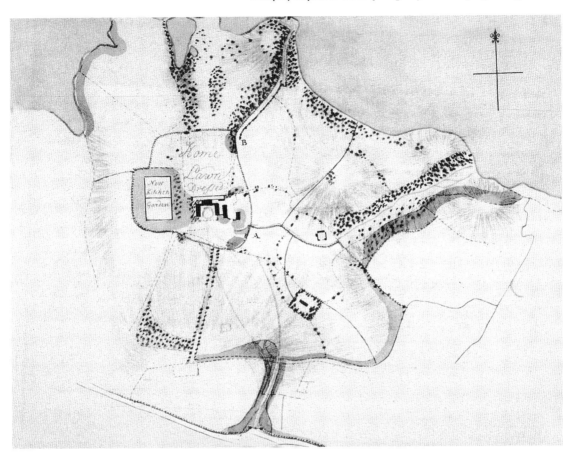

39 *The estate map in Repton's 1792 Red Book for Antony illustrates his obsession with aristocratic privacy; the drive, a public road, must be screened, but triple views down to the Lynher estuary must be opened up.* Bristol University Special Collections

> The Terrace must be considered as a remnant of the ancient stile, and with it there is no impropriety in terminating the two ends by correspondent buildings. I have in the following drawing supposed a reposoir to be formed by the same arcades and pavilions which I advise removing from the north front.[13]

Neither the lodge nor the pavilions were built, and the arcaded cloisters survive untouched on the north front.

Ignoring its more obsequious projects, the Red Book for Antony concentrates rightly on the enhancement, by planting and felling of trees, of the views from the house out over the Lynher estuary to the north. 'A continuity of wood, and also a continuity of water' was the avowed aim with water more important than wood.[14] The carefully water-coloured estate map is the key (*39*). All hedges were to be swept away but a choice selection of hedgerow trees would be retained. A few lines of hurdles, almost invisible iron fences, were 'to prevent improper roads or foot paths and to secure the privacy of the Grounds'.[15] Between them Brown and Repton created a cult of aristocratic privacy which has endured into the twenty-first century with adverse social effects.

Always sensitive to optical illusions of perspective, Repton wanted to reverse the tree situation on the 'hanging slope above the terrace',[16] a much shorter terrace, it should be noted, than the superb half-mile long platform of shorn grass created for Antony by Sir Reginald Pole Carew, the nineteenth-century garden genius. Repton's new Kitchen Garden blocked out any such western extension of the existing north terrace; Repton's eye was on the estuary. He proposed a vast home lawn where Prideaux had drawn a formal garden. Trees at point B would hide the offensive public road to the ferry, 'three miserable elms' were to be felled, 'a large mass of evergreen oaks should be suffered to present themselves'. These ilex trees are distinctive toning landscape notes in the northern views today. Repton wished to extend the apparent length of the northern slopes by having small trees in the distance, large trees on the nearer fringes. At the back of Jupiter's hill (named after a ship's figurehead) 'a glade of lawn should be introduced to shew the turn in the shape of the ground'.

It is easy to tire of such subtleties, but Repton really was 'painting' the view with trees, as an artist paints with oils, and his composition enjoyed today, with its three focus points on the estuary and the further shore, is extraordinarily satisfying in detail and in broad extent. If the trees do not, as he urged, show water under their lower branches and 'hide the ouze at low water',[17] the water still wins out in the conflict for attention with the woods, and the three focussed vistas are implicit in his estate map. His patron wisely rejected Repton's proposal to throw the proto-Gibbsian forecourt garden open on its fourth side. It remains a rare cloister approach to an English country house as proposed by Gibbs, cheap warm brick and *Magnolia grandiflora* softening that terrible icy purity of unadorned granite. Repton's map proposed a dog-leg approach drive to the house from the south down an avenue which would have allowed visitors to take in the whole forecourt from a distance. A nineteenth-century drive slides in at a more subtle angle, after the deliberate monotony of the 1930s lime avenue on that 'offensive' public road.

Catchfrench was a less important station on that 1792 tour,[18] the owner, Francis Glanville, was an obscure Tory MP and the house itself is pleasantly open to the north, where its terrace overlooks the valley of the Seaton, but it is otherwise sunken in a sea of trees that were sighing like sea-waves on my visit. That leafy enclosure provoked Repton, once he had staged a ritual demonstration in favour of parallel approach drives, one for gentry and one for trade,[19] into that previously mentioned earth-moving project. And, surprisingly, it works. A climb up out of the trees leads, via steps in that masonry skull of fifteenth-century ruins that peers so gruesomely into the back premises, and suddenly there is a wide west lawn, sunshine and the view that Repton planned, at the expense of fifty cart-loads of earth transferred: 'I ascertained with sufficient exactness, that a stake

40 *This skull of fifteenth-century ruins has been allowed by antiquarian sentiment to survive in the back yard of Catchfrench with two small gardens planted in its dark, roofless rooms*

6 feet high placed on top of this swell, would appear above the outline of the distant hill'. Those fifty loads were just enough to lower a lip of meadow in the 'swell' between the main hill and a clumped knoll. Repton intended the view to focus on a picturesque cottage, but

> the improvement of this scene does not arise merely from the introduction of the distant cottage, tho' very picturesque in itself, but from the variety in the outlines of the landscape which instead of being parallel will become beautifully contrasted.

This is a prime case of the classic foreground, middle ground and background; the effect today is still liberating, particularly after those memorably Gothic ruins.

Repton ignored the skull of ruins (40). Today they are softened by two tightly enclosed garden garths, one with Japanese anemones and hydrangeas to enliven their gloom, the other with two stone water basins, creepy but undeniably atmospheric. The Reptonian enclosed garden at Catchfrench is the Quarry Garden, the site of which he must have seen at least five days before Lord St Germans' awesome quarry garden at The Craggs on the Port Eliot estate stunned him into generous praise for a 'Sublime' garden achievement. A path winds down steeply north-east of the house through beech trees edging an open glade. Then unexpectedly, a tunnel under a Tudor-style arch leads dark and ferny into a small quarry of more ferns with a few exotic shrubs flowering funereally against the dark walls. There is nothing to do once a visitor has braved the tunnel except to brave it back again, but it is a modest preparation for Port Eliot and The Craggs.

Before Port Eliot and the climax of his Cornish pilgrimage came Trewarthenick on windy, east-facing uplands near Truro, an un-maritime inland corner of the county. The Red Book for this house[20] is impressively exact in its prescriptions and the Gregors, who lived here from 1640 to 1921, obeyed his directions to hide everything savouring of 'the yards and outhouses of a mere farmer … even the poultry and pig yards'[21] uphill behind the house to the west. That has created a near-village complex of ancillary buildings, a big, walled Kitchen Garden and a dower house that has its own mini-walled garden of bamboos, pampas and tall classical columns.

Eastwards down the hillside Repton had planned a new drive with a lodge for John Adey to build. The Gregors had other ideas, but they were impressed by the blast of treescape jargon on the Red Book's estate map:

> The deep recess at M will produce a play of light and shade in that outline when view'd from the opposite side of the lawn…the deep recess or bay in the plantation L will open the concave shape of ground in that direction…The plantations will be of sufficient depth to admit covered walks to be cut thro' them hereafter, which may burst out at the best points of view.[22]

Reading the jargon now conveys the intensely precious optical enthusiasm of those years of the Picturesque, the refinements of the age of the Claude Glass. How Repton would have revelled in Feng Shui if only it had been introduced! So the Gregors planted the trees as directed and they still function as Repton said they would. However, in between his hidden 'Conveniences' up the hill and the subtle plantations down the slopes runs the present direct entrance drive, not so much a drive as a broad band of scenic gardening, Victorian to the south, more recent near the road. It might be expected to open with a lodge. Instead visitors drive straight off the main road into a haphazardly delightful belt of smooth, hilly lawns with specimen trees, *Cordyline australis*, pampas, hydrangeas, even a small lily pond with gunnera. But all the way along it, to the left, is parkland clumped as Repton proposed (*41*), and bounded, as he suggested, with broad swags of woodland that tactfully terminate the park, but not the horizon. Brownian park and

41 *Shelter belt, tree clumps and grazing sheep present the epitome of Reptonian devising at Trewarthenick*

fussy bourgeois planting juxtapose attractively. To the right the hill closes all vistas within fifty yards. Repton offered no treatment for this area.

When the house swings into view, backed by the towering Irish yews that are a Trewarthenick excellence, it impacts again as Repton required, stark, grey and high-pedimented, with enormous long Regency windows. Its grey stones have been cut laboriously in shape to imitate brick. Three shallow terraces front its gravel walk, the colonnade of yews has been cut down into dark green Irish cauliflowers in order to open up the view, which is so fine that the severe pruning is excusable. The Gregors did everything on a scale of giganticism to accord with the house, and beyond it is a vast, empty lawn backed by fine specimen trees of 1860s vintage, a continuation of the drive's random arboretum with Turkey, English and Sessile oaks the dominant notes, then golden yew, Lawson cypress, Douglas and Noble fir, ash and sweet chestnut. It is an easy introduction into the garden worlds that Repton spanned, from the eighteenth-century Picturesque to the nineteenth-century Gardenesque, the time of the coastal redwoods.

A hefty punctuation of big stone ball finials changes the mood, and the Spring Garden begins. Down in a dell monstrously oversized cushions of rhododendron: 'Cornish Red', Crossbill, 'Lady Alice Fitzwilliam' and *williamsanium* brood away in extreme old age, hiding, as Repton would wish, the grey Kitchen Garden wall. Wisteria has tried to smother one of the great clumps in vain; and there the plantations, which Repton was hopeful, could be induced to colonise the hill top, are doing just that. He will have heard of Lord de Dunstanville's experiments at Tehidy, using the pinaster as a 'nursery' tree to support the growth of less sturdy spruce, birch and sycamore on his cliff top park near Camborne.[23]

On the last stage of his 1792 trawl Humphry Repton came to Port Eliot at St Germans, where he seems immediately to have been torn between reverential awe and abject flattery. Even now that very private house can bring out the 'Humphry' in a visitor and inspire feudolatory; it is so beautiful, so historic and so romantic. What other great house in England has a tame cathedral on its front lawn and is inhabited by a peer who is the twentieth in a male line from the John Elyot who acquired it, after some smart footwork, during the Dissolution?

Not surprisingly the Devil has visited Port Eliot in person. When the loutish twin-towered church was an active priory, one of its monks, a man called Dando, was a keen hunter. Even worse, he hunted on Sundays, and on one fatal day, famished after a long, fierce chase, he was resting at St Erths and unwisely cried out for 'food in hell rather than hunger on Earth'. Whereupon the Devil rode up with refreshment, clamped Dando onto the back of his hellish steed and galloped straight into the deepest reach of the Tiddy estuary, still marked on maps as 'Dandy's Deep'.

The park around the house must be Repton's and, to be fair, the Lords St Germans', masterpiece, it is so effortlessly Picturesque in the true sense of that term: picture worthy, varied and Claudeian. Nature may have been unusually generous to the Eliots, giving them that Claudeian ideal of the sea interpenetrating by tidal creeks a lively variation of little hills. But they have had to plant trees, drain the 'ouze' and heighten the hills by Reptonian devices. A key passage in his Port Eliot Red Book,[24] which is, incidentally, bound in brown leather, reads:

> the woods of the valleys should seem to climb the hills by such connecting lines as may neither appear meagre nor artificial, but following the natural shapes of the ground, produce an apparent continuity of woods falling down the hills in various directions.[25]

The result has been a landscape not so much 'improved' as made perfect, an English Eden rather than an Eden Project. This is Cornwall's finest park and, private as it is, anyone can steal an enchanting aerial view of it simply by taking a train from Plymouth to St Germans, sitting on the right-hand side and looking down from that absurdly elegant and aristocratic thirteen-arched viaduct that spans the Tiddy creek (*42*). This is in itself the handsomest garden building in the county; even its embankment has been planted with ilex. There, down below, girdled, if the tide is in, with shining water, is a sizeable fraction of Port Eliot's grounds: its Battery of coastal canon, the Battery Cottage for its canoneer, clumps of lordly pampas, the thatched Boathouse and the present Lord St Germans' Pleasure Ground with its beech Maze and temples on a small hill.

To create the Great Lawn that extends north of the house, making a picture for the hills to frame, Edward, Lord Eliot, created 1st Baron in 1784, had first to

42 *The most handsome garden building in Cornwall is, arguably, the railway viaduct across the Tiddy estuary at Port Eliot. Some horticultural philanthropist has planted ilex on one of its embankments*

raise a long earth dam and drain the stinking ooze of the tidal inlet that fronted the garden ranges of the house. Repton's explanatory map of the park (*colour plate 11*) shows this in place and he was obviously irritated that this improvement had already taken place. He pettishly insisted: 'there is evidently a deficiency of that kind of Park or lawn which modern gardening expects as an accompaniment to a large mansion'.[26] His patron had cleared a large, flat area of water but, from Repton's detailed before illustration, the windows of the house now looked out north to a ragged group of farm buildings or warehouses with commonplace low hills beyond the dull sector of drained land. His solution was impressively subtle and the view looking north today (*colour plate 12*) is very close to what Repton proposed when the slide was pulled back. As an artist he painted with woodland and gave each plantation he was proposing a letter. The proposals which produced the present subtly satisfying vistas to the north were:

E But as every plantation loses much of its dignity, if the neighbouring ground be seen above it, there will also be a necessity for planting part of the Great Furze Park, … which will crown and unite the grand mass formed by these several plantations A, B, C and D.

F Is a plantation to hide the head of the fresh water pool, which as an object of necessity and convenience ought as far as possible to be made an object of beauty in itself.

G Surrounds the farm yard [Lithiack] and gives an interesting line of connection with the Craggs.

H Extends that connection towards the water, uniting into one fine mass of hanging wood, the plantation of The Craggs, and that on the steep banks of the river.[27]

Repton felt himself up against a near equal with Edward and in a clever gesture to prove his superiority threw in a lesson on optics, entitled 'Axis of Vision', into his Red Book for the park, a lesson he liked so much that he would reproduce it in his *Observations*. This was Repton changing his hat, no longer Repton the Artist, but Repton the Scientist. He was examining the question, quite relevant in a garden: at what distance does any object appear at its greatest height? After claiming as a fact, which seems to be far from self-evident, that when we look straight ahead our angle of vision above the horizontal is less than that below,[28] he provided a chart demonstrating at what distances a man whose eyes were five feet five inches from the ground, would have to stand away from a tall object, let us say a sixty-foot church tower, to see it entire without raising or lowering his head. The church at Port Eliot, for instance, is too close to be absorbed by someone standing on the south lawn without looking up and down. It works much better visually when viewed from Repton's favourite spot in the park, 'the tumulus', as he curiously calls it, on The Craggs. He meant a covered Seat now lost, on a ledge above the quarry.

The newly drained area may have surprised him by the ambitious nature of the project, the sizeable earth dyke that Edward had constructed. But what had really impressed him into an abject admission of inadequacy was Edward's treatment of the quarry in The Craggs at the far end of that 'deficient' lawn. He wrote:

> The bold and masterly stile in which the rock scenery of Port Eliot has been handled would make it presumptious in me to suggest any hints on the subject. In viewing the sublime horrors of the Craggs, I confess my powers are subdued; and like the conquered magician, I break my wand in presence of superior skill.[29]

This was an unusually generous response to an existing garden feature. The Red Book includes a fearsome view inside the Quarry Garden showing a great spike of rock jutting up inside an arena of cliffs: sublime in the Burkeian sense. It is approached along a narrow gorge overhung with trees, much gloomier than the small Quarry Garden at Catchfrench. So Cornwall was quite sophisticated enough to have had its own native tradition of the Sublime and Beautiful before Repton imported one.[30]

43 *Delighted by the overshadowing trees, loud waters and genuine late medieval baptismal shrine at Menacuddle, the Rashleighs of Menabilly laid out, after 1795, a garden with zig-zag paths, rustic seats and a goldfish pool*

This tradition is easy to believe if two strange gardens, St Nectan's Kieve at Trethevy, near Tintagel described in the Introduction, and Menacuddle, less than a mile from St Austell, are remembered. Menacuddle is milder and more endearing than the Kieve, but has the same combination of loud water, rocks and overshadowing trees. Here though, there is a genuine medieval chapel built to the memory of a baptismal pool of the Age of Saints in the river that flows past (*43*). There were flowers in the shrine on my visit. Gilbert described the scene at length:

> The view from the ruin is much confined, and yet extremely beautiful. The waters, after having quitted the fall, roll through a narrow dell, darkened with leafage, and strewed with enormous rocks. At the end of this perspective, the opening arches of Menacuddle Bridge let in a partial light; all above is an immense mass of shadow, extinguishing every distant object.[31]

44 *In his 1793 Red Book for Port Eliot, Repton contrived to make the house in his view before the intended improvements look like a vaguely classical tenement.* Bristol University Special Collections

45 *After Reptonian improvements the House and Priory Church at Port Eliot have been combined into a sumptuous Gothic whole. No changes are urged for the visually strategic hill behind the house.* Bristol University Special Collections

Burke had written and Repton quoted him in his Port Eliot Red Book: 'You ought to pass from the greatest light to as much darkness as is consistent with the uses of architecture'. Repton had urged the building of a covered seat on The Craggs, ignoring, curiously, the fact that one had been mentioned there already in a survey of 1784.[32] The present Earl of St Germans has discovered on the lip of the cliff in The Craggs quarry a circle of cobblestones for such a seat, whether of Repton's time or earlier is not known.

Menacuddle proved irresistible to the grotto building family of the Rashleighs of Menabilly. Gilbert recorded that after 'the difficulties attendant on raising coppice wood, in a situation so barren and exposed', the same problem Lord de Dunstanville had faced at Tehidy, 'Charles Rashleigh, esq. was at last rewarded for his unwearied exertions' and the trees grew.[33] He continued:

> There is a variety of intricate walks carried through the inclosure; also ponds, stored with fish of gold and silver hues. The upper walks stretch over the steep acclivities, in zig-zag directions, accompanied by rustic seats, formed of rough blocks of wood, covered with moss, and entwined withy ivy. Opposite a rustic building called the Hermitage, stands a pedestal, capped with an urn, bearing a profile likeness of the late earl of Mount Edgcumbe.[34]

Perhaps the proper place for Menacuddle and St Nectan's Kieve was in the previous Arcadian chapter, along with the Zig-Zag at Mount Edgcumbe and the Wilderness paths of Moditonham, but they explain The Craggs at Port Eliot. In Cornwall the sheer topography of the county often called forth the Savage Picturesque garden with little need for outside influences. Even Ethy, a confident, flat-faced Baroque villa, poised above the tidal creek at Lerryn, was subject to a nautical Picturesque treatment when Admiral Sir Charles Vinicombe Penrose, rich with prize money, descended on it in 1798. Admirals are accustomed to pace the poop-deck, the fore-deck, the stern-walk or whatever. It was a ritual of the service and Ethy, though otherwise a true sailor's reward, had no deck to walk upon, so Admiral Penrose, mindful perhaps of the Hall Walk at nearby Polruan, had a ship's terrace constructed on the edge of the grove at Ethy overlooking the ebb and flow of Lerryn's tides. It is raised on either side with stone walls, flanked by beech under-planted with laurels and extends about a hundred yards long with a 'prow' at one end and a 'stern' at the other. It is the essence of the Picturesque movement that the scene, salty in Ethy's case, inspired the gardener's response.

Indeed Port Eliot drove Repton himself into a most Gothic mood. One of his illustrations, without the usual slide, shows the proposed Gothic Boathouse, which was to have a salt bathing pool and an attendant's cottage, framed in the mouth of a frightening cave, a gross exaggeration of an existing quarry. Cleverly, he produced a before and after view of the house and the church (*44 & 45*). In the before view, the house looks like a decayed classical workhouse, dwarfed by the west front of the church. With the slide pulled back, the house has not

46 The elegant Orangery at Port Eliot with its bowed Doric porch was in place by 1790, well before the Repton visit. There is a hint of Robert Adam in its design

only been given a splendid Gothic trim, but is now linked very convincingly to the church by a cloister range. That commission for John Adey Repton was never awarded but, encouraged by Repton's drawing, the Eliots brought in Sir John Soane between 1802 and 1806 to affect a workmanlike Gothic re-cladding which succeeds admirably.[35]

Such a change was not enough for Repton; he wanted the whole town of St Germans to be Gothicised, the School and the Court House in particular. He urged that 'the new stables together with every other building in the town, by assuming the Gothic stile, would become part of the same magnificent and picturesque *whole*',[36] while a classical gable on the north front 'at present disgraces that side of the house'.[37] The gable is now Gothic. Unexpectedly Repton failed to mention the Hermit of The Craggs. He was one of two brothers who both fell in love with the same girl. The jilted one of the pair retired to a cave in The Craggs and came up to the house each morning for a bowl of soup. Presumably he poached for the rest of his sustenance. But then Repton tends to avoid features where he has been outpointed. He ignored the Orangery (*46*), an airily elegant classical structure entered through a bowed Doric porch and commanding an attractive, hidden Walled Garden with a gardener's bothy. It was already there in 1790, a recent addition when Repton visited,[38] and is today a sun parlour with a chaise longue. One of the many charms of Port Eliot's gardens is that they are still a very evolving concern. For no recorded reason the Eliots generally missed out on the mid eighteenth-century Arcadian phase of gardening, but the last and the present Earls have compensated richly by their new Pleasure Ground on the hill beside the house. This will have its proper place in a later chapter.

The most satisfying approach drive today is not the one next to St Germans church but another up the road. This leads through an atmospheric retainers' suburb before diving through trees into a wide stable yard and between the twin, machicolated and solidly handsome stable towers. Soane devised these, obedient to Repton's Gothic urge, and they are most un-Soaneian in character with a cobbled yard and a channel for urine. After this brooding mood-setter the drive runs out into the great lawn, stripped, as Repton demanded, of all dividing hedges. An arboretum closes in and a little stream, the Slatterbourne, runs under a rustic, ivy-covered bridge. It has stepping stones and then, like Coleridge's Alph the sacred river, falls into a grid and disappears. House and 'cathedral'[39] show up superbly against a dark background of trees with no built link, only a yew hedge. Several *Magnolia grandiflora* climb up the house walls to battlement level. On the lawns are urns and a very low terrace wall divides the garden from the park proper, affording a correct foreground feature when viewed from the house.

Far out, beyond the Great Lawn are two *ferme ornée* complexes near The Craggs: Penimble and Lithiack. One building at Lithiack is castellated and has a Soaneian air. Lithiack's Dairy has a lovely tiled room with orange and blue borders around pictures of fishes. It sounds more like a copy of Queen Victoria's Dairy at Windsor than a Repton creation. An American visitor, Elihu Burritt, walking from London to Lands End and back in 1868, described it as 'supplied with a fountain of pure water [which] throws up a beautiful spray and making the most congenial atmosphere for such a place'.[40] European Union regulations controlling milk production have now put it out of use.

Repton made his tour of Pentillie and Tregothnan sixteen years later, in 1809, when much jolting on public vehicles and one road accident had saddened him and probably lessened his drive to alter and reform. It is obvious from his Red Book of Tregothnan that he had deviated from Brown's style of landscaping but, fearing to take his master on, he turned pettishly and snobbishly against Brown's followers:

> It is not surprising that many of his foremen became his successors, these persons having arisen from the same low class of society, it deterred men of higher pretensions from being confounded with such rivals or associates.[41]

He then launched a sidelong barb at Brown himself:

> their great master who often did more than perhaps he could explain his reasons for, and

produced beautiful effects of which he hardly knew the cause. Yet from the multiplicity of his concerns he was occasionally apt to degenerate into an uniform system and became a mannerist.

From the impressive optical analysis in the Port Eliot Red Book it is apparent that Repton saw himself as a landscape scientist as much as a landscape artist. Spiteful as his attack may have been, there is some truth in this 'mannerist' jibe:

> Brown's belts and clumps were easy to imitate and his mechanic followers have uniformly adopted them, and treated all plans exactly by the same recipe, making no difference between the mountains of Wales or the flats of Lincolnshire.

He then proceeded to some outrageous generalisations about the topography of Cornwall. Whereas other counties had, he claimed, 'those undulating forms … which may be described as convex and convex lines flowing into each other', in Cornwall 'the hills are without valleys and may rather be described as convex lines dropping into ravines some of which are filled with water and some with wood'.[42] Quite what he intended to do to remedy this fault is never stated. It seems from his complaints about the drives at Tregothnan that his real problem was that Lord Falmouth had already done what Repton himself would have liked to do, but:

> I must observe, that nothing can be truly delightful where danger is evident, and that those parts of the drive which are too steep or too narrow, or which from the appearance of a precipice require some regard for safety, should be more immediately remedied … a drive of pleasure should be free from horror: we expect the *beautiful* rather than the *sublime* of Nature in our gardens and pleasure grounds.[43]

This was the exact opposite of what he was praising seventeen years earlier in his response to The Craggs at Port Eliot.

At Tregothnan there was, as at Port Eliot, the existing natural drama and visual variety of the site, a long, lofty peninsula richly wooded, with the River Fal on one side, the Truro River on the other, both tidal. The village of St Michael Penkevil, trimly estate in character, sits across the public approach road, but mile after scenic mile of driveways run around the river shores and offer private ways of entry. Desperate to make some kind of mark on an already Picturesque layout Repton complained that:

> at present during a ride of many miles through a wood of great extent and constantly varying its course, there is little variety in its scenery, it is a continual succession of water glittering below, among the tangled branches and trees hanging down the steep sides of a rocky bank, and though such scenery is for a certain time delightful yet we become impatient of its uniformity.

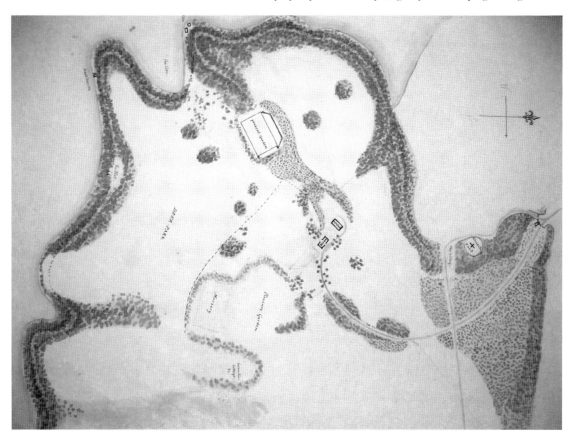

47 *Tregothnan and its grounds from the Repton Red Book showing the untidy jumble of ill-coordinated planting along the various valley sides and no shelter belts to the exposed west.* By kind permission of Lord Falmouth

So the drives were too beautiful. The solution was to vary the planting, as Brown had always done, allowing sudden glimpses of that 'water glittering below', then closing it off with trees. It seems a feeble complaint but, as will be seen later, John Nash did just that to the upper drive at Caerhays Castle and it still works admirably.

There was to be a punishment for this fastidious fault finding. It was Repton's fate at Tregothnan yet again to suggest a Gothic reshaping which his son might carry out, but which would be given in 1816, not long after the preparation of the Red Book, to William Wilkins. This could be paralleled by what happened at Pentillie Castle, so the Pentillie Red Book of the same year probably made similar Gothic recommendations. Happily Tregothnan has kept Wilkins' highly photogenic pinnacles to crown its hill while at Pentillie they have been demolished. It was the 4th Viscount Falmouth, later the 1st Earl, who commissioned Repton.

The usual estate map (*47*) shows the Boat House, The Flat, the Deer Park, Pleasure Garden, Present Garden and Nursery. It is evident that in the years

48 *Repton's Gothic proposal for turning the 1650s' house at Tregothnan into a Regency castle with arcaded conservatory. As so often his ideas were ignored and the eventual commission went to William Wilkins.* By kind permission of Lord Falmouth

since he serviced Port Eliot, Repton had moved from his Picturesque, basically Brownian, garden styling towards the Gardenesque, that style of richly sentimental flower bedding with trellises, arches, fountains and endless large flowerpots. The 'before' and 'after' views tell the tale (*colour plates 13 & 14*). One view down to the Fal with trees on the right has three people struggling with umbrellas against what is clearly a strong wind. When the slide is pulled back all is calm. Roses and camellias are flowering in a foreground of pots, the view is more open, but there is a new shelter belt of trees and even the deer sit tranquilly. This view can be matched today with the shelter belt protecting the house from westerlies. In another view, this time of the house from the Fal, the building is of the 1650s. With the slide pulled back the house is castellated, though more soberly than Wilkins was to redesign it, and there is a heavy wall for the Kitchen Garden. A second close-up view of the 1650s house goes Gardenesque when the slide is pulled back (*48*). A conservatory is added to a house now Gothic, there is an orangery to the right and there are flowering shrubs in front of the house in place of lawns.

In garden history terms this, for all its negative complaints, is a very important Red Book. It means that in 1809, long before Victoria came to the throne, while the old mad king still reigned and Waterloo had yet to be fought, all the garden changes that John Claudius Loudon would be advocating and, in 1832, actually coining the word 'gardenesque' to describe, had been accepted by the turncoat Repton, a garden designer who truly spanned two very different garden centuries. Tregothnan was as much a garden on the cusp as Port Eliot was a garden of the Arcadian, though at The Craggs it turned Savage Picturesque. It may seem a harsh judgement, but Repton was at heart a vulgarian, ready to adapt to capitalist pressures. In the nineteenth century, as a result of the Industrial Revolution, Britain could produce virtually any kind of garden artefact in tiles, mosaics, wood and stone: bird baths, conservatories, fountains and ornamental ironwork. Repton opened his arms to them all. More threateningly for Cornwall's garden future, in the new century plants from all across the Empire could be brought in. These would, in most counties, be grown in heated greenhouses, but in very nearly sub-tropical Cornwall the range for open air planting would be much wider. The gentry would venture into exotics and soon they would be cross breeding their flowering bushes in a competitive frenzy.

Walking the acres of Port Eliot it comes as a refreshing surprise to find that this beauty is very largely native and that the rhododendrons, azaleas, camellias and magnolias that infest most of the county's gardens, substituting with their garish colours for thoughtful planting, firm vistas and memorable buildings, have no place in the park of the Earls of St Germans. Exactly what happened when another near-perfect Picturesque layout was overwhelmed by the train-spotter plant fanciers, can be experienced at Caerhays Castle, near St Austell.

Caerhays went up in 1808 just before the fall in Picturesque values of composition, and was designed by Humphry Repton's onetime associate, John Nash, the Prince Regent's favourite architect, for John Bettesworth Trevanion. Two drives lead to its courtyard, one from the Upper Lodge, one from the Lower Lodge, which is down almost on the beach of Porthluney Cove. The lower drive is short and visually satisfying; the upper drive is long and has a reasonable claim to be the most rewarding in a county of great drives which has always preferred the linear garden to the spatial. The Trevanions bankrupted themselves by building the Castle and laying out its approaches. Their estate was bought in 1854 by the Williams family, who would later lay destructive hands upon Werrington. In this chapter our concern is only with the Caerhays of the Trevanions and their theatrical genius of a drive designer, John Nash.

In its half-mile length the upper drive of Caerhays presents a running film strip of views, all worthy of, and presumably inspired by, the Claudeian eighteenth-century aesthetic. First comes a boldly-castellated Lodge brightly chequered in pale and dark brown stone. The alternate dark chequers are composed of thin shales packed together and it works more by its colour than by its outline. That slim turret on the left is a Nash signature; it will be repeated on the Castle itself, elegant, theatrical and impractical as it is too thin to contain anything but a stair, so a stair to nowhere except a Gothic broom cupboard! The note is playful.

49 *A view from the upper drive at Caerhays Castle over John Nash's carefully composed lakescape to the seashore at Porthluney Cove*

The drive begins its rich unfolding. Flanking it on the right is a steep, splendidly wooded hillside with the usual post-1854 under-planting of shiny camellias, bamboo and rhododendron. All the interest lies to the left, looking out over a fertile valley to another carefully wooded hill, the bushes on this left side are artfully planted to reveal a succession of distinct vistas. Another valley opens up the vistas much more boldly, but then attention is diverted to the right into a small gloomy quarry where tree ferns flourish in the moist shadows. To the left hand a widening lake appears with an island and one exquisitely groomed pine tree, as in a Chinese screen print. The lake expands with a second island clumped with pampas. Then, just before the drive forks, left for the servants, right for gentry, a full-tilt Claudeian composition unfolds (49). This was initiated by Nash, but perfected, at considerable expense, by the Williams family who employed a group of local men to dig away a fold of hill that was blocking the balanced perspective of the view. The islanded lake is still in the foreground, but behind it in a wide bay confined by modest cliffs a line of white breakers is roaring in across the dark sea.

The left-hand fork leads to a tall single turret, unexplained and without apparent function, followed by a high, grey terrace wall superbly lined with giant magnolias. The right-hand gentry drive seems as if it is approaching an armed city. A gate yawns in a high, fortified wall that hurries up the steep right-hand slope in a flurry of towers. Through the gate across long lawns is Caerhays Castle (*50*), composed to defy expectations of order and obviously magnificently false. The whole visual experience of this drive has been enlivening; a lesson in how much can be packed visually into an unfolding curve.

In contrast the Lower Lodge is lower, squat, grim and suggestive of a gun emplacement. From the moment of passing it the Castle is in full view, with sumptuously pale stone complexities against dark trees that Repton would have enjoyed for the surprising variety of billowing gloom that they offer: depth rather than mere background. It is almost contemptuous in the way it gives everything up at once, with no distractions after the cosseting indulgence of the upper drive. The one gives a picture, the other gives an educational process in awareness, and that is what the Picturesque Movement was all about: noticing and judging the world in a series of views to be rated aesthetically. The two dangers were exclusive arrogance and being a bore.

50 Nash's brilliant architectural proposals for the approach to Caerhays Castle bankrupted his patrons, the Trevanions, but gave the house the air of a medieval city

6

Nineteenth-century gardens outside the magic circle of the plant-spotter dynasties

Whenever the term 'Gardenesque' comes up it always seems to require definition.[1] Most people can recognise a formal seventeenth-century layout or an Arcadian park, but how easy is it to spot a Gardenesque garden? The term can include the complex geometrical flowerbeds of The Downes at Hayle or that wonderfully melancholic Pinetum at Boconnoc, so any definition is likely to be inadequate. J.C. Loudon invented the inadequate descriptive term in 1832 for a deeply inadequate period of English garden styling and it is no coincidence that he was the author, in 1822, of an *Encyclopaedia* of gardening. By 1822 there was such an encyclopaedic welter of garden technology available and so many new plants had already come on line that gardening, which had begun as an art for the inspired amateur, had become a science for the trained technician and careerist. It was during the nineteenth century that rich garden owners, like rich house builders of the same period, lost their sense of direction and aesthetic sequence. They became what we now refer to as train-spotters or anoraks, anxious only to include in their gardens any expensive garden toy or to collect every available species of a particular plant.

It was telling that in the November of my Cornish garden year I visited two very different gardens in the same week. Port Eliot was the first, with not a flower in sight and not, that I can recall, a single shining leaf of camellia or magnolia except that *Magnolia grandiflora* sprawling lazily over Soane's Gothic walls. It was so beautiful in its composition of woods, lawns, water, and that one perfectly sited Doric Temple-Changing Room by the swimming pool, that it was heart catching, very near to a garden sublime. Then I went to Trebah, one of the big three, or four, or five, plant-spotter, valley gardens on the Helston River, that are distinguishable one from the other only by their ever busy restaurants.

And I walked along a camellia avenue, bush after shining leafed bush, each with a nametag, but there was nothing to distinguish one from another. It was not a garden so much as a zoo of plants, staked out next to each other, a true plant-spotter's collection: no compositions, no sense of vista control.

Some people collect the numbers of diesel locomotives, some devote their leisure hours to a complete holding of the postage stamps issued by Trinidad and Tobago or, if they are ambitious, the twentieth-century French Colonial commemorative stamps. That is the Gardenesque mindset: a double row of camellias, planted one on either side of a path with no views, no temple background, just a plant museum; for a few months those bushes will be overwhelmingly radiant with white, pink, red and variously flushed waxy flowers, but there has to be an open question hanging over them. They are part of a hugely successful tourist industry. Was it 30,000 or 60,000 visitors that Trebah attracted in one year? The answer is 60,000. But are these valley paradises great gardens? It is the question at the heart of any chapter on the Cornish Gardenesque. Does a great collection of flowering plants and shrubs make a great garden?

The subject is far more complex than it appears. In the three centuries between 1500 and 1800 Cornish gardens usually deviated a little from those of most English counties in the way they interpreted a fashion of garden styling. Geography, geology, climate or, though harder to prove, the social angle of the local gentry, all account for those slight Cornish idiosyncrasies. But then, when we come to the nineteenth century and the Cornish interpretation of the Gardenesque, that deviation becomes a gulf. The average English county slid, as Repton slid, from Brownian to Picturesque to Gardenesque and, for the greater part of the nineteenth century, played the variations on heated greenhouses, conservatories, trellis work, rose arches, multi-spouting cast iron fountains, bird baths, cast metal maidens and Japanese cranes, crazy paving and the regimented flowerbeds planted out to keep pace with the seasons in glaring ranks of salvias, asters, gladioli and similar predictabilities.

Cornwall did indulge, in a desultory fashion, in that standard Gardenesque, and this chapter will be devoted to several interesting, though never heart-stopping, examples of the style. Parallel, however, with these modestly greenhouse-centred gardens are the epic, astonishing and nationally celebrated plant-spotter gardens that give the county a three or four month extension to its tourist season and are, in themselves, a major industry and employer. The gardens, to name a few: Penjerrick, Trebah, Glendurgan, Trewithen, Trewidden, Caerhays, Tregrehan, Trengwainton (51) and Heligan are national treasures, factories of exotic blooms, memorably colourful, an inspiration to uncounted thousands who go back home to grow camellias in pots in their back gardens. They are not so much greenhouse-centred, like the standard Gardenesque layout, they are the creation of men and women who have realised that on the south coast of Cornwall, given the right protecting valley or shelter belt of trees, a greenhouse is not needed. Miniature, sub-tropical microclimates are to hand for those wise enough to take advantage of them.

51 *The plant-spotter's paradise of Trengwainton is enlivened by a wooden Chinese Bridge, a much-needed note of architectural interest amidst the flowering exotics*

They have, therefore, no natural place in this chapter; they are a branch of the Gardenesque which has grown far greater than its parent tree. They are the county's wonderful Garden Renaissance, not beyond criticism, for they grew out of Cornwall's flawed past garden history, but they are a true cause for celebration. They are there for our specialised enjoyment, and most of them open their arms wide to paying visitors. It is simply my perverse personal reservation that, because they are rather dull for half the year they are not in my ranking of great Cornish gardens as are: Port Eliot, Mount Edgcumbe, Barbara Hepworth's sculpture garden at St Ives, that south cliff garden at St Michael's Mount, Eagles Nest at Zennor and Penheale. I have purposely left Tresco Abbey out of both lists; it is certainly a plant-spotter's garden and certainly great in national ranking, great enough almost single-handed to keep a heliport working. To me it is never quite part of Cornwall and I have never forgotten or forgiven that magical, frightening flight out into sea mists over an ocean as 'wine-dark' as anything in Homer. Never again, but what a garden experience!

One of the many unsatisfactory side-notes to the true Gardenesque is the difficulty of knowing exactly when it began. If the obsessive collection of exotics is a marker then Henry Compton, Lord Bishop of London, was collecting magnolias in the 1680s, taking advantage of his chaplains ministering in Virginia.[2] The first camellias came in 1739 and the villainous, invasive *Rhododendron ponticum* arrived from Gibraltar, surely a station of transit, in 1763. Penjerrick, oldest and most deliciously run-down of the great Fox dynasty of Falmouth's gardens, was being planted initially in about 1790.

If, however, greenhouses and conservatories are the key to Gardenesque status then William Mason, priest, fellow of Pembroke College, Cambridge, a Yorkshireman and a poet, has a fair claim to have founded that dubious garden style with the lame, but clever and perceptive poem, *The English Garden*, which he wrote in separate parts in 1774 and published in four volumes in 1777, encouraged by his friends, Thomas Gray and Horace Walpole.[3] Repton's garden practice was largely based on Mason's poetic precepts. In that Red Book for Port Eliot, Repton quotes Mason's first book to explain his tree planting for those sublime vistas down the great lawn:

Rich the robe,
And ample let it flow, that Nature wears
On her thron'd eminence: where're she takes
Her horizontal march, pursue her step
With sweeping train of forest; hill to hill
Unite with prodigality of shade.[4]

While Repton's frequent allusions to breaking the line of a wood come from Mason's advice:

Stay then, thine hand;
And try by saplings tall, discreetly plac'd
Before, between, behind, in scatter'd groups,
To break th'obdurate line.[5]

All of this advice could still be considered Brownian. It is in Book Four of the poem, when Alcander, a youth straight out of Bernardin de St Pierre's *Paul et Virginie*, takes charge, that an ambitious Gardenesque greenhouse, a precursor of the Great Stove at Syon House and even the Crystal Palace, occupies centre stage:

High on Ionic shafts he bad it tower
A proud Rotunda; to its sides conjoin'd
Two broad Piazzas in theatric curve,
Ending in equal Porticos sublime.

Glass rooft the whole, and sidelong to the South
'Twixt ev'ry fluted Column, lightly rear'd
Its walls pellucid.[6]

Port Eliot already had an elegant orangery in its secret garden before Repton's visit in 1792. Mason's advice had been taken. But Repton was in time to urge the Gothicising of Port Eliot's twin *fermes ornées*, Penimble and Lithiack, with that elegantly fish-tiled Dairy as Mason had proposed:

'Draw we round yon knowl,'
Alcander cry'd, 'in stately Norman mode,
A wall embattled; and within its guard
Let every structure needful for a Farm
Arise in Castle-semblance, the huge Barn
Shall with a mock Portcullis arm the gate,
some Tower rotund
Shall to the Pigeons and their callow young
Safe roost afford; ... his Dairy too
There stands of form unsightly: both to veil,
He builds of old disjointed moss-grown stone
A time-struck Abbey.'[7]

As a result, between 1804 and 1806 Sir John Soane would be castellating not just the farms, but also the stables of Port Eliot. So the Gardenesque helped to precipitate the Victorians into their practice of making most buildings look like what they were not; the Houses of Parliament being a classic example.

Again and again Alcander's garden for Nerina, whom he has rescued from a shipwreck, unlike Paul, who failed to rescue Virginie from her shipwreck off Mauritius, sounds coyly artificial and Gardenesque:

So here did Art arrange her flow'ry groups
Irregular, yet not in patches quaint,
But interpos'd between the wand'ring lines
Of shaven turf which twisted to the path....
Leading the Eye to many a sculptur'd bust
On shapely pedestal, of Sage, or Bard,
Many an Urn
There too had place
And now each flow'r that bears transplanting change,
Or blooms indigenous, adorn'd the scene.[8]

So annuals, that bane of gardeners, would have their place in the Gardenesque just as Mason had decreed in 1777. Hot-house fruit, another nineteenth-century

Gardenesque obsession, one that Gilbert gloats over in almost every house entry of his *Historical Survey*, were another fixation handed down by Mason:

> A glittering Fane, where rare and alien plants
> Might safely flourish; where the Citron sweet,
> And fragrant Orange, rich in fruit and flowers,
> Might hang their silver stars, their golden globes,
> On the same odorous stem.[9]

When that American Elihu Burritt visited Port Eliot in 1868 he was more impressed by its hot-house fruit than by any other aspect of the gardens except the Dairy. In the Peach and Vine Houses, which survive now as a sun parlour, he remarked: 'It was pleasant to see trees heavily hung with large luscious peaches in the middle of June [the earliest had ripened on 26 May and been sent to the family in London], all fully ripe, and breathing out that peculiar savour so delicious to the sense'.[10] Keats of the *Eve of St Agnes* begins to emerge as an equally fruit conscious Gardenesque poet.

If these remarks begin to sound confused and savouring of the greengrocer then that is accurately of the period: luscious, self-indulgent, gardens verging on bourgeois vulgarity as, if we are honest, does most Victorian country house architecture. The best way to absorb the hit-or-miss aesthetics of the Gardenesque is to take in the confusions of its Cornish gardens chronologically, always remembering that the parallel theme of the great plant-spotters' gardens is developing alongside, though that will be explored in the following chapter.

The first seminal meeting of the plant-spotter dynasties, the Foxes, the Williamses, the Gilberts and the Bolithos was held in Pearce's Hotel, Truro on 18 May 1832.[11] That was when they founded the Cornwall Horticultural Society; and the first two incoherent but significant Gardenesque gardens were taking shape at much the same time. John Vivian was in the chair at that first committee meeting and Sir Richard Vyvyan, 8th Baronet, had begun to reorganise the eighteenth-century grounds of Trelowarren in an undirected way in 1820. As Richard Carew had pointed out in 1602: 'all Cornish gentlemen are cousins',[12] and cousins can be highly competitive of each other. In 1830 Christopher Wallis bought Trevarno and began a major reorganisation of its grounds. Trelowarren and Trevarno lie within a few miles of each other and, with the former straining to escape from an eighteenth-century Arcadia, and the latter surging confidently toward the age of garden technology, they present an accurately conflicting picture of Cornish gardens in the 1830s. To compound the chaos it does no harm to remember that Tullimaar, on the hillside above Perranarworthal, had just been built in 1829, for the bourgeois owner-manager of a gunpowder factory, Benjamin Sampson, with confident Italian terraces overlooking what was then a tidal estuary.[13] If Gardenesque gardeners hankered after any firm garden model it was the Italian. Terraces could project statues, urns, steps and balustrades, all satisfyingly expensive and showy.[14]

52 *The broad, green terrace parallel to the Gothick Chapel at Trelowarren is a survivor of Sir Richard Vyvyan's Arcadian Garden, which is recorded on an eighteenth-century estate map by Dionysius Williams*

Time and again in the 1780-1840 period woodland gardens were attempted with flowers planted in deep shade by the side of paths. Deep shade suits very few flowers and Mason was being most impractical. As at Moditonham's Wilderness the serpentine paths at Trelowarren's Pleasure Grounds have lost their roses and their honeysuckle. In an inappropriate stroke of formalism, typical of the Gardenesque's Italian hankerings, Sir Richard Rawlinson Vyvyan laid out a massive flight of formal steps with vases up to the soft green Georgian terrace where a wide, straight avenue, axial to the old house, slices through the serpentine woodland (52). Then, as if responding archaeologically to the house, he created three walled gardens, one large and botanical, but the others cosily clustered against the seventeenth-century house core, including a Melon Garden and Lady Clara Vyvyan's Garden, which works delightfully today.[15] The Botanical Garden, very much in the spirit of the nineteenth century, was intended to instruct, with plants laid out to the systems of Linnaeus and Decandolle, and in its centre there was to have been a temple housing a library whose entrance 'will be formed by two folding iron gates, the pillars of which will terminate in busts of the founders of the two systems'.[16] It is not known how much of this scheme was actually achieved; today the enclosure is laid to grass and acts as a caravan and camping park.

As if these enclosures were not random enough, there is the crenellated wall and the visually insistent, but pleasantly playful, castle turret. How were they all meant to work together and what was Sir Richard's stylistic vision? His grounds included the most impressive fougou in the county, a viewing Mount climbed by a spiral path, Hannibal's Park, a paled and ditched field close to the house, and a wrecked Grotto in Trecoosehill Wood. Yet Trelowarren's central garden area never coheres to form a justification for the sprawling spider of drives that lead into it through belts of trees from arbitrary points of the compass. There is a long, attractively picturesque drive that was laid out in 1846 to the quay at Tremayne to meet Queen Victoria's yacht, which never sailed up the Helford River for its proposed reception; and then there is the 1833 Italianate Ilex Avenue winding up casually between stately dark trees, and the Gweek drive with a pretty *cottage ornée* Lodge; as if the direct way in from the Double Lodges on the St Keverne Road was not enough. Instead of complaining about the way Trelowarren's gardens never quite deliver, it is wiser to enjoy the chaos and absorb the distractions that must have been bemusing the Vyvyans in those early years of the century.

Trevarno does not make the mistake of spreading its Gardenesque offerings so widely. It concentrates its Gardenesque features and has recently crowned them with a most rewarding Garden Museum, highly appropriate to grounds which are a kind of stylistic museum in themselves. Trevarno has been given, by successive nineteenth-century owners: Wallis, Wallis-Popham and Bickford-Smith, every feature a Victorian garden should have, with conservatory-greenhouses in a Walled Garden at its heart. These overlook, beyond three terraces, a stone-rimmed, rectangular lake that ends in a disappointingly shallow cascade. This busy, resourceful garden then makes up for it with a version of King Arthur's Round table in stone, a dramatic Savage Picturesque Rockery (53) and a rockwork Grotto which, with its twin rivulets, would have won Alexander Pope's praise a hundred years earlier.

That formal lake has wild, informal islets, one sinister with gunnera to deter invaders; while, to focus attention from every point on this steep, south slope, a wooden Boathouse has been built (54), like a Gothic chapel, with decorative bargeboards. Until recently this Gardenesque hillside was even more authentic, with bedding of annuals on the 1880 terraces. The glasshouse complex is still richly in period with Muscat and Black Hanbury vines growing in the appealing wreck of glass and delicate woodwork, the whole fronted by a solid, granite Gothic potting house. This atmospheric area deserves thorough restoration: it needs the scent of ripening peaches and a tropic glimpse of orchids trailing down from its roofs. Immediately above the Vine House is a mysterious spiral tunnel of yew, which the Cornwall Gardens Trust survey team has hopefully dated back to the Middle Ages.[17] It would be splendid if they were right, but nowadays these datings need to be scientifically proven.

Trevarno has been fortunate in that its earlier nineteeth-century Gardenesque has been made exotic with an over-planting of the later half of the century. Easy-going camellias have taken over the terraces from the tiresome demands of annuals. Its many garden buildings: Bothy, Dovecote, Gazebo, Icehouse, Loggia,

53 *A Rockery and matching Grotto in the Savage Picturesque manner stand at the head of Trevarno's severely rectangular lake near a stone version of King Arthur's Round Table*

54 *Delicate Gothic bargeboards and a turret lend Trevarno's Boathouse the air of a waterside chapel, as unexpected on that trimly bordered lake as the Round Table*

Rotunda, Ruin, Summerhouse, Boathouse and portico columns dismantled from the house, lie among lush plantings of magnolia, tree ferns and the usual rhododendrons. These cluster moistly round the end of the lake where *Taxodium distichum* on one of the islets looks across to a *Sequoiadendron giganteum* that is properly gigantic, and a small waterfall trickles from a leat into a Bog Garden near the Pet's Graveyard. Oddly I find it hard to imagine Trevarno's garden in sunshine; it is made for Victorian shade.

The twentieth-century additions are incongruously open and formal, with a long Croquet Lawn developing into an Italian Garden gravelled when it should be crazy-paved, and there is a recent summer planting of ceanothus, meliosmas, sorbarias and tetradiums. But the slope above it is beautifully wooded and that white Edwardian Summerhouse is a fine visual contrast, working like the Boathouse down below. After Trevarno one is left thinking how difficult it is for a garden to go wrong when it starts with a valley site. Yet in many ways Trevarno works much harder, with all its Gardenesque trimmings, than do the plant-spotters' gardens in the Helford River valleys and it proves more memorable as a result. I confess to a prejudice in favour of Trevarno; in typical Gardenesque over-generosity it offers so much so compactly.

Pencarrow, more precisely dated to 1831 than Trevarno, which sprawls across the century from the 1830s onwards, is a Gardenesque layout on its best behaviour. Its drive is one of the most enjoyable in Cornwall, comparable with Lanhydrock's marvellous station drive. Walk them both if possible. They are meant to be absorbed from open carriages, not closed motorcars. Pencarrow's drive starts with saucy twin Regency Lodges in the *cottage ornée* style and then sports the original, and now enormous, *Araucaria araucana* which Charles Austin christened 'Monkey Puzzle' when Sir William Molesworth showed them off to him. Most impressive is a solemn grove of beeches around an Iron Age hill fort that puts a kink in the otherwise straight drive. The beeches have been pollarded and grown into a Disneyesque and most un-beech-like profusion of main branches. On the last reach of the drive, which is walled in by the 15th Baronet Molesworth's camellias and azaleas, an unofficial right turn can lead dramatically to the wide bowl of the Italian Garden (55) with rising woods on every side except the west, where Pencarrow's polite 1760-5 classical front acts as a sober foil to the drama of its Gardenesque layout.

Pencarrow's best garden features were created between 1823 and 1855 when the most distinguished and lively of the otherwise staid Molesworths, Sir William, the 8th Baronet, was in charge. He had an important career in Parliament and ended up as Colonial Secretary before dying quite young. His rockworks are very Savage Picturesque, in spirit more mid eighteenth-century than nineteenth; the sylvan walk to the American Garden and the lake is Reptonian in feeling while the great Italian Garden already mentioned is Williamane of 'Sailor' William IV's brief, cheerful, 1830s reign. This last area will have been a bland arena in the Brownian manner before Sir William laid out shallow semi-circular terraces

55   *Sir William Molesworth, the 8th Baronet, transformed the grounds of Pencarrow between 1823 and 1855. This Italian Garden is a typical feature of the reign of William IV, the 'Sailor King'*

centred on its non-figurative fountain. It was described in 1842 as planted out 'with the newest sorts of Dahlias, and of the choicest Pansies, Verbenas, Petunias and Alstromerias',[18] making it Gardenesque at its finicky worst, with only frail fencing to ward off rabbits. Today a stately punctuation of urns has replaced the flowers and stresses the Italian.

A whole scree of giant granite boulders was hauled from Bodmin Moor by grateful tenantry after Sir William had eased them through the grim years of the Corn Laws and, between 1831 and 1834, the gardener, Mr Corbett, built the dramatic Rockery. The boulders now make the arena's enclosing slopes look improbably fierce, like a 'clitter slope' on a Cornish moor, but a crooked passage leads in between them to a small, welcoming Grotto of crystals. Twycross saw Pencarrow in 1846 and recorded:

> The gardens and shrubberies have been laid out by the present proprietor, and are much admired. The garden before the southern front of the house is in the Italian style, with terraces of grass, and in the form of an amphitheatre. In its centre is a fountain made of granite, the basin of which is copied from that in the Piazza Navona, at Rome. On its eastern side is a rockery, in imitation of the neighbouring tors, and composed of rocks of time-worn granite, with shrubs interspersed; dense masses of American plants, with lofty trees in the background, crown the rockery.[19]

An illustration in the *Journal of Horticulture* for 1878 shows a later planting of camellias, rhododendrons, pieris and yuccas.[20] Sir William must have been intensely proud of this feature as in about 1846 he had himself painted with his favourite dog, Garth, sitting in the Italian Garden[21] with the Rockery looming behind him (*colour plate 15*).

Above the Rockery a picturesque route leads off uphill, passing on its way to the lake a handsome stone cross taken from some roadside. Halfway along it the path divides, one branch climbing steeply to a so-called American Garden. To be authentic this should have flowering trees and bushes from the Appalachians. If they were ever planted they have been crowded out by native trees, but the path is worth taking for one quite prodigious oak, pollarded so severely that it looks like a knobkerry, yet still clings onto life. A stream garden has been laid recently along the main path in memory of the late 15th Baronet, Lt. Colonel Sir Arscott Molesworth St Aubyn who restored the grounds after the Service's occupation during the 1939-45 War. Mole's Garden, as it is called, still smacks too much of bark mulch, but the lake, black and reputedly very deep, restores the Savage Picturesque air. Yellow water lilies grow freely, suggesting that it is perhaps not unfathomable. An eighteenth-century Molesworth might have set the lake off with a temple; but we are in temple-grudging Cornwall and the nineteenth-century Molesworths merely circled it with a path. There is an Icehouse, but would Cornwall's gentle climate ever have allowed the lake to ice over? Tree fanciers will want to hunt down a Swamp cypress, a Deodar cedar and a Japanese cedar – all Sir William's and now overwhelmingly mature. Pencarrow's trees are well above the county's extremely high average standard. Back at the house there is a pretty Gothic Seat in the garden wall and a very Cornish tunnel made of slates. Much of the art on the walls of the house is illuminatingly of this mid Victorian period.

Boconnoc comes across as an Airedale terrier among Cornwall's parks: big, good-looking, but a bit rough. There is no arguing about its size, more like a small county than a park, or its looks: river valleys, hanging woods, a chain of lakes, or at least sizeable ponds, and two small forests. If Cornwall had its own proper duke, instead of a royal duke living in London, Boconnoc would be the ideal ducal base; but over the centuries, park and garden-wise, it has never quite got its act together. In other counties Capability Brown's influence is often a mixed landscape blessing, manicuring elegance about him. He never crossed the Tamar, and Repton was not invited, but if either of them had got to work on that promising but tangled countryside they could have worked wonders.

Boconnoc is the archetypal Cornish linear park of drives, anything from seven to nine of them depending on who is counting. One most rewarding ride comes in from Braddock church, climbs up to the 1771 Obelisk to Richard Lyttleton[22] with its two classical altars,[23] then swoops down past the civil war entrenchment and Lawn Lodge to the house. Another from Park Lodge on the west plunges down in to a valley with heart-stirring glimpses of a large herd of beautiful

56 *This small lake with its willow planting is a rare note of careful landscaping in the generally rough-and-ready park of Boconnoc*

57 *The very grand, but waterless, Cold Bath and Bath House of 1804-7 to the rear of Boconnoc house is of a piece with the forlorn charms of this vast park*

fallow deer, passes a lake with self-conscious willows (56) and then comes up to the house. That is Boconnoc's problem. There is something anticlimactic about the house in such a major park. Its eight-bay centre fails to justify its Venetian-windowed wings; and where are the gardens? The front lawn has a sunken tennis court that must once have been a bowling green. There is a small rockery on the bluff that supports the pretty little church. Hidden away behind the house, where there could have been terraces overlooking the Lerryn is the 1804-7 Bath House and Cold Bath (57), now dry and overhung with camellias and magnolias.[24] A lion's head should spout water and when the current restoration is complete perhaps it will again.

The Stewardry Walk leads north past a quarry Grotto with a 'Roman' sarcophagus with ferns. There is a 1791 Cascade, and above the stables, towards the Pinetum, the remains of a terrace with a circular pool and stretch of wall. In George Fortescue's 1870s album of early photographs the wall is seen supporting an elaborate Orangery with twin cupolas.[25] The Pinetum is a Gardenesque feature, a collector's garden. *Pinus patula*, that most strokable of conifers, features largely, and one redwood seems to have an apprentice's proving piece like that beech at Enys, a weirdly projecting limb. The planting was done around 1840, and there is undeniable rugged charm to it all. The poet Thomas Gray, a guest of the local vicar Mr Forster, used to come 'and pore upon the brook that babbles by'.[26] William Mason was so fond of the Lerryn that he wished he had included it in the third book of his *English Garden* poem. Characteristically the park hosts an annual Steam Festival; perhaps that is the time to experience it, snorting with steam harvesters: rough. It also hosts the Cornwall Garden Society's Spring Flower Show.

Boconnoc's Pinetum was planted in 1840, William Andrews Nesfield was called in by Edward Carlyon to design a Gardenesque setpiece for Tregrehan in 1843.[27] With balustrading, steps, urns, statues, a fountain pond and a French-style *parterre de broderie*, it was a concentration of the style at its most artificial.[28] Now the parterre has gone, replaced by a flowery lawn more yellow and white with buttercups and daisies than green with grass. The other Gardenesque furnishings remain, but children's toys scatter the lawn and a little blue swimming pool centres it.

Simply to remember the gardens at Tregrehan is cheering. How much Nesfield had to do with the grounds to the east of that flowery lawn is not exactly recorded, but his style: colourful, eventful, crowded and geometrically ordered is everywhere. So much more happens in the Gardenesque at its best that can be remembered and called up than in a plant-spotter's garden, even in its flowering prime. The house, a handsome but severe seven-bay Ionic villa, looks down a long, south-facing slope from a broad ledge of hay fields and mature woods. Entrance is through a strange roofless area of abandoned grain mill and apple store, a sequence of shady garden rooms, but then full light and colour burst in. A wide avenue of creamy *Cornus capitata* flanks beds of white roses firmly outlined in clipped box (*colour plate 17*). If bronze leaves can ever be radiant then *Acer palmatum* trees are, seen against the long commanding line of a white 1846 greenhouse that sets the whole garden's exuberant tone.

An avenue of *Cordyline australis* was in full flower on my visit (*58*), and to walk it was like being sprayed with an expensive men's aftershave. Until this chapter I have restrained my surprise and pleasure in this astonishing palm, which is not botanically a palm at all, though it looks like one, but a member of the lily of the valley family, which explains its heavenly yet quite un-floral scent. The Maoris eat its tips and make porridge from its pith, which seems sacrilege to me. I had never come across it before my Cornish journeys, or perhaps I was not near it at the right time in June to have its fragrance wafted down every other street and every Cornish garden, municipal and private. West of the Tamar it is called the Cornish Palm; east of the Tamar it is the Torbay Palm; it actually comes from New Zealand, and should gratefully be named from that country.

To return to Tregrehan the much blessed, that Cornus avenue leads to a fat cherub standing on a shell supported by three dolphins twining their tails, it is backed by those blazing bronze Acer trees, and Tregrehan is heavily populated in

58 *To walk down this fine avenue of Cordyline australis at Tregrehan was like being sprayed with expensive aftershave. These trees are New Zealand's best gift to Cornwall*

the true Gardenesque fashion with statuary and urns. On the wall by the white greenhouses *Abelia floribunda* droops cerise flowers; a cork oak by a pink camellia and a copper beech makes another uninhibited colour confusion, Monterey pines give background silhouettes and, because plants here are so well labelled, I discovered the name of my most esteemed Cornish exotic bush, which I had seen but not named at Lanhydrock. It is *Kalmia latifolia*, pink and with exquisitely whorled florets. According to my notes, which I find hard to credit, the sitting-out area, modern but Gardenesque in spirit, is planted with courgettes in box-hedged beds. At that point severity takes over with a soaring avenue of forty-foot yews guarded by the angry looking statue of Molossan hound, quite unlike the resident Labrador.

The avenue, which is positively funereal in all this colour, leads back to Nesfield's formal enclosed garden and the house. He intended the parterre to be separated from the entrance forecourt by yew hedges 'kept clipped and grown in such a manner as to cause arches over communicating walks'.[29] Now the planting has gone, but four statues of the Seasons still stand on corner quadrants of the lawn (59). They look Art Deco in their linear stylisation but are of the 1840s, not at all early Victorian in feeling, though the urns on the balustrading

59 *Nesfield's parterre and yew hedges for the garden forecourt of Tregrehan have gone, but the 1840s' Statues of the Seasons from that formal layout now guard a swimming pool*

are indulgently rich with vine leaves, goat's heads and Pan pipes. Entirely un-shaded and sun soaked, like everything else at Tregrehan except the yews, they do need Nesfield's original fussy parterre to be authentically Gardenesque, but the children would not enjoy the swimming pool much if it was restored. When a gardener has been notably successful, as Martin Mattock was at Enys, I like to mention the name, and Tregrehan's presiding genius, New Zealand like the cordylines, is Tom Hudson.

Nesfield was also commissioned to design a French-style *parterre de broderie* for Tregothnan as a foil to the newly enlarged house, recently completed in 1845-8 by Lewis Vulliamy for the 2nd Earl of Falmouth. Until recently it was unclear as to what Vulliamy designed around the house and what Nesfield achieved in the gardens. Vulliamy was responsible for the arched Gate House Lodge at Tresillian Bridge, which is the entry to a four-mile scenic drive along the Tresillian River, but the railed and walled forecourt to the house with its heraldic gatepiers would seem to be by Nesfield, who drew it out along with the designs for the parterre.[30] This was planted to the rear of the house on the terrace overlooking the Fal and was criticised in 1877: 'One turns from this pleasant scene [of the Fal] with regret, for, most unfortunately, the terrace is not in harmony with it…[it] is now occupied with circles of Box embroidery and spar of various colours.'[31] This gives a good idea of what the Tregrehan parterre must have looked like in its prime. Nesfield's layout has since decayed and has been recently replaced.[32]

The most impressive Gardenesque layout in the county is at Lanhydrock where a geometric garden (*60*) was laid out on the east-facing slope between the Jacobean main house and its Commonwealth Gatehouse.[33] Until recently it had been assumed that George Gilbert Scott, who was altering Lanhydrock for Thomas James Agar-Robartes between 1855 and 1864, was responsible for the garden, and that it was executed by his chief assistant, the Liskeard-based Richard Coad. But the Trust's House and Collections Manager at Lanhydrock, Paul Holden, has discovered a garden design by the London architect, George Truefitt, which proves that Coad merely modified Truefitt's original Italianate conception of a walled enclosure with steps, gravel paths, sentinel Irish yews and geometric beds.[34] Coad was more historically aware than Truefitt and produced a simple, stepped and pierced wall with an embattled enclosure punctuated by pinnacled obelisks to accord with the architecture of both the house and the Gatehouse; the wall is dated 1857. Neither Coad nor Truefitt make any mention of the original planting schemes, and the layout may well have been planted up by the Head Gardener, Joseph Bray, in consultation with Anna Maria Agar and her daughter-in-law, Juliana Agar-Robartes.[35] The gardens were further altered in 1881-6, again overseen by Coad, and they now present an historically confusing, eclectic mix of Italianate and Jacobean revival. But then the Commonwealth Gatehouse presents blind Renaissance arches to the outside world and similar, but old-fashioned, Gothic arches to its parent house in a parallel, binary balancing trick of stylistic uncertainty.[36]

60 *George Truefitt's Gardenesque Italian concept for the forecourt of Lanhydrock was realised by George Gilbert Scott's assistant, Richard Coad. The Gatehouse is Commonwealth in date and Coad's pinnacled wall accords well with it*

There is some measure of stylistic confrontation between the flat, stale classicism of Pencalenick's nineteenth-century façade and the garden that was created to front the house and, with the best of visual intentions, to enjoy views of its estuaries. As built in 1883, for Michael Henry Williams by that lacklustre architect, J.P. St Aubyn, the house was meant to look out over three grand terraced levels to the river, with Tregothnan beyond. All that is lost now as a thick growth of self-seeded ash with the usual sub-jungle of *Rhododendron ponticum* grew up under military wartime requisitioning, a period as an Italian prisoner-of-war camp and lastly a residential school for children of special needs, who must have a marvellous time hacking out dens in the rhododendron jungle. A 1950 survey of the gardens discovered that of twenty-five exotic shrubs flourishing in 1897 only eight, hardy species such as rhododendrons, bamboo, magnolias and akebia were still struggling for life. Few of the cultivated herbaceous plants were left on those overgrown terraces.[37]

Chymorvah marks a descent down the social scale, as it is a pair of semi-detacheds, one of them an hotel, one a private house, set back a safe distance from the cliff edge at Marazion. Each semi has a long, narrow strip of garden at its back, walled off from each other but sharing at the bottom a semi-detached Gazebo pleasure pavilion high on the very edge of the cliff and commanding one of the greatest sea views anywhere along our coasts. St Michael's Mount is perfectly placed in the middle ground and the Newlyn coast streams away, soft purple in the background. For some reason, possibly because they are expected to fall eighty feet down onto the sands at any moment (*61*), no one uses these perfect rooms for picnics or for writing. Each room has sash windows and, while their parent semis, built for two related mine officials, are solid granite blocks of the 1860s, the Gazebos have, in their cornice and their wrecked ironwork, a Regency dash about them. The hotel's garden is the epitome of Cornish holidays, a happy sequence of wind chimes, a small lily pond, smelly black ducks, lawns for sunny tea-times and the boiler house of a ruined greenhouse. Next door has retained more of its Gardenesque structure with four of the garden enclosures marked off completely from each other, usually by those flowering escallonia hedges that are as Cornish as the cordylines. It is all very modest and matter-of-fact, but it is good to be reminded how class-versatile the Gardenesque can be. It adapts equally well to terraced two-storey houses, one class lower than these.

It is questionable whether the last garden of this chapter should be placed in with the Victorians or with the later Edwardians, but its date of 1867–8 anticipates the reign of Edward VII by thirty years so it has to take its chronological place here. At the same time it can be noted as the Gardenesque reaching forward to the stately aristocratic yew hedges and walled enclosures of the Arts and Crafts revival. The gardens of The Downes are otherwise only Gardenesque in one feature: their flowerbeds, and most of those had either been replaced by lawns or

61 *The semi-detached Gazebos at Chymorvah are perilously poised on the cliff edge looking out to St Michael's Mount. In their Regency details they seem older than their 1860 parent houses*

disappeared under a growth of weeds, brambles and bushes on my visit.

One pleasant relic of the days of heavy industry at Hayle is the number of Roman Catholic institutions: convents, hospitals and chapels in the Trelissick Road. They could be the result of an influx of Irish labour to take the place of smitten and poisoned Cornish nonconformists. In the heart of this Catholic hospital land is The Downes, an attractively asymmetrical house of suburban Gothic aspect built by Edmund Sedding for an antiquary, William John Rawlings, who had invested successfully in Hayle's industry.[38] Its gardens were laid out by Sedding's brother, John Dando Sedding, to his earnestly expressed principles that 'Art and Nature should be linked together'.[39] To achieve this Sedding argued that:

> it is essential that the ground immediately about the house should be devoted to symmetrical planning, and to distinctly ornamental treatment; and the symmetry should break away by easy stages from the dressed to the undressed part, and so on to the open country, beginning with wilder effects upon the country-boundaries of the place, and more careful and intricate effects as the house is approached.[40]

Sedding illustrated this 'appearance of graduated formality'[41] in his seminal 1890 *Garden-Craft Old and New* by a perspective view of part of the garden at The Downes (*62*), which shows the original layout of geometric flowerbeds, arcaded yew hedges and domed pavilion.

For many years after Rawlings' death the house was a convent. How concerned the nuns were with the garden's upkeep is not clear, but the new owners, Hazel and Bryn Danson, have returned much of Sedding's labour-intensive terracing and paths to pristine order leaving a large area, roughly a half of the grounds, in a formidable tangle of almost impenetrable growth. So walking the grounds today is a curious dual experience of trim clarity and brambled ruin. First comes a shaven sea of lawn, all just a little out of scale for what is essentially no more than a big suburban villa. Sedding had his eye on the Hortus Palatinus behind the Elector Palatine's great schloss at Heidelberg, but Hayle and Heidelberg was an over-ambitious union. A broad stone-flagged terrace, Jacobean in styling, continues the grandiose pattern and then, on the right of a wide, axial way lies discipline, while on the left there is chaos, with weeds surging around well-grown trees and bushes. There is one aspect of this garden that never seems under control: its skylines are unpredictable (*colour plate 18*). There are lines of scrawny eucalyptus, Chusan palms rear up alien heads at unplanned places, a lovely Monterey pine dominates by the sheer elegance of its branching crown. Where Sedding had planned thick, firm yew hedges in arched and disciplined division, the axial way now marches between the notorious Leyland cypresses which lead, not to a domed Palatine pavilion as in the original design, but to a good replica of the Gothic St Germoe's Chair, a chantry chapel in the churchyard wall of Germoe. It was an admirable nationalistic gesture to point out that the fifteenth-century Cornish could design an original Gothic pavilion, but that, together with the Leylands, does cross the visual wires, as do the escallonia hedges, pink and pale green, so unlike Sedding's proposed yew-dark barriers.

Down the far end of the garden, where vistas out to sea might be expected there is a high wall with an interesting range of practical garden structures. They have brick and slate floors, water tanks and small stoves ready to heat up the warm beds; and there is a bothy or apple store waiting for gardeners to brew their tea and eat their midday cause. As a survival of nineteenth-century working conditions they would be an asset to any museum, and it is to be hoped that one day they will be restored and returned to productive use.

The curious feature of this garden is its determined isolation from what could be a fine view. Probably when it was laid out in 1868 the outside world was so full of poisonous smelting fumes and smoking chimneys that a garden oasis from industrial ugliness was a necessity. But there was the sea. There is no feeling in The Downes of a seaside garden even though it is within the sound of breakers. It was an interesting experiment in formal isolation and Pett claims it as 'one of the most historically important gardens in Cornwall'.[42] Tourism can breath life into most wilting institutions, and tourists could be led away from run-down post-industrial Hayle to make their way through the hospital premises into this remarkable garden on the cusp between Victorian Gardenesque and Edwardian Arts and Crafts. I hope they can, because in terms of 'hard' landscaping in a county of 'soft' gardens, The Downes is without a rival.

62 *John Dando Sedding's proposed garden for The Downes, Hayle, from* Garden-Craft Old and New. *His domed classical temple was replaced by a replica of the medieval St Germoe's Chair.* Bristol University Special Collections

7

The Edens of the Quaker plant-spotters

These are the gardens for which Cornwall is rightly famous; the nineteenth-century was the county's golden age of daring horticultural experiment. Where the 50th parallel of latitude cuts into the coast of northern Quebec near the Pentecost River the pine trees are stunted and fail to grow to any height. Cornwall lies for the most part even further north than the 50th parallel, which cuts its way across the Lizard peninsula. Yet Cornwall, as a direct result of bold horticultural enterprise in the nineteenth century, is full of gardens that bristle with bamboo, have skylines of palm trees, groves of camellias and thickets of bright flaming Chilean fire bushes. The county is by no means sub-tropical, yet it can confidently assume subtropical airs. Thanks to Cornwall, England feels that it can at least dip its toes into the Mediterranean and have a share in the warm South. As King Arthur retired in his wounded old age to Lyonesse: 'Deep-meadow'd, happy, fair with orchard-lawns/And bowery hollows crown'd with summer sea',[1] so every year in our time hundreds of retirees come to Cornwall in quest of that same vision, to spend the evening of their days in a different climate. Because of its garden profile, the Royal Duchy is a psychological extension of everyone's concept of England, not a northern land of cold and harshness, but a country that contains its own boundaries, a holiday home of surfing and soft, warm nights. It is not important that much of its garden air is an illusion, that the Chusan palms that lend the image of a South-Sea island to so many Cornish coastal landscapes can survive 8,000 feet up in the Himalayas and withstand temperatures of -20°c.[2] The illusion is what matters; and the great planting dynasties of the nineteenth century: the Foxes of Falmouth, the Bolithos of Penzance and the Williamses of Caerhays, demonstrated that, with Chusans, phormiums, *Cordyline australis*, a few tree ferns and a towering Monterey pine, anyone could conjure up the tropics and proceed to the rich, self-indulgence of camellias, magnolias and half the world's floral riches. All thanks to experimental curiosity, a Quaker confidence in God's bounty and the Gulf Stream.

If a founding father, or at least a founding family, is required for this great expansion in British garden thinking then Robert Were Fox II (1789-1877), and the Fox family, shipping agents and industrialists of Falmouth, are likely candidates. At Falmouth, where the Foxes' firm acted as consuls for no fewer than thirty-seven nations, a shipping agent would have regular friendly contact with sea captains sailing into that busy, prosperous, deep-water harbour. And if one of those agents was, like Robert Were II, a scientist, a fellow of the Royal Society with a large garden at Rosehill in Falmouth's mild microclimate, then most captains would be ready to oblige by bringing back from the Far East and Australia exotic plants for naturalisation. Robert Were had leased Rosehill, where the Falmouth College of Art now stands and scraps of his garden survive, from Lord Wodehouse in 1821. Soon he was growing orange and lemon trees and date palms in the open and had naturalised 300 plants in the ground close around the house. What caught the imagination of his fellow garden enthusiasts was the report that from one tree in one season he had produced 400 oranges and, better still, picked 123 lemons from one tree in one day.[3] By raising vistas of many branched cordylines alternating with bamboo and the *Chusan Trachycarpus fortunei* he had brought images of the Pacific right into Falmouth harbour.

What made Robert Were Fox's achievements so influential was that he was a member of a clan of devout Quakers and that two of his brothers and a cousin were equally keen gardeners. Alfred (1794-1870) created Glendurgan and Charles (1797-1878) created Trebah, cousin George Croker Fox III (1784-1850) gardened at Grove Hill and Goonvrea, while Robert Were Fox himself made Penjerrick famous.[4] Ironically Penjerrick today is an idyllic, little visited jungle, as natural and Quaker-friendly as Robert would ever have wished. His brothers' gardens, on the other hand, are nationally celebrated, concentrations of horticultural expertise, serviced by car parks, restaurants and shops, while any number of un-Quakerish devices are deployed to seduce overweight visitors and potentially bored children around the steep, testing paths of their valley circuits.

This question of Quaker beliefs and the function of a garden is a fascinating one. We pay our substantial entrance fees and walk around Trebah, Glendurgan, Caerhays or any of the more successful tourist draws in Cornwall's astonishing ninety or more gardens listed in the current Tourist Board brochure. But are we enjoying their original vision, or the skilful anticipation of what the average modern visitor requires? By happy accident of itinerary my first two gardens of this nineteenth-century plant-spotter group were not two of the 'big beasts', but two relatively unchanged gardens by the two rival figures of that first age: Robert Were II's own experimental grounds at Penjerrick, where I saw no other visitor, not even an owner, in the rewarding hour I spent struggling through a wilderness of riotous growth. The other was Sir Charles Lemon's very different, very private, garden at Carclew. Before attempting any analysis of the Quaker's garden psyche, two brief descriptions are in order.

The drive to Penjerrick is long, straight and stony, leading in typical Cornish fashion, not through a park, but down a green field, with woods well back on either side. Before reaching the house a notice tells visitors to park beside the drive, then dive down left through a little wrought-iron gate (*colour plate 19*), by an honesty box, into the wood. Blossom breaks out and an overgrown terrace leads right past the remains of a fern-planted Grotto and several semi-circular beds, until the house, a pleasant sub Arts and Crafts suburban villa of 1935, sidles in unannounced. The property had been in the family since the eighteenth century, but the grounds, apart from the terrace, came under no particular control until Robert let his son, Barclay Fox, loose on them in the mid 1830s. Barclay died in 1855, long before his father, and Robert and his elder daughter, Maria, were then responsible, landscaping with what the *Gardeners' Chronicle* described reverentially in 1874 as 'the most exquisitely cultivated taste'.[5]

Certainly the steep view down to and across the deeply sunken public road that divides Penjerrick's garden in half, is theatrical and cleverly narrowed to make it seem longer. A splendid copper beech on the right adds gravitas and contrasting colour. Rooks caw, under-planted rhododendrons colour up the shadows, wild garlick, solomon's seal and fritillaries are wild-English and almost Chiltern. Then, with a high, wooden bridge, like one over a railway line, the garden leaps across the road into the Wilderness and vegetation closes in. There was once a Swiss Cottage by an upper pond which Barclay and his father Robert were digging in 1837. Pett mentions a '*cottage ornée* listed grade II',[6] so I and a friend divided our ways and plunged into the truly authentic, subtropical jungle that has grown up there; battering our separate ways through rattling phormiums, squelching gunnera swamps and past tree ferns that sometimes posed fetchingly by shrunken puddles (*63*). Often we would hear each other crashing in the distance but, for an amusing ten minutes or so, completely lost each other and our sense of direction, if ever there was one on that 'exquisitely cultivated' waste. If the Swiss Cottage exists I could not find it and we guessed that the Revd. Pett may have got as lost as we did and took it on trust from the Garden's Register. One sad result of this rampageous overgrowth is that the view from the terrace no longer ends, as it originally did, with yellow sands and the sea. Penjerrick's garden is a ghost and there is little evidence that it ever had much earthly form; so it does raise questions about Quaker gardening. In a letter of 1890 which Sarah Fox (Alfred's wife and Robert Were's sister-in-law) wrote to her son, George, to explain the planning of Glendurgan, she makes a very revealing admission about what has become one of the best-known and most visited gardens: 'There was no original design for the grounds but it gradually worked into what it now is'.[7]

The Fox family lived in a world more of seventeenth-century than nineteenth-century religious devotion. It involved marrying within their own sect, cold-shouldering brother Joshua for marrying an Anglican, conducting their baptisms on the beach at Durgan, seeing visions, caring for the poor of the parish, the education of the children in particular, whipping naughty sons,

63 *The atmospheric jungle of gunnera, tree ferns and muddy puddles is what remains from the pioneering, post-1835 valley planting of Robert Were Fox and Barclay Fox at Penjerrick*

refusing to take a hat off even to Queen Victoria, and suffering regular raids from bailiffs for refusing to pay their tithes to the established Church. God permeated every aspect of their being; but a wealthy Quaker tends to live in an aesthetic limbo imposed by simple living. A vainglorious show of ornamental architecture is forbidden, but do the same rules apply to a garden? Is that perhaps an area of neutral aesthetics? Since God made a garden as Man's first environment, are plants and trees morally safer than bricks and stones? Can a simple house be set in a richly ambitious garden? If so was Penjerrick once richly ambitious, and were Trebah and Glendurgan also rich gardens?

A park with winding artificial drives and geometrically-patterned beds was unacceptable because it could be seen as a symbol of sinful pride in ownership. Garden buildings in deceiving imitations of churches, castles or, worse still, heathen temples, would certainly be wrong, and in this respect Quakers would be thinking in line with the general Cornish avoidance of garden buildings over the eighteenth century.

How much care then, ever went into the composition and design of the great Quaker gardens? Sarah Fox claimed that there was none, but on several occasions at Trebah, Charles Fox had sixteen helpers working with loudhailers, ladders and flags plotting where to plant a tree that was likely to grow tall in future and block the view. There was clearly a grouping together of plants in the same genus. It resulted in that train-spotting sequence of camellias mentioned earlier, and in that later, depressing level swamp of hydrangeas in the lower reaches of Trebah, just where the garden should be making some response to the seashore. Bamboos and Monterey pines are architectural enough to lend form to areas where they are growing. At Trebah the Bamboozle, by its noisy brook, creates an event, as does the nearby grouping of tree ferns, lily pool and open sky that composes well from three angles: accident or design?

Was there, at the back of the Fox family's gardening, the notion of creating, in a lowly human scale, models of the first Garden of Eden by concentrating God's floral riches from around the world within the heaven-sent microclimates of Falmouth? Whatever the motive, those plant-spotter gardens that the Fox, the Bolitho and the Williams families were planting across Cornwall, forty in all by one cousin connection or another,[8] were truly innovative garden forms, neither park nor garden, but whole tracts of country given over to rare imported trees, bushes and plants, exempt apparently from the design rules and decorative buildings of the gardens of two preceding centuries: no balustraded terraces, no formal canals, no parterres, no folly buildings. Was the formal Gardenesque style dead or still being practised alongside the plant-spotter gardens by members of the same horticultural society? The answer lies in the gardens behind the gutted, romantic wreck of Carclew, Cornwall's most handsome ruin.

It is possible to sense, in the minutes of those earliest meetings of the Cornwall Horticultural Society,[9] the brooding presence of Sir Charles Lemon, the master of Carclew. Other aristocrats were present, the Duke of Leeds from Godolphin, the Earl of Falmouth from Tregothnan and Lord de Dunstanville from Tehidy; but none of them except de Dunstanville, who had planted successful woodlands above the cliffs of Tehidy, could match Sir Charles's commitment to gardening. His family had made their money from tin mining but settled at Carclew, in their resoundingly Greek Revival house, to be Truro's resident aristocrats, hence Lemon Quay and Lemon Street. It was Sir Charles's father, Sir William, who had given the gardens of Carclew their controlling terraced form, but the almost overwhelming floral richness of those terraces, that pit of flowers that still blossoms today at Carclew, was created by Sir Charles with the help of his scholarly gardener, William Beattie Booth, an authority on camellias.[10]

It was Sir Charles who had the idea of offering a medal to the ship's captain who brought in the most exciting new plants, and Sir Charles who employed in minor garden roles the young Lobb brothers, William and Thomas, sons of his gamekeeper, John Lobb. The two boys went off, inspired by the forward looking horticulture of Carclew, to work for the great Veitch nurseries of Exeter.[11] William

Lobb may have done more to change the actual profile of English gardens than any other plant hunter, if only by bringing back thousands of seeds of the Monkey Puzzle, *Araucaria araucana*, and the *Sequoiadendron giganteum*, which we insist on calling Wellingtonias, even though the Americans wanted to name them after George Washington.[12] As if those were not enough to spike the English skyline, he poured, very profitably, into Veitch's stock, the seeds of the noble fir (*Abies procera*), the western red cedar (*Thiya plicata*), Douglas' giant fir (*Abies grandis*), several other showy conifers and a number of west-coast flowers. Those middle decades, the 1840s and the 1850s, were the boom time for Victorian planting of specimen trees and, like them or not, they are mostly still growing, some with a possible one or two thousand year life span, and the growth potential to soar up to two-thirds the height of Salisbury Cathedral's 404 foot spire. All that from a Carclew gardener's boy! Thomas, Williams' brother, made for India and South-East Asia, aiming for delicate orchids and rhododendrons with similar success.

Today Carclew's garden has gone through a most peculiar reversal of directions, but still remains more than worthy of Sir Charles and the Lobb brothers. The house was gutted in 1934 and since then the service buildings at the far end of the terraced garden sequence have been made into a pleasant modern house which now controls, over a cut-down wall, the wild luxuriance of the flowery terraced pit. As a result, a visit to the gardens, which are sometimes open for charity, begins at the top of the terraces where they were originally supposed to end when they were viewed from their lost parent house. I was taken around by Penny Scott-Barrett and her son on a memorable morning visit which happened to be my first introduction to the stunning flowery profusion which is quite common in this favoured part of the county.

The first view was unforgettable, like looking down into Dante's circles of hell that had been transformed into the circles of heaven. Red and yellow azaleas and rhododendrons gave the prevailing swirls of colour around the sides of the arena; and the rectangular Higher Pond at the bottom was hardly visible as water because it was so solidly covered with yellow iris and kingcups. Distinct notes of hard architectural gardening showed up among the flowering bushes, with terraced lawns, monolithic, granite gatepiers with pagoda caps and ball finials and ironwork, all most unlike the Quaker gardens further south along the sea coast. The skyline was as hyperactive as the arena, with yews, beech, ginkgo, sequoias, Lucombe oaks and that Cornish signature, the Monterey pine. This last had been discovered by David Douglas, but it was William Lobb who brought a treasure of its seed cones back for Veitch to popularise from the firm's new premises on the King's Road in Chelsea.

What made that Carclew visit easy to recall was the compartmentation of the arena. The two, or, by another count, three terraces with six subdivisions created their separate gardens linked down steps with muted Art Nouveau leaf-shaped ironwork balusters. There were walls of white roses, *Cornus chinensis*, a little holy well, a cherub in a circular pool, a Rococo-style gnomon of Bath stone, a seat

1 *Heaths and harebells on a slope overlooking St Michael's Mount have taken over the pre-Roman courtyard houses at Chysauster*

2 *Less than three feet high, the walls of the supposed 'garden' on Tintagel's most exposed plateau are more likely to have bounded a medieval hurling court or bowling green*

3 *Writing in 1602, Richard Carew admired Sir Reginald Mohun's Hall Walk at Polruan for its views 'on the fair and commodious haven' of Fowey*

4 *The gracefully curvilinear parterres of clipped box within the cob-walled garden at Rosteague could be 350 years old: a unique survival*

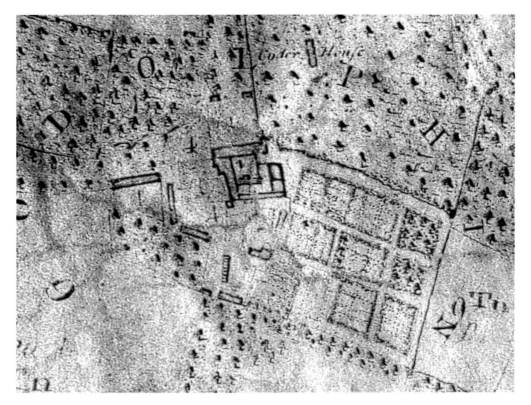

5 *The 1791 estate map of Godolphin was drawn for the Duke of Leeds from a 1786 survey and shows late seventeenth-century planting in the nine earlier enclosures of Jacobean date*

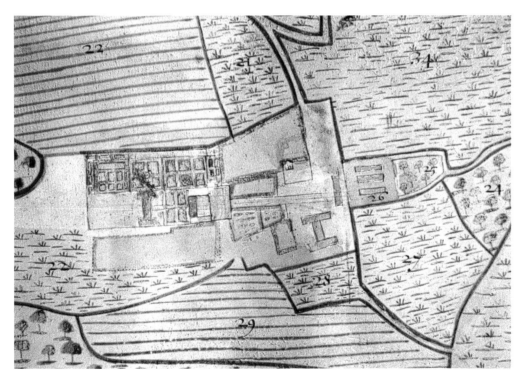

6 *Ambitious but ill-conceived, the formal gardens of the Earl of Bath's seat at Stowe, near Kilkhampton, drawn here in Joel Gascoyne's 1690s estate atlas, lasted a bare thirty years.* Cornwall Record Office

7 One of the twin, two-storey early eighteenth-century garden pavilions in the finely textured decay of Enys, Cornwall's lost, but happily not yet found, Arcadia

8 The Italian Garden at Mount Edgcumbe was laid out in 1785 by George, 3rd Baron and later 1st Earl, as an enchantingly inappropriate tribute to Ariosto

9 With its delicate relief of a sea nymph and a four-masted ship, this, one of two Coade stone panels, is set into the side walls of a viewing pavilion in the grounds of Sir John Call's lost Whiteford House at Stoke Climsland

10 The grounds of Chyverton are a rare Cornish essay in the park style of Capability Brown by a Truro lawyer, John Thomas, working in the 1770s

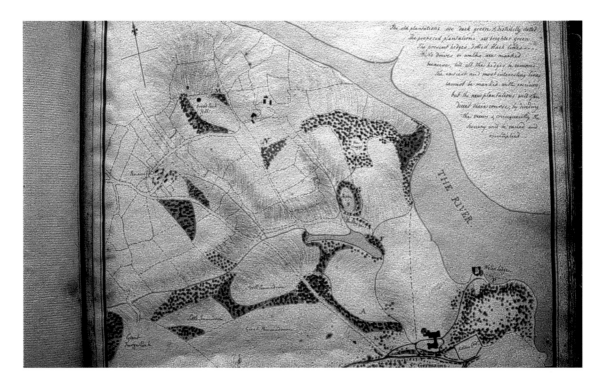

11 *The map in Humphry Repton's Red Book for Port Eliot demonstrates with satisfying clarity how he intended to dramatise an existing topography by planting sweeping curves of woodland along ridges of land facing the house.* By kind permission of the Earl of St Germans

12 *This view of Port Eliot's Great Lawn looking north from the house illustrates Repton's planting of shelter belts against prevailing winds as presented in his intended alterations on the estate map*

13 *Repton's persuasive artistry: looking west from Tregothnan to the Fal estuary before his recommended planting of shelter belts against the prevailing winds.* By kind permission of Lord Falmouth

14 *After Reptonian planting: the slide is pulled back and all at Tregothnan is calm with the contours firmly framed as his Red Book of 1809 proposes.* By kind permission of Lord Falmouth

15 *Sir William Molesworth sitting in his Savage Picturesque Rockery, a picture of a proud landowner with his dog Garth by Alfred Edward Chalon of about 1846.* By kind permission of the Molesworth-St Aubyn family

16 Jack Siley's *1960s Berniniesque Tritons* enlivened the Higher Pond at Carclew, which has now grown almost solid with iris and kingcups.

17 *A welcome formality of creamy cornus, white roses and bronze acers in the Walled Garden at Tregrehan*

18 *Order to the right of John Dando Sedding's central axial way at The Downes, Hayle, tangled chaos to the left. This 1868 layout anticipates some of the features of post-1892 gardens, but terminates in a Ruskinian medieval structure, not a Jacobean-style pavilion*

19 *Entry to the refreshing but overgrown plant jungle of Penjerrick where Robert Were Fox and his son, Barclay, pioneered the Quaker valley gardens of exotic profusion in the 1830s*

20 *Modelled on a Regency maze in Sydney Gardens, Bath, the Maze in Alfred Fox's Glendurgan creates a much needed event to which visitors can relate in the long sequence of flowering bushes and trees*

21 *Black water and sinister gunnera at Trewidden are relieved by the bronze tail of a whale which, when first installed, wriggled and spouted water*

22 *David Wynne's statue of Gaia, the Earth Goddess, is surrounded by the flamboyant fertility of Tresco Abbey's pastiche of a sub-tropical garden*

23　*These miniature menhirs and dolmens are the best joke in a mock 'Rococo' garden created late in the nineteenth century and restored in the late twentieth to entertain guests at the Long Cross Hotel near St Endellion*

24　*Looking down on the three terraced levels of the cliff garden on the south face of St Michael's Mount with the Walled Gardens in the middle ground; this view explains how agapanthus can seem to hang directly above the breaking seas*

26 Above: *Barbara Hepworth bought the Trewyn garden in the middle of St Ives in 1949 and, advised by Priaulx Rainier, planted it to create a flattering background for a concentrated group of her boldest sculptural forms.* Bowness, Hepworth Estate

25 Opposite: *Created by a succession of three owners between the 1880s and the 1960s, the garden of Eagles Nest on a headland above Zennor uses plants to dramatise granite boulders rather than the other way round*

27 *A thin film of water flows down William Pye's Water Cone of 1996, sited aggressively but successfully on a very grand late nineteenth-century terrace in the French chateau style at Antony*

28 *After a long, tentative dalliance with Modernist garden designs Cornwall plucked up its courage and in 1997 began the most Modernist garden in Britain, Nicholas Grimshaw's Biomes for Tim Smit's Eden Project: a master stroke for the tourist industry*

carved with a horse and a lion, the usual but always delightful *Davidia involucrata* or handkerchief tree, and at every stage, camellias, azaleas and rhododendrons, the background bushes which in this part of Cornwall are taken for granted.

A raised, dry, water chute came in on the left, like a hangover from a tin mine and then at last the Higher Pond, so dense with flowering plants that it was a temptation to walk on it in order to make a closer inspection of the muscular stone tritons (*colour plate 16*), rising high out of the leaves and lending a Florentine note to the heady chaos. Penny Scott-Barrett would not, I think, mind if I described the lake verges, and indeed the whole arena, as being in a state of glorious dilapidation, the very best condition for a garden to be in. The Ionic temple (*64*) with frail seat and a wrought iron dome is a 1930s addition; and its delicate charm makes the point that even the most successful garden is improved by a little architectural punctuation like this to focus a view.

When that Cornwall Horticultural Society was formed, one of its worthier aims was 'for improving the condition of the poor, by the distribution of prizes

64 *This frail 1930s' Ionic Temple gives a much needed focal point to Sir Charles Lemon's gloriously rich 1840s' planting at Carclew*

to cottagers'. This meant that at their first exhibition, held at Truro on 29 June 1832, only a month after their inaugural meeting, vegetables, strawberries, currants and raspberries featured heavily. Apart from the prize for 'Best Stove Shrub', the flowers mentioned were restricted to ericas, pelargoniums, China roses, Scotch roses, ranunculuses, carnations and 'Heartsease bouquets'. But George and Charles Fox were both present, as was a William Williams from the rival clan. The Chairman, the man who had taken the initiative of calling the Society into being, was John Vivian of Pencalenick, whose gardens are now little more than a memory of blocked views and jungle choked terraces.

George Croker Fox III (1784-1850) raised the horticultural tone impressively four years later in 1836 when he was awarded the silver Banksian medal of the affiliated London Horticultural Society 'for the best description of the largest number of plants considered tender in the possession of and under the care of the competitor'. George was the cousin of the brothers Robert Were, Alfred and Charles. He gardened at Grove Hill House in Falmouth and Goonvrea, above Perranarworthal. Little survives on either site.

Sir Charles Lemon, whom one imagines as smouldering sulphurously in the background, fired back the next year, 1837, when he was awarded the same silver medal, 'for an account of the largest number of new and hitherto undescribed plants which shall have flowered in the possession of the competitor'. So honours were even. Not being philoprogenitive, Sir Charles founded no dynasty, but he has left a notable garden.

Looking back on the visit to Carclew and comparing that layout with the Quaker valleys visited soon afterwards it was the concentration of the planting, all on an earlier, late eighteenth-century formal layout by Sir William Lemon, that made it so impressive. At Glendurgan and Trebah very much the same bushes were flowering, in a much neater, though not necessarily better, order, but they are spread out over a longer valley along a circuit with alternative paths and many side vistas. In retrospect they are remarkable achievements, sited next door to each other and disturbingly interchangeable. I often have to refer to my notes made on site to find out which one has the Maze (it is Glendurgan), which one has a Camellia Walk close to the house (they both do); which has the children's names to make certain paths and areas memorable (it is Trebah, under Tony Hibbert's successful direction since 1981; the National Trust at Glendurgan is more genteel). After two visits to both gardens, one in the spring flowering, one in late autumn, it is impossible not to feel admiration for a Puritan vision achieved. But it is difficult not to want to slink off around the corner to the next valley at Carwinion, which is only Fox by the marriage of one of their daughters to a Rogers, and enjoy there the Quaker simplicity enduring, un-commercialised, homely and rough. The National Trust has to take a lot of criticism from people who are really grumbling snobbishly about the kind of visitors who patronise its properties with a horrid, awed reverence. What should be marked up to the Trust's credit is the little noticed fact that they run both Carwinion and Glendurgan and allow the two valley gardens to develop in totally different styles: authentic Quaker at Carwinion, glamorously lavish at Glendurgan.

In his fine memoir of Glendurgan, the present Charles Fox quotes a letter to his great grandfather, George Fox, from his sister, Lucy, written as recently as 1923, to congratulate him on his return to live at the house:

> I have such a strong sense that it is all in the Divine Guidance that Glendurgan
> should be blessed once again with thy management & oversight ... so I am
> singing songs of thanksgiving all today.
> Thine fondly
> Lucy.[13]

These gardens were conceived as the green churches of people who found stone churches too confining to express the Creator's spirit. How does the National Trust safeguard that? The answer is Carwinion, but financially the Trust probably cannot afford more than one garden like Carwinion.

Physically linked at the coast to Glendurgan, Carwinion's unassuming house is sited down a long drive from Mawnan Smith village. Facing the front door in a steep island slope of bamboo is an antique, outsized garden gnome, weather-beaten down to its brown terracotta (65). There is no guardian in a sentry box

65 This antique Garden Gnome sits amongst shrubs at the front door of Carwinion, welcoming visitors to that least changed of Quaker-style gardens

issuing tickets and no restaurant and shop, although Cornish cream teas can be served on the terrace and the lawn. Six ponds, some very small, run like beads down a valley of meadows and woods. Somewhere along its paths, but needing to be hunted down, are clumps of the usual plant-spotter standard features: gunnera, camellias, a Fernery in the old quarry, a Secret Garden so well concealed that I never found it. In between these predictabilities there are welcome bucolic spaces of old Cornwall, with primroses on my visit, and, poking up everywhere, the bamboos upon which Carwinion endearingly prides itself. They were planted by the Rogers, who have remained happily in charge after the Trust was given the garden. Probably the Trust told them: 'you must have a feature and if you won't have Queen Elizabeth rose beds, how about an exhaustive collection of bamboos?'

The bamboos are indeed exhaustive, though hard to take seriously. There are fifty species in the Walled Garden alone, an interesting example of the encyclopaedic Loudon tendency, Cornwall's special version of the Gardenesque. They have all been planted since 1986, which proves how easy it is to become expert and authoritative on a narrow line, as in Glendurgan's camellias or Caerhays' magnolias. Entering into the relaxed spirit of that casual, open, green valley I identified *Chimonobambusa quadrangularis*, which speaks for itself, and the dramatic black bamboo, *Phyllostachys nigra*; they are all clearly labelled and there is a modest two-page introduction to the grounds with a plan. The rocky beach was pleasant; there were some tree ferns, and I searched out the forty-five-foot *Drimys winteri*, which flowers for six months and still had a few ivory white blooms; it is the tallest in Europe.[14] Odd facts like that help a visitor round these 'soft', un-architectural gardens, but should one need to go around any real garden with a guide of helpful facts to hand?

Carwinion's neighbours, Trebah and Glendurgan, must once have been much the same, but now they are professional performances, taking themselves much more seriously as factors in the county's vital tourist industry. It would be invidious to prefer one to the other as they both deliver exactly what visitors want; starting with ample car-parks, ending with large restaurants and tempting shops. In between they offer the flowering bushes at every turn of the immaculately kept non-slip paths.

Interestingly both gardens are edging towards hard gardening. Realising that old people struggling up so many steep slopes need visible destinations where they can sit down, the Trust at Glendurgan has cleverly thought up a Quaker substitute for a garden temple: a School Room. It is sited perfectly against trees, a white, faintly Regency Gothic structure so politically correct as to deserve a preservation order in some future age. 'Why rebuild the School Room?' a notice asks, and promptly answers itself: 'The project has enabled us to maintain involvement with the local community and continue the learning theme for education groups.' There follows a pious, potted history: Alfred Fox's wife, Sarah, built it in 1829 and taught there herself until 1842, when Sir Joseph Pease MP built the big stone School Room down on the beach, now a Trust holiday cottage. In Sarah's day the valley was full of apple and pear trees, a major change of function, and the old School Room became a cider house that doubled as a donkey pound. The donkeys carried fish to Falmouth: all child-centred facts. Few signs of that bucolic past survive, but the view from the recreated School Room composes well behind a little stone marker: a big Scots pine, tree ferns, beeches, a splash of water and, in October, a gallant rearguard action by hydrangeas, that great standby in these essentially spring gardens.

There is one designed garden feature in Glendurgan, more Elizabethan than Gardenesque and it has been there, surprisingly, since 1833, though replanted in 1991. That is the Maze (*colour plate 20*), which sprawls, impressively visual, up one side of the valley, so that visitors can be observed from the opposite side patiently trying to find their way out again. A maze appealed to Quakers because it could be interpreted as a moral problem with choices to be made in the paths of life. Glendrugan's Maze is unusually spiteful as it has four dead-end clearings where steps have to be retraced. It is a copy of a lost maze in Sydney Gardens, Bath.

Trebah's venture into hard gardening is the thatched Alice's Seat (*66*), a cosy memorial to Alice Hext who, with her husband, was probably responsible for most of the present rich planting of exotics between 1907 and 1939, before

66 Alice's Seat at Trebah is, like the Ionic Temple at Carclew, another proof of how the richest collection of flowering exotics still needs garden buildings to pull them together. Alice Hext introduced flamingos to Trebah in the early twentieth century

which time Trebah was like Carwinion. Alice's most impressive introduction was the Mallard Pond for a flock of flamingos, not a Quakerish gesture, but then neither was that Cider House at Glendurgan. The Hibberts have given Trebah a number of other features. For the children there is Tarzan's Camp, The Paraglide to equal Glendurgan's Giant's Stride, and Fort Stuart, a sandpit. A Zig-Zag, a Fernery, a Stumpery, a Vinery and a fern-shaded Koi Pool keep adults on the move, while every path has been personalised on the lines of 'High Harry', 'Badger's Walk', 'The Bamboozle' and 'Lizzie's Lane'. While 'Dinky's Puddle' is cringe-making, that water next to the Bamboozle, Peter's Bridge and the Apollo Pool does compose almost architecturally with tree ferns and lilies. It was sadistically satisfying in that autumn Trebah to see the entire ugly swamp of *Gunnera manicata* lying smashed and shattered. Those thorny leaves look so permanent yet apparently they need to be cut back viciously.

These Helston River, plant-spotter gardens gain greatly in drama as well as shelter from their deep valley sides but, given shelter belts of trees, the same plants flourish equally well on the gentle open slopes of the Bolitho gardens, Trewidden and Trengwainton, behind Penzance, and at Trewithen, near Probus, which was largely George Johnstone's creation on very open ground. While all three must be classed in the plant-spotter category not one of them relies on a mere parade of species in a plant zoo, but all work hard with events and diversions to entertain on a circuit walk. Trengwainton has an unsatisfactory plan requiring a return on virtually the same course as the outward walk. It is likely to be of the least interest to children; but all three gardens have splendid mature specimens of flowering trees; Trengwainton, for instance, left me a permanent admirer of *Magnolia campbellii*.

As usual in the county Trengwainton and Trewidden make a feature of their drives. Trewidden's is deep-delved between high Cornish stone hedges and overhung by hydrangeas and fuchsias. The garden, oddly disconnected from Trewidden House, was not begun by Edward Bolitho until the late 1880s, these Penzance gardens belong chronologically to a later generation than the Quaker, Falmouth group and, therefore, take more pains to charm. This one is a happily contrived wood, helpfully signposted and numbered to lead visitors around a maze of trees.[15] Uniquely, in my experience of Cornish gardens, it offers no outside views and not many open clearings. A plantswoman owner, Mary Williams, left the grounds with 300 different species of camellia, the kind of boast in a garden that makes me fear the worst: the plant-zoo obsession. But there are feature-clearings of memorable character to make up for interminable glossy green leaves. One moves in permanent shade on any one of three or four mapped-out routes and the principal pleasures can come in any order.

There is one very dark pond. All Trewidden's waters are black and dangerous looking. This one has the diving back and half-raised tail of a small whale (*colour plate 21*), a Christmas present to Alverne Bolitho's son, Thomas, from a godfather. When it was first installed the tail not only wiggled but spouted water. Now it composes perfectly with an island of Japanese Acer and a small stone pagoda in a miniature field of white flowers. Big blue and green dragonflies haunt the unreflecting waters. Another random incident in this delightful maze is a *Magnolia hypoleuca* with a wide, gnarled trunk, the champion tree for size of its class anywhere in Britain. I realised as I read the notes that I was falling into the plant-spotter's trap of: now read on to your next interesting anecdote. This one was planted in 1897 and, in the usual grudging style of magnolias, refused to flower until 1911.[16] Quite near to it was an unattractive monster, a *Butia capitata* or Jelly palm from whose sap palm wine can be made for its lucky owners. Then there is a bomb crater where a landmine floated down in the Second World War and devastated many trees, notably a still-living, bomb-damaged sycamore. Another sinister black pool lies in a rock garden made with stones from the local Bolitho tin mines. The Rhododendron 'Saffron Queen' was named to honour Mary Williams by her own nickname, but Cornish gardens are full of shrubs named after ingenious hybridizing gardeners.

Lastly, these camellia-crammed paths lead to Trewidden's real distinction. It is another pit, a relic of open-cast tin mining, deep enough to allow aerial views down onto a tremendous, prehistoric-looking forest of tree ferns: *Dicksonia antarctica*. The rusting rails that support the crumbling sides of the pit are railway lines from those Bolitho tin mines. Penzance is the tree fern capital of England; nowhere else do these improbable trees look so confidently at home in their green, sunless shade.

After Trewidden, Trengwainton is likely to be a slight disappointment but, if approached industriously, it has its rewards. Elegant twin Lodges raise the tone of its entrance. One is mock Regency of 1994 with concrete lintels, the other is of 1820. The Italianate house which they protect is a mere side distraction to a long garden based on two parallel drives. One has been turned into the Long Walk, the other, which shadows it distractingly all the way, is the new drive for wheeled traffic. Thomas Bolitho was responsible for this strange duplication and it was his nephew, Lt Colonel Edward Bolitho, who inherited in 1925, who had to make the best of it.

A first impression on the Long Walk is one of tree ferns and hydrangeas ranged along a little stream. The hydrangeas are in acid soil shades of blue, never pink or red, and small side tracks lead off into the shallow tree belts on either side. For a time the mature trees carry the attention, but the path climbs steadily with no outside views, no incidents and it needs to be rethought. Eventually it leads to a small Chinese Bridge (*51*) with a limited vista across a bright green pond to a seat. The path bends left there into a wide lawn with a distant view of the house. Those round-arched Italian windows give any building a melancholy air and Trengwainton looks not so much tearful as grey and exhausted, clearly not interested in entertaining visitors. A broad, raised Terrace bordered by agapanthus leads away from it. Until the famous gale of 1990 this was backed by holm oaks, but only one has survived. A white Summerhouse and a white arch terminate the end of the Terrace and an immense view sweeps down from it across open fields to the sea and St Michael's Mount. Turkey oak, beech and alder try to make up for the lost holm oaks, but the Terrace lacks a sense of purpose. Aware of this, the National Trust has employed a local artist, Joe Hemming, to create an octagonal slate toposcope. This sits somewhat uneasily on the open field, boxy in profile and needing a canopy, but the mermaid, farm implements and fish carved on it offer a conversation point. This is where the unsatisfactory planning of Trengwainton strikes home. The only way back is by the Long Walk or the drive parallel to it. Someone needs to design an alternative viewing loop; it is a challenge for the National Trust. Surely there are gardens hidden away behind that mournful house, some area to give a sense of having arrived before walking back the same way?

A real consolation prize are the Walled Gardens back near the Lodges. These exude Victorian industry and brilliant planting. Brick walled, they present a chain of isolated plant worlds: Foliage Garden, Fuchsia Garden, Kitchen Garden, Middle Walled Garden, Campbellii Garden and Veitchii Garden, each one a treasure of warm, sheltered colour. It is worth visiting Trengwainton just for these and for the tastefully designed new Tea Room and not bothering about the Long Walk. Lt Colonel Edward invested in Kingdon-Ward's 1927-8 plant hunting in Assam and, with his head gardener, Alfred Creek, used these safe enclosures to nurture the rarities that Kingdon-Ward had brought back. These must be hunted down from their name-tags in April and May, not in high summer. I warmed to the antique-looking *Metasequoia glyptostroboides* from China in the Veitchii Garden. It is important to walk backwards and forwards between the Veitchii and the Campbellii or it will never be clear which tree of that 1927-8 period is which. Then it is best to retreat to the Fuchsia Garden, which is far less taxonomically taxing. The walled area, with the Kitchen Garden's sloping beds to catch the sun's every ray, is not for casual sauntering; horticultural expertise is hard to acquire, there is so much of it and the Latin names rarely offer easy mnemonics. The guidebook over-praises the *Osmunda regalis* clump growing by the old Dipping Pond in the Kitchen Garden. It might flourish more regally growing near the little stream in the Long Walk.

There comes a point with these plant-spotter gardens when, having seen one it is difficult to raise enthusiasm for the next eight. That is their basic flaw. They rely on the plants rather than their setting. The first garden is staggeringly, voluptuously beautiful, wafted perfumes and perfect waxy blooms; but then the second, third and fourth of the same come up and rapture fades to mere appreciation. That makes me wary in writing about Trewithen, far away from the sea, up on the breezy heights near Probus and quite unlike Trewidden, but it seemed to plant its magnolias out more appealingly even than Caerhays, the magnolia capital of Cornwall, and offers a richer variety of grounds and satisfying contrasts.

Trewithen behaves like a normal English – as opposed to Cornish – house. Baroque in fenestration, but Palladian in its spreading wings, its entrance court

67 *The bronze Magnolia Fountain plays at Trewithen in a broad avenue of real magnolias created after storm damage had left wide gaps in the garden.*

faces east down a wide avenue of trees, formal and assured. That axial formality is joyously repeated, largely by accident, on the west, garden front. Trees were requisitioned and felled during the 1914-18 War and Major George Johnstone, who had inherited a dull garden in 1905, took the opportunity to lay out a 200-yard straight lawn leading to the pleasantly smug nine-bay garden front of the house. He then planted its sides with an imaginative range of *Magnolia salicifolia, M. kobus, M. stellata* and *M. campbellii*, with *Reevesia pubescens*, Kashmir cypress, *Viburnum betulifolium, Acer triflorum* and a twin woodland of flowering delights.[17] The result is that rare creation, a major formal avenue of gloriously informal colour, a cheerful parody of the dark avenue on the other side of the house. The present owner has a taste for ambitious wickerwork, and light-hearted viewing platforms of this stuff rise up out of a sea of petals. Even the bronze fountain is in the form of a huge green magnolia (67). Next to this is a superb *Magnolia wieseneri*. A cross-axis to the right leads past the Cockpit, an old quarry planted with primulas, meconopsis and azaleas. In a generally level garden it is pleasant to have some area on which to look down.

Conscious of this the present owners have begun an ambitious restoration of the Eagle Ponds out to the west. A wild track leads out through woodland down into a valley which in 1745, when the estate was owned by Thomas Hawkins, had three distinct shallow waters linked by little cascades.[18] These are being restored; a log bridge leads challengingly across them and there are water-loving plants, *rodgersias*, *astilbes* and *ligularias* with Swamp cypress and, higher up, dogwoods. Most gardens would benefit from the refreshing contrast between formal and half-wild gardens that Trewithen enjoys. As if that were not indulgence enough there is a sumptuously planted and very private walled garden next to the house with *Ceanothus arboreus* 'Trewithen Blue', *mutisias*, *berberidopsis* and *schisandra* climbing its warm brick walls, a pergola, lily pond and rose beds. Trewithen has everything except a cliff garden.

The other great magnolia garden, Caerhays Castle, has sea views in plenty and its visually organised drive has been described in an earlier chapter. The Williams dynasty came originally from Scorrier near Redruth where they had made their money as mine managers. An air of cool efficiency hangs over their garden enterprises. They still own Scorrier, which has a quartz Grotto, a conservatory and a Folly Dairy, very typical Cornish garden buildings. The Trevanions of Caerhays bankrupted themselves building the Castle to Nash's brilliant but extravagant design, so Michael Williams II was able to buy the empty shell cheaply in 1854. His grandson, J.C. (John Charles) Williams was the genius who made Caerhays nationally famous, first by sponsoring so many of the most successful plant hunters, then by systematic hybridization of rhododendron, azaleas, camellias and hydrangeas, all carefully recorded from 1897 to 1934 in a Garden Book.[19] Easily the best known of his triumphs, the cross between *Camellia japonica* and *Camellia saluenensis*, will send camellia enthusiasts scurrying on a pilgrimage to the one-time ladies toilet in the service and reception area; more of that later.

Of his sponsored hunters, George Forrest introduced *Primula vialii* in 1906, *Gentiana sino-ornata* in 1910, three brilliant rhododendrons: *R. haematodes* (1911), *R. sinogrande* (1913) and *R. griersonianum* (1917); the fabulous *Magnolia campbelii subsp mollicomata* came in 1924 from the temperate forest of Yunnan and north Burma.[20] An intense concentration of flowering shrubs covers the hill behind the Castle, not by any means all of them are magnolias. Caerhays is pioneering the movement to extend Cornwall's prime flowering time well into the public holiday period of July and August. *Magnolia dealbata* and *M. delavayi*, *Styrax japonica*, *Hoheria glabrata* all help a little. It may reflect the owner's preferences but I found the Caerhays plants unusually, even stimulatingly, sweet scented. After reading so often in accounts of Cornish gardens of the triumphant pairing of *Camellia saluenensis* and *Camellia japonica* to produce the *x williamsii* camellias it was a mild thrill to see the two original, rather seedy plants growing outside the old toilets. Readers may have gathered that camellias are not my favourites.

The garden at Tresco Abbey is not in Cornwall, but in another county, Lyonesse perhaps, subject to severe flooding. As the helicopter comes in from Penzance the original extent of this flooded county is exactly mapped out by the pale blue water of the shallow area between the islands. Landing at Tresco is on a grassy plot a hundred yards or so from the stone-walled hedge and line of trees bounding the Abbey gardens. Its presence impacts as visitors walk thankfully away from the throbbing helicopter: so much succulence and brilliant chemical colour ooze out of the granite garden wall. It is as if Augustus Smith, when he settled in his retiring and angular new house there in 1838, had done a Diaghilev, said '*Etonne-Moi!*' to his gardeners, and they had done just that, and never stopped astonishing us since.[21]

While awarding gold medals of merit to Augustus for his ambitious vision, he was a bachelor with no other distractions. It should be stressed that his plan, to create a series of exotic gardens with plants from several sub-tropical areas lying side by side on a square slope of land rising quite steeply from south to north, was in the great Cornish tradition pioneered at Mount Edgcumbe where several European gardens flowered alongside each other.

His uncomfortable looking Abbey house lies up high in the north-eastern quarter above the old Abbey ruins and the future Succulent Cliff. The Top Terrace and the Long Walk both run east–west and the south–north Lighthouse Walk divides the whole slope into roughly four quarters. That top north-eastern circle was taking shape by 1850, the Succulent Cliff by 1859. Kew, under Sir William Hooker, had been generous though doubtful of success. The Hop Garden, eventually a circle of yews, followed in the south-east quadrant and the Top Terrace was centred on Neptune's figurehead at the top of the Lighthouse Walk. A pebble garden in the shape of a Union Jack is a reminder that Smith was thinking in Gardenesque terms; indeed the Valhalla is also a typical Victorian museum in concept. Mexico, Australia and South Africa all had their garden areas with dramatic profiles of the taller plants, agaves especially.

Augustus died in 1872 leaving Tresco to his nephew, Thomas Algernon Dorrien, who developed the narcissus farming for which the Scillies were long famous. Arthur Algernon Smith Dorrien succeeded in 1918. Most of the liveliest 'hard' garden features have been added in the visitor-conscious days since 1950. What is so satisfying about this Tresco garden is the assurance it gives that our long straggle of islands, which begins on the bird-haunted cliffs of treeless Shetland, could produce a tropical humming bird of a garden like this. It exudes utterly un-English colour against a skyline of Mexico or the Indies, yet it is British. From the path around the walls to the entrance, David Wynne's 1990 statue of romping children gives a first glimpse of the scale and the ambition of the garden. The Lighthouse Walk runs ruler-straight uphill through dark, alien tree shapes, palms and aloes, to Neptune's Steps (*68*). That and the Long Walk which crosses it half way up the steep slope are the guiding axial lines of Tresco. Lighthouse Walk ends high up above it all at Father Neptune, Long Walk ends in the Roman Altar. Tresco works in much the same way as the gardens of the Villa Gamberaia outside Florence. Both are aligned on an inspired natural geometry in a confined site loaded with incidents, terminal features and tall, thin tree shapes. Tresco has a fair claim to be one of the top five gardens in Britain because it aims high with great assurance and never stumbles but often surprises.

68   *Neptune presides appropriately at the top of Lighthouse Walk, one of the two great controlling axes of Tresco Abbey Gardens. Palms, aloes and alien tree shapes cluster around him.* Brian Earnshaw

Each of the two principal straight walks has seven or eight brilliant episodes of colour and shape. Long Walk opens with the Abbey ruins, its provincial Gothic arches carrying an encrustation of ice plants and succulents like some lovely disease of the stone; the tallest arch is out-pointed by the palms and aloes behind it, *Cordyline australis* was in full scent. If anything could be changed it would be the clearance of the anticlimactic finches and sparrows. Small brown birds seem entirely out of place in all this colour; an importation of kingfishers and jays would be more in keeping. At the far end of the Long Walk, just before the authentic Roman Altar, there is the Mediterranean Garden. That has the dazzlingly garish Shell House mural by Lucy Dorrien-Smith of Renoir-like flower vases executed in shell and stone mosaic, an instance of defiant bad taste in a tiled pavilion above a spouting lead fountain. To one side is the Cactus Fountain, like Trewithen's Magnolia Fountain, but less friendly, and down below that on the bottom edge of the garden is Valhalla. There again praise has to be reined back, but even in cautious retrospect that gallery of twenty or more figure heads from ships wrecked on the Scillies seems to be a collection of naïve art superior to the very impressive but faux-naïf art in the Tate St Ives collection: direct, beautiful, memorable.[22] The combined effect of them was that of a festive Baroque, half indoors, half out in the open air. It seemed almost unfair that such a superior garden should have accidentally collected a fine art gallery as well as everything else.

A cooling experience after so much colour is the Aloe Walk which climbs uphill from the Roman Altar. It is lined with the white trumpets and long leaves of *Amaryllis belladonna* and ends in a perfectly contrived group of dark bushes above a flight of steps. Another pleasure is the impossibly elegant *Araucaria heterophylla* from Norfolk Island, a tree behaving like a fern yet still a conifer, no stumpy tree fern but a Platonic perfection of the tree-fern union. Then memorably, back in the centre of the garden near the Abbey ruins is Gaia the Earth Goddess (*colour plate 22*).

Gaia is intensely sexual, but in this garden she can get away with it. The statue is in a rocky circle with aeoniums around it. Whoever decides what grows on Tresco Abbey has a warm feeling for aeoniums. That Shell House has a bed of them, one on each side of it, brown and lustrous and shameless. Most Cornish gardens risk a few of them, Tresco has virtual hedges of them and Gaia is in the right place in this distinctly feminine-feeling garden, all rampageous fertility. One of the excellences of the garden is its occasional flowing over into bad taste, or at least questionable taste. That Succulent Cliff on the way up to the mostly hidden Abbey House is like a colliery bank crumbling under the weight of fleshy cacti in a dreadful confusion of strident colours; it should be growing in Namibia. The idea may have been that after passing the Cliff, the Abbey itself would look relatively attractive.

After a few hours of the garden it is a relief to get out into Tresco proper and find that the rest of the island, apart from the miraculous mature woodland above the great Pool which somehow survives the full force of the Atlantic gales, is rather suburban, dull and overpriced. Sensibly perhaps no one has tried to live up to that garden.

8

The great gap in Cornish garden history

To claim that there is a void in Cornwall's garden development during the Edwardian period looks, initially, like the most arrant nonsense. Taking the Edwardian span generously from about 1885, when Victoriana as we understand it was beginning to mellow, to 1914, when the Great War ended Edwardian imperial confidence forever, there was never an actual time when gardens were not being planted and planted ambitiously in the Royal Duchy. But they were for the most part soft gardens and the rest of England during the Edwardian years was hard gardening more brilliantly than at any other time in its garden history, with the possible exception of the Arcadian gardens and parks of 1730-70. Cornwall, so taken by the ease with which flowering exotics could be induced to flourish in its mild climate, gave little or no thought to the superb revival of late Elizabethan and Jacobean garden forms: terraces, twin pavilions, balustraded walks with seats, sundials and geometric topiary work, chiefly in yew, with which other counties were experimenting with historicist daring.

The reason was probably a matter of aristocratic attitudes. Cornwall, being Celtic, has rarely taken aristocrats seriously, and the splendid formal gestures of revived Jacobean gardening are like stage sets that demand to be used with self-conscious hauteur. England's *douceur de la vie* period was the Edwardian.[1] It was then that money from an Empire covering a quarter of the earth was flowing in to an elite class whose refined arrogance had barely been shaken by the Boer War or Lloyd George's budget battles with the House of Lords. Among a group of European great powers England was still the greatest, and a sublime confidence infused our ruling classes in their last years of unquestioned power. It seemed natural during that contemporary naval and mercantile dominance to revive the garden forms of another age of historic success, when the Armada was wrecked and James I established Virginia, the core of an English-speaking North America. If we think of the tone of Kipling's writing: its confidence in an imperial destiny, its contempt for lesser breeds without the law and its awareness of a glorious historic past that was the mood in which Sir Reginald Blomfield projected hard architectural gardening in his *The Formal Garden in England* of 1892. He had chosen his time perfectly. Lutyens, Thomas Mawson, Francis Inigo Thomas and the other architectural gardeners were all eager to give the upper classes the perfect garden stages on which to perform their arts of leisure, dalliance, sport and aesthetic posturing. Hard landscaped Edwardian gardens in Gloucestershire and Dorset, favourite counties for those weekend parties made possible by improved rail and road communications, were laid out as theatres for artificially superior behaviour, time-trips back to Elizabeth and James, formal but innovative, artificial but imaginative.

The Quaker simplicities behind Cornwall's soft gardening of exotics were essentially anti-aristocratic. Those rival dynasties of Falmouth and Penzance were recreating God's Eden, not aristocrats' arbours for adultery. The Souls – that inner elite of Edwardian society – gathered around the great hostesses like Lady Desborough, Lady Elcho, Violet, Duchess of Rutland, and elegant political fops like Arthur Balfour, had a reputation for being dangerously sexual in their relationships. They haunted the bedrooms of other men's wives, and arranged meetings between lovers in sheltered yew arbours and discreet garden pavilions.[2] That was very far from the nonconformist, Quaker approach to social intercourse. In Edwardian Cornwall adultery was not fashionable so gardens designed for assignations were not required. J.D. Sedding did, however, as noted in the Gardenesque chapter, come very close to a hard-hedged and terraced garden at The Downes in Hayle twenty years before Blomfield published his persuasive book.

Edwardian-style gardens in the county can be numbered on the fingers of one hand. Penheale appears to be an alien masterpiece, one of Lutyens' great garden achievements. Place at Fowey has the completed wreck of a possible Mawson scheme, Long Cross has an amusing parody of an eighteenth-century 'Rococo' garden and at Tivoli Park, in the woods on the south bank of the Lerryn creek, there are amusing fragments of a small Edwardian pleasure garden; but that is more or less the complete tally.

Tivoli Park may be a very minor Edwardian essay in gardening, but it has a peculiar forlorn charm that makes it well worth searching out, though seekers can easily pass within yards of it and not notice it, so entirely has it been swallowed up in young woodland. As a social phenomenon it is closely linked with another public garden, the Larmer Tree Gardens on the Wiltshire-Dorset border.[3] Both were products of that hopeful interlude at the end of Victoria's reign when the bicycle had conquered both the roads and the social isolation of country villages, but when motor cars had not yet shattered the rural quiet with a mass invasion from big towns. H.G. Wells captured that time perfectly in his non-science fiction novels and in Cornwall, Frank Parkyn, who had made a fortune in the china clay industry, was philanthropic and poetic enough to believe that a small park of fanciful architectural gardening on the south bank of the Lerryn could serve as the focus of an annual people's festival of water sports. He lived across the river in Penquite, a Georgian house now turned youth hostel, so he seems to have been a keen yachtsman with ready access to boats.

His regattas did not survive the Great War of 1914-18 and, in the Cornish way of things, young trees quickly took over his Tivoli. But in another hopeful period, using money left over from the local Coronation celebrations of 1953, the trees were felled, regattas were held again and Tivoli revived for a time. However, by 1968 the impetus had flagged, the trees sprang up again and now Tivoli is a hunt-the-thimble garden. A track down the south side of the Lerryn creek passes old sail lofts and flowery cottage gardens. When this Piggy Lane crosses a side creek by a bridge the woods immediately ahead are Tivoli's shrouding sheet. A strange Gothic mini-crypt leads off into the trees, but the best way in is the next clear opening. Dimly between the slim sapling trunks a monstrous fountain bulges up (*69*), set in a deep, dry basin, its bulbous base circled by wheels of quartz. Next to it is a broken wall of uncertain purpose. Further on and easily missed is the empty bed of a cataract that once raced down under the ruined arches up in

69 This monstrous, bone-dry fountain in the heart of a thicket is the principal surviving feature from Frank Parkyn's Edwardian pleasure ground, Tivoli Park at Lerryn

the wood. The place must once have been alive with water music, now there is just the rustle of leaves. And that is the end. Steps will lead back down onto the creek-side at that Gothic crypt, which may once have had a park function.

A few other gardens, such as Sir Charles Hanson's Fowey Hall, on the hill above the harbour town, make slight Edwardian gestures, but one balustraded terrace, a flight of steps and a solemn grove of Monterey pines is not enough to rank as a true architectural Edwardian garden. The terrace leads nowhere, there are no garden pavilions and the paths on the slope below the Hall's porch merely amble among bushes.

Place, in the same town, but lower down the steep hillside, is a more serious garden proposition in the same vein of Monterey pines; but when Thomas Mawson advised the Treffry family on what they could do to give their astonishing Regency Gothic castle a setting worthy of its challenging towers and overstated machicolation, either they did not offer him enough money and a binding contract, or the narrow site defeated his creative reach.[4] It is indeed a testing garden terrain: a narrowing sliver of land sloping to a low cliff above Fowey, that most winning of Cornish harbour towns. It was, presumably against Mawson's advice, that the Treffrys planted it with that handsome but aggressive grove of Monterey pines that today tends to overwhelm everything else on the slope. Before Mawson's visit there was already a main terrace drive running from the house along the lip of that cliff to take carriages down to the ferry over to Polruan.

At his best Mawson was a very good garden designer, bold, unpredictable, a town planner liable, therefore, to make major city gestures in quite modest gardens. In 1906 at Leweston in Dorset he sent a Fascist 'Glade' roaring down through woodland to where a grand exedra-shaped piazza with colonnaded viewing pavilions could look out arrogantly across a view.[5] After 1920 at Boveridge, in the same county, he began to edge towards the square, angular designs of the Art Deco. His paths, canal and parterres are patterned around equally geometric pools and tie these compositions tightly around the house.[6] At Place he suggested no such firm gestures. His garden field ran along a lovely river view across the harbour from that inspired Elizabethan Hall Walk, noticed in an earlier chapter. Surely he should have handled that view, focusing on it with sudden clearings; but he, or whoever carried out his advice, did no such thing.[7]

The garden relates neither to Place house nor to the river. It begins half way up the drive where a flight of steps, not made of his favourite concrete, rises for no strategic reason up into a Crescent Garden of magnolias centred on a stumpy sundial. The steps continue axially out of this, but then lose their way to the next objective, a brick and timbered, faintly Arts and Crafts Summerhouse (70). In his *The Art & Craft of Garden Making*, Mawson expressly disparages wood as a material for such pavilions.[8] This suggests again that the Treffrys were cutting costs as they improvised around suggestions he had made on a single visit, but its open verandah is similar to the Garden House he designed for Cringlemire,

70 *The Summerhouse in the grounds of Place, Fowey, is post-1908 in date and carries a faint air of Arts and Crafts integrity. It is a survivor from an extensive formal garden laid out possibly to the advice of Thomas Mawson*

Windermere.[9] Nothing excuses the wandering uncertainty of the paths leading, via another circular bed, from the Crescent Garden to the Summerhouse, which in fact stands some way off that hesitant axis. Then there is no logical link sideways down and from the Summerhouse to the other main feature of this quite limited garden. This is a Sunken Garden with a central rectangular basin; above it is a raised pergola of angular, granite plinths, which once supported wooden posts, standing on a small terrace. Some concrete steps do lead up to this from the main Terrace-Drive and the cotoneasters of its original planting still flush red.

All these ill-linked features lie on a slope of rough grass which should, by the standards Mawson displayed in several layouts illustrated in his *Art & Craft*, have been level with straight linking ways.[9] When Mawson designed a woodland walk it wandered sinuously,[10] but his main gardens are formal work on firm, straight connections. The Treffrys' interpretations of Mawson merely amble from one point to another. Would Mawson, designing a Tea Garden below the main Terrace and blessed with a superb harbour view, have endowed it with nothing more than a line of plain wooden posts acting as a shelter? It seems unlikely. As for that main Terrace itself, which is a shadow of the Hall Walk across the water, later growth of trees and bushes may have cloaked and confused its original planting, but it runs for much of its way, before diving down to become a drive, with the harbour views largely hidden from it. Mawson could hardly have resisted creating topiary alcoves or planting hedges that revealed sudden glimpses.

Early photographs show the garden almost exactly as it is now but treeless, with neither the Monterey pines nor the present bushes. Architectural Edwardian gardens required the direction and orchestration of well-clipped topiary. Place seems never to have had this, nor the vital link of steps to connect the lawns immediately around the house with that long finger of garden above the main Terrace. Mawson wrote: 'Tall hedges of Yew, Laurel, or Holly form substantial divisions, but years must elapse before such hedges can be effective. And here the common or garden trellis will prove the temporary substitute'.[12] The Treffrys may have taken him at his word, hence the trellis in that Tea Garden and the bare slopes shown in the photographs. But they never got round to the hedge planting. Considering the memorable excellence of the house and the interest of the view, chances were lost here. The main Terrace must predate this formal layout as it dives under the road below the house to reach the harbour at a castellated gateway, not at all in Mawson's manner.

If it is permissible to stray briefly from one county, Cornwall, to another, Dorset, I must admit to a genuine nostalgia and sense of absence at this point, as I remember all the intricate, surprising formalities and strong individual character of gardens like Mapperton, Chantmarle, Kingston Maurward, Waterston and Athelhampton. It was at Dorset's Abbotsbury gardens that I felt the same sense of loss, the absence of direction that I have often experienced in Cornwall at Trebah, Glendurgan, Trengwainton and Trewidden. That was because Abbotsbury, like these Cornish gardens, relies upon a few Chusan palms or a venerable Caucasian wingnut and then just a mass of flowers and flowering bushes to carry a visitor along more and yet more wandering ways. Cornwall has its undeniable glories, but it missed out badly when it concentrated on its exotics and ignored its hedges. It was a relief in that small west garden at Chymorvah to be groomed and directed even in that limited space by firm walls of escallonia.

Nothing makes that argument for hard gardening more persuasively than Penheale; but then the inspired additions to Penheale Manor were not only by that great architect, Sir Edwin Lutyens, who created the stony splendours that lie behind the Viceregal Lodge at New Delhi, but Penheale is Lutyens at the top of his form, responding to existing Cornish ranges of distinctive beauty.[13] What might Lutyens have conjured up if Lord St Levan had let him loose on the south-east grounds of St Michael's Mount, as Hudson let him loose on Lindisfarne's Holy Island? But at least Cornwall seems to have in both the Manor and the gardens at Penheale a creation of Lutyens' splendid prime.

Penheale's twentieth-century garden cannot be divorced entirely from the Manor itself, a complex of six buildings ranging in date from the late sixteenth century to the eighteenth. Sir John Specott, of a wealthy, and presumably sophisticated, Somerset and Devon family, bought it around 1610 from the last of the Cornish Grenvilles; and Sir John's son, Paul, moved in after his father had built the fine stable range in 1620. Dates matter at Penheale because Paul, who erected a riotously elaborate Corinthian hall screen between 1637 and 1640 also built in absolute contrast a cool, simple Doric Loggia on the inward face of a new Gatehouse and Porter's Lodge range. This is so close in design to the celebrated but undated Doric loggias at Godolphin that it either inspired Godolphin's early classical experiment of bringing the garden into the house or, more probably, it copied Godolphin. The main entrance range to the house which faces the Gatehouse has a date of 1636 over its doorway, so a date for the Loggia in the 1630s seems reasonable and suggests a similar or slightly earlier dating for the double loggia at Godolphin, one of Cornwall's very few pioneering architectural ventures and one closely linked to Cornish garden thinking at this period.

Lutyens responded skilfully to Penheale's existing complexities and beauties: the main range, Gatehouse range, stable range and Pigeon House, only ignoring the confident classical former farmhouse. Consequently, Penheale's gardens are equally complex and not easy to absorb from a printed account.[14] This festival of highly individual and unpredictable buildings had become by 1920, when Colonel Norman Colville bought it, a run down, near ruinous set of farm buildings and lodgings. Colonel Colville, who was a Scot, came down to Cornwall for health reasons, seeking a milder climate. At that time Lutyens was working on Castle Drogo in the next county. That would explain the Arts and Crafts castle of angular grey-green Delabole stone that the architect then proceeded to add as a south wing to complicate an already unusually rambling manor house. Lutyens' reputation is currently riding high and all accounts of his south wing at Penheale extol its subtle union of contemporary and Jacobean. For his gardens too there can be nothing but praise except to question who actually designed the gardens, Lutyens or Colonel Colville.

It will seem disloyal after all the enthusiasms of earlier chapters, but I love and admire Penheale's gardens because they are so un-Cornish, so aristocratic, so controlling and so mercifully free of the county's predictable flowering bushes. There are rhododendrons and azaleas discretely tucked away in the oak woods around the great south Canal and the Colonel did try his hand, or his gardener's hand, at rhododendron and camellia hybrids. Aware of what was being planted at Castle Drogo, Colonel Colville called on Gertrude Jekyll's advice for the planting at Penheale and, while she never came out here to inspect the site, the Rose Garden above the main house and the Gatehouse range in the upper walled enclosure was re-laid to her instructions.

In his seminal text, Sir Reginald Blomfield had urged a rich scatter of stone pavilions to raise a garden's tone; but Penheale already had so many that all that had to be done was to wind the garden rooms and surprises winsomely around these existing detached ranges and thereby circumnavigate the Manor. Then, Blomfield's aim that the garden should be 'considered in relation to the house, and as an integral part of a design which depends for its success on the combined effect of the house and garden' would be achieved.[15]

The existing gardens at Penheale had been conventional in planning. There were already two grass lawns between the main house and its colonnaded Gatehouse range and, on the east front beyond the upper, so-called 'Elizabethan' Terrace, which must date from the 1630s, was a central path running east, pointing to Dartmoor and lined with herbaceous plants. Colonel Colville, in flight from Scotland, was naturally attracted to Dartmoor. Consequently, while the 'Elizabethan' Terrace has, in most un-Cornish fashion, a lavish show of summer flowers in those two flanking herbaceous borders, the view east was, on the Colonel's direct order, framed in 1925-7 by impenetrable yew hedges. These resemble similar barriers at Castle Drogo and defy entry until the visitor has walked north up the Terrace to find a way into the maze of sheltered garden rooms hidden behind that wall of yew. First comes a camomile lawn, recently planted replacing vegetables, ready to exhale its perfume whenever trodden upon. Someone has decided against that self-indulgent nonsense and a chain of stepping-stones has been laid across the lawn so that not a leaf need be crushed. There follow, by narrow gaps and puzzling turns, a series of yew rooms. One contains a swimming pool, perfect for sunbathing. Eventually the persistent explorer will emerge on the far side of the yew hedges where a second Terrace runs parallel to the first, commanding wide views of Devon. At the south end of the lower Terrace moon steps lead down to the Canal, which is lined with oaks and an under planting of rhododendrons. A sumptuous clump of royal fern grows at the foot of the steps and, while the Canal might not be long enough for Versailles, it would be quite grand enough for Hampton Court, and it is overlooked by a huge brick-walled Kitchen Garden. There was an island planted with bushes and a Monkey Puzzle marring the formal vista, but that has gone.

The best way to direct a reader-visitor at this point is to walk them back up the steps between the south edge of the yew barrier and the north end of the Canal, onto the upper Terrace again. With flowers on both sides and the mellow mullions of the house on the left, a walk along the Terrace to the point where earlier the yew wall opened grandly, will lead to steps up left into that memorable court with the five bays of the Doric Loggia on the inner face of the Gatehouse. Its symbolism is still potent. Here are no fortifications, but an Italian garden of Charles I's reign. It is a structure, contemporary with Inigo Jones' Queen's House at Greenwich, and built by Paul Specott in the unfashionable wilds of the Royal Duchy. The planting around the colonnade does it justice. There is a yellow Banksian rose facing an even brighter yellow *Dendromecon rigida* from California; pink, daisy flowered *Mutisia oligodon* twines up a column, blue ceratostigma and perovskia grow at the columns' bases. *Crinodendron hookerianum* with drooping crimson bells does well here.[16] Steps lead up from this historic court to the upper enclosure with its two Rose Gardens, the sunken one by Jekyll (*71*) with beds enclosed in box hedging. Now it is time to turn left to explore my favourite

71 *The Rose Garden at Penheale with its nine box-edged compartments may have been planted up to a design by Gertrude Jekyll. The Walled Garden and its twin Gazebos are probably Caroline in date*

area of the garden where Lutyens cleared away some old granite farm buildings, but left the very high wall dividing the area into two with its conical capped Gazebos towers as in some manoir of the Touraine. The wall is a tangle of white hydrangeas, clematis and climbing roses. A small wooden door opening through it is the only way from one enclosure to the other, which is entirely sheltered with a small pool and an island of gunnera; this must have been what Colonel Colville wanted from Cornwall: an equable climate, calm waters, no winds and rich planting.

The comparison with manoirs in the Touraine is apt because James Colville, the Colonel's son, showed me a map of 1769 with a Rococo cartouche and a delicately drawn vignette of the complex at that time.[17] This records Paul Specott's Caroline Walled Garden with its two Gazebos and the pool. Stretching away to the south is the rectangular Canal; Cornwall, being old-fashioned in gardening styles, was still laying out seventeenth-century formal gardens in the early years of the eighteenth. Enys did exactly this. So the gardens around Penheale Manor are not the result of a Lutyens-Jekyll collaboration, but an imaginative orchestration of an existing seventeenth and early eighteenth-century complex by the owner, Colonel Colville.

There only remains that vast Kitchen Garden which could have supplied a regiment with loganberries and a brigade with onions. But it is worth wandering back along the second drive to an architecturally rich yet informal area where the Barton, far too gentlemanly to be a simple farmhouse, is smothered in roses and looks across to the 1620 stable block and the more vernacular, less daring, north face of the Gatehouse. The geometrical Pigeon House seems to have been Lutyenised at some stage and a servant's range out in a meadow to the west has marks of that architect's imaginative tinkering. Only St Michael's Mount can put on a show of architectural invention to equal Penheale. The celebrated Lanhydrock is completely outclassed. Unfortunately Penheale is a private house, open only rarely for charity, but well worth a long journey to experience. The directors of the great Quaker gardens in the south could profit by copying some at least of Penheale's enclosures and surprises.

Closer at hand, of the same date and equally private, are the Pleasure Grounds at Port Eliot. The Elyots have tended to design their own gardens, and it was Granville John, the 7th Earl, working post-1925, who devised on the hillside next to the house a little Arcadia that savours more of the 1740s than the 1920s.[18] Winding circuits of paths, some brick, some slate, with lonicera hedging, lead to the Temple Garden, a three-columned portico of 1932, snug in its small glade; then, via a laurel screen, to a Japanese Pond Garden with a stone lantern and gunnera. Beyond this a Gothic pinnacle from Westminster Abbey commands a view over that quarry which Repton drew. Above it there is a Maze of harsh hexagons which has recently been replanted in beech after a fire by the present Earl. Its patterns of escape can be altered by swinging iron gates, which could be described as cheating, like the Earl's Bowling Green, which is circular. All these pleasantly whimsical features are hidden among the trees. The 7th Earl's cleverest stroke was the Temple Swimming Pool (*72*) of 1930 which creates the perfect Picturesque 'side-screen' feature to Repton's landscape when that is viewed from the house.

Like the 7th Earl, Captain Allardyce, his almost legendary contemporary, had absorbed the spirit of mid-eighteenth-century Arcadias. He, however, parodied them rather irreverently at Long Cross, in St Endellion parish on the north coast. What is misleading about the Victorian Gardens at Long Cross is that they were only styled 'Victorian' by those who restored them as a pub attraction in the 1980s. When Captain Allardyce created their maze of hedges and their miniature eclectic events in the last years of Victoria's reign, he was looking back nostalgically to an age in the middle of the eighteenth century when a park, not a garden, but a whole generously wooded and watered park, could deliver a series of charming folly buildings to delight walkers or carriage riders. As a concept, his gardens are a whimsical but well-informed comment on English garden history, a concentration in three acres of what 150 years earlier would have covered fifty acres or more.

72 *In another instance of the way a well placed, firmly designed garden house can raise the whole visual tone of a landscape, this 1920s' Swimming Pool Temple completes the view north from Port Eliot. Repton failed to suggest such an essential foreground marker*

Those three acres are a wide cornfield away from the cliff edge, so there is no nonsense here about sublimity, though every so often a tiny prospect tower with a castellated frill will pop up out of the hedges and a climb up three or four steps will give a maze-treader a good view of that cornfield. Nor are the ranked flowering bushes of the south Cornish coast forgotten. Cordylines spray out their perfumes, there is a magnolia or two and one tall Monterey pine asserts its profile, while escallonia hedges offer green barriers hiding, in the best Lutyens' tradition, the next eclectic surprise to the last possible moment. There is a small pool called 'Frog's Delight' with arum lilies and an islet of six palm trees, a fortlette, a house for sheep, with the custodian cropping the grass outside, a round pool for goldfish with a statue, a bravely jetting fountain, urns at the end of brief formal vistas, a corner 'for horned pets' that illogically includes ducks and guinea pigs with the goat, a full-sized and convincingly antique pigeon house and, best of all, the Prehistoric Garden (*colour plate 23*). This last is a brilliant commentary upon Celtic humbug. It has lines of shapely but diminutive menhirs and a stone with a hole in it, through which, if anyone can manage to crawl, they are guaranteed to become fertile. If, that is, they have not ricked their back in the process.

It is easy to laugh at Long Cross, but it should be considered thoughtfully. It is a cartoon with all a cartoon's exaggeration and liberty to criticise. Taken together, these two sharply contrasted gardens, Penheale and Long Cross, make a fair point on what is lacking in the better known gardens of the south coast tourist circuit.

9

In the lee of the plant-spotter storm – twentieth-century gardens

As mining and fishing have dwindled and tourism has become the county's staple industry, Cornwall has had its quiverful of twentieth-century gardens. There is a rich profusion of them, but not an easy profusion to set out in an orderly account of influences, fashions and evolving forms. To take, for instance, gardens associated with artists. Is there any useful link between Eagles Nest near Zennor, where granite boulders and the brilliance of the light from the Atlantic Ocean inspired Patrick Heron, and Barbara Hepworth's studio garden in St Ives, where her abstract sculptures create a setting for plants, or the Japanese Garden by Robert and Stella Hore at St Mawgan, where a national garden artistry rather than a single artist is involved?

That tidal wave, a horticultural tsunami of tender flowering bushes, which swept away any Edwardian hankering after hard architectural gardening has still not entirely ebbed away a hundred years later. In this context the gardens of Tremeer, near St Tudy, are a case worth considering.[1] In 1946 Major-General E.G.W. Harrison retired from the army and settled in the pleasantly severe Arts and Crafts house of 1899 that he had bought just before the war broke out in 1949. He intended to hunt and dabble in painting, but the gardens were in a poor condition and, while tidying them up, he became hooked on the pleasures of hybridization, keeping a careful record in separate books on camellias and rhododendrons. In his first entry of 1946 he fertilised *R. euchaites*, a sub-species of *R. neriiflorum*, with the pollen from *R. beanianum*. Nine years later, in 1955, one of the seedlings of that cross produced dark red flowers and was registered in the Rhododendron Stud Book as 'Sunshine'. The General was on his way to becoming a successful breeder.

In 1961 he married Mrs Roza Stevenson, the widow of the chairman of the Royal Horticultural Society's rhododendron committee. By that time the General had 1000 rhododendrons and 300 camellias. His new wife brought a dowry of more than 200 rhododendrons with her from Tower Court, Ascot. In 1965 she died. By 1975 the General needed a new book to record his rhododendron crosses; he was also still crossing camellias. By 1978 he had had enough and retired from Tremeer, where he had grassed over the formal Victorian beds and created a maze of flowering bushes with winding paths around a small, new lake. Rhododendrons predominated but he had planted a range of other plants including hostas, primulas and heaths.

In Arthur Hellyer's account of the General's time at Tremeer, he makes no secret of his admiration for the Major-General and the way that, though losing between thirty and fifty rhododendrons to honey fungus every year, he gardened gallantly on. To me, an outsider to the county, but familiar with garden experiments going on in counties like Dorset and Wiltshire, the story is obsessive and gently depressing. New directions were needed, Modernism could have been a positive influence, but hybridization was becoming a meaningless fixation in the county. This chapter will trace, therefore, ignoring unavoidably at least twenty beautiful but not innovative gardens like Tremeer, that faltering time between 1920 and 1991, the year when Tim Smit began to realise the power of an idea at Heligan.

The oddity of this time of hesitancy is that it opened in the 1920s with two of the most brilliant gardens in the county, both of them rock and moorland gardens, one being Eagles Nest, the other those terraces on the south-eastern face of St Michael's Mount. These two are of such startling and often abstract beauty that ten or twenty similar responses to a challenging natural site would, in an alert garden society, have sprung up on Cornish coasts and quarries. But Headland at Polruan, the only worthy successor, would not be planted by Jean and John Hill with Peter Ball until 1974.[2] It sometimes seems that a rhododendron bush rather than St Piran's somewhat sinister black-and-white cross should appear on the county's national flag. The rhododendron would, of course, have to be hybridized!

The garden at St Michael's Mount, visited, one would estimate, by less than one in ten of the Israelite host that troop each summer's ebb tide across the stones of the causeway from Marazion, was perfected by the 2nd Lord St Levan in the 1920s, but had a much longer ancestry. Any number of authorities, such as Bishop Pococke in 1750 and Borlase in 1758, mention a garden on that improbable, apparently exposed south-eastern face of the rock. Only Christopher Hussey, who mentions no source but is usually scholarly, claimed that in the early eighteenth century, three terraces, the standard Italian formalism of the seventeenth century, were contrived by 'two old Miss St Aubyns'.[3] When the buildings on the Mount were nearly a ruin in 1736 the 3rd Baronet, Sir John St Aubyn effected some repairs, so possibly the two old ladies were his aunts. By a fortunate climatic freak, a ground layer of air is dense enough to act as a buffer to send any strong winds up the cliff, leaving the terraces of the Walled

Gardens in a magical, invisible greenhouse (*colour plate 24*). The medieval nuns of St Michael's convent would surely have discovered this heavenly gift centuries earlier; the planting, however, is of the 1920s.

The gentler north face of the Mount is relaxed, with sloping lawns and two umbrella pines. A slightly absurd avenue of *Agave americana* leads around the east side to the sublimities of the south face. The sublime requires an element of terror and the snaking terraces edge into the vertiginous. It is worth making the effort to visit in sunshine with a high sea running to enjoy the intense sequence of very steep steps, tiny lawns, eruptions of flowers and sudden sun-heated enclosures that lead up to the Sea Gull Seat. There the garden ends; round the corner to the west bracken and unshaped cliffs take over. Here the clearest image is of sky blue agapanthus dangling over white breakers upon black rocks (*73*). Up above, the crudely theatrical battlements of Piers St Aubyn's Victorian additions flaunt themselves. Between wild sea and wilder Castle the silvery granite is sculpted into imitations of masonry where flowers grow at outrageous

73 *Given clear skies and a wild, stormy sea, not an impossible combination in Cornwall, the gardens of St Michael's Mount can touch the horticultural sublime*

angles. There are deep bronze aeoniums big as dinner plates, a *Clematis armandii* smothers a sheltered seat. A little pavilion fronts the Tortoise Lawn on the middle terrace and a path hangs over it for aerial views. One wrought-iron Wellhead commemorates a St Aubyn golden wedding (1916-66). Somewhere there is a secret family way down from the Castle and St Michael's cave, but it is not for visitors. This light-soaked stepladder of a garden delivers in miniature everything that Tresco Abbey gardens promise but never quite deliver. There is exotic colour here in the eye of an untamed sea: myrtle, bottlebrush, a spike of furcraea nine-feet high, cordylines for scent, mesembryanthemums for their disturbing un-English blaze of colour, huge climbing geraniums, *Leptospermum scoparium* and borage running wild. An unlikely opportunity has been taken and persuaded into a memorable experience utterly unrelated to the mainland. Is it a criticism of Cornwall's gentry gardens that only Eagles Nest and, in a minor suburban key, Headland garden at Polruan, offer the same sublimities elsewhere in the Duchy? Do Cornish gardens tend to ignore the sea?

On the Mount the garden climbs and clings; at Eagles Nest the garden drops, and any visitor has to drop with it. In both it is the vertiginous threat that alerts the senses and makes the experience of a visit so intense. Zennor seems neither North Coast nor South, it is West Cornwall, but like a chunk of Bodmin Moor or Dartmoor rising beyond St Ives. Eagles Nest is a grey, gabled and slate-roofed house substantially extended from the original cottage in the 1880s.[4] It lies next door to the Old Poor House, originally the parish workhouse, in a wind-flattened huddle of sycamore and ash on an otherwise bare promontory up above the village and the sea. This is a true house of the four winds, no freak trick of air shelters this garden from the elements; lumpen boulders of granite strew the heathy ground. Back in the 1880s Professor Westlake whose wife, Alice, was a painter, cleared enough rocks to extend the house and begin the garden and to coax trees to grow. The sycamores that arch now across the short drive from the main road may well be of his planting, but the inspired gardener who brought the grounds to life was the Liberal politician and League of Nations enthusiast, Will Arnold-Forster. He arrived sometime before 1920 with his first wife, Ka.[5] She was a friend of Virginia Woolf and had been a girl friend of the gay poet, Rupert Brooke. Virginia Woolf visited and coveted the house,[6] while for five years Gertrude Jekyll owned the Old Poor House next door. Jekyll had planted a quarry in Switzerland and there is an old quarry at the Old Poor House that she may well have planted up. It would be surprising if she did not influence the Arnold-Forsters in their subtle planting of the great boulders around Eagles Nest. Is this a Cornish Jekyll garden by proxy?

To the right of the entrance drive is a rough lawn where boulders lurch behind ilex and pour in a monstrous torrent of elephantine shapes down the steep hill behind the house (*colour plate 25*). Left of the drive, separated from it by a hedge of griselinia and escallonia, is the only clear space for the Kitchen Garden and greenhouse. Flanking this towards the Old Poor House and its retaining wall of pines is the Long Garden, a shady avenue of camellias and azaleas, enclosed by Cornish walled hedges and terminating in a stone bench. To its rear through a mini-monolithic stone arch is the stone-walled Camellia Walk, then comes a raised lawn and the exhilarating experience of the vertiginous Boulder Garden tumbling down behind the house. Here the Arnold-Forsters created eighteen enclosures for plants, many tender, to thrive. A wooden ladder (*74*) leads down into this giant's bonsai garden where tiny beech trees and sycamore cower behind impending stone. The rocks are miraculously alive with olearias, including *Olearia x mollis. 'Zennorensis'*, a glossy leaved Arnold-Forster creation, camellias, scented azaleas and pink, white and purple heaths. In one cave garden below a little precipice a Chilean fire bush flowers like a mad honeysuckle,[7] gentians and white violets grow from cracks in the stone hedges; hydrangeas behave as usual, the reliable workhorses who fill the summer months with mauve.

One vast rock, the Snuff Box, towers above the rest, a permanent challenge to visiting children and, apparently, George Leigh Mallory who was able to climb it on all four sides. He disappeared on Everest in 1924; his widow was the second Mrs Arnold-Forster. Every move involves cautious steps from one insecurity to another. Random slits of openings catch the eye, with vast views down over Celtic fields and four huddled farms to the dazzling reflections of the famed Atlantic Cornish light. Always the garden has to be treated with caution,

74 *The essential thrill of Eagles Nest lies in its verticality and an abiding sense of physical peril. One rung of this wooden ladder down into the Boulder Garden is missing*

and an awareness that there must be, in all the distraction of ferns, lichened branches, cotoneasters and senecio, a hard climb back up to the level ground where cyclamen will flower in autumn and spring, and the camellias will fill the Christmas vases. It was in one of those farms of Tregerthen that D.H. Lawrence and his Baroness Frieda settled for a time in 1916. 'When I looked down at Zennor', he wrote, 'I knew it was the Promised Land, and that a new heaven and a new earth would take place'.[8]

Patrick Heron bought Eagles Nest from the Arnold-Forsters' son Mark in 1955 and found inspiration in the rugged coastal terrain there for his abstract paintings of luminous colour in rocks and sea-washed light. 'To have', he wrote, 'the rocks and the bushes illuminated from below, from a glittering reflector which is over 600 feet beneath one, and many miles wide – is a special experience'. Heron's 1958 charcoal drawing of Eagles Nest with its familiar swiftness of line and 'a wiry spareness of means that encompasses volume and measured distance'[9] is the frontispiece to this book. While Patrick soaked up the Atlantic light his wife, Delia, a keen plantswoman, tended the garden, and their daughters, Susanna and Katharine, continue to maintain this extraordinary horticultural eyrie.

By that time Barbara Hepworth had begun the third of the great precursor gardens in the middle of St Ives, the only one of the three that can be described as by association Modernist, the first two being basically plant-spotter's gardens in pioneering natural settings. She bought the Trewyn property as a studio and garden from Mr Trewhella of Trewyn House in 1949 after she had been living in Cornwall for ten years. It was elaborated into a dwelling with workshops by further purchase. Douglas Pett, very bravely, gave it no place in his encyclopaedic study on the county, considering it, with justification, to be neither a park nor a garden. It hangs like a leafy mantelshelf above one of the back alleys of St Ives: a unique complex with the artist's workshops, very much as they were on the day of her death, crammed with half-finished carvings and moulds of plaster, all opening out onto the small elevated garden, equally crammed with palms, camellias, flowers, grasses and a pond of white water lilies. In her planting Dame Barbara was advised by a musical composer, Priaulx Rainier, and it has to be said that while the small garden has been positively stuffed with bronzes and stone sculpture (*colour plate 26*), some, like 'Four-square (Walk through)' of 1966, overwhelming in size, the planting holds its own against the Hepworth competition.

Personally, and where abstract art is concerned all opinions are subjective, I enjoy the area enormously, while being no particular fan of Hepworth's sculpture, and visit it often. There is a rare and instructive pleasure in being able to sit in a conventional, elegantly simple room full of rather smaller Hepworth pieces and then going straight out into the 'Garden', which it surely remains, and experiencing how a wide selection by the same sculptress works out in the open competing with natural forms. By a very slight measure of comparison they come over more completely, in my view, indoors against white walls and on a polished wooden floor.

The small pond in the garden is a survivor of Mr Trewhella's garden and in Dame Barbara's time the prevailing colour of the garden was provided by blue cinerarias which have been allowed to die off; but the wall in the left-hand corner is kept pale blue. Most movingly the garden includes the sculptress' bedroom complete with white bed (75). It was there, like some mythical phoenix, that she consumed herself in fire, accidentally by falling asleep while smoking in bed. One wonders if she ever appreciated the June perfumes of the *Cordyline australis* that lie exquisitely heavy in the garden today.

As far as influence by example goes this is not a true Modernist garden. A good, conventional urban garden full of exotic plants enlivened by Modernist sculpture is not the same thing. So neither of these three undeniably great gardens: St Michael's Mount, Eagles Nest and the Trewyn Studio set an inspiring Modernist example to the county. That would account for the timidity and predictable planting in the county by the National Trust at Trerice in 1953 and

75 *Among the flowering plants and brazen sculptures of Barbara Hepworth's Sculpture Garden this little bedroom cabin is a reminder of how closely Hepworth lived, and died, with her creations.* Bowness, Hepworth Estate

Trelissick after 1955. Trerice is a prettily gabled manor house of the Arundells built in 1570, the kind of property the Trust would have accepted in the 1950s before they set their sights high, but probably not today. Its terraced gardens and forecourt are acceptable, but not authentic, nineteenth-century restorations. In his account of it, Pett damns it with delicate precision in his last line: 'There is an interesting museum of lawnmowers'.[10]

Trelissick, accepted in 1955, is a major property where it is easy to criticise the Trust's subsequent garden policy, but less easy to suggest how they could have done better. The house has a satisfyingly pure neo-Greek Ionic portico by P.F. Robinson of 1825. Far more important from a garden point of view is a matching Ionic Palm House attached to its south-east side. Unfortunately neither main house nor Palm House is shown, so the Trust was left with an interesting service area centred on a French Gothic stone Water Tower and exceptionally beautiful wooded grounds, with walks overlooking the Fal estuary and the glorious Regency Gothic pile of Tregothnan across the water. But how long would visitors be satisfied by walking around a view with only sidelong glances at the forbidden main house?

The Trust's answer has been by conventional enrichments of flower beds and by careful development of the plant-spotter camellias, rhododendrons, occasional tree ferns and flowering cherries with which Ida and Ronald Copeland had endowed the grounds in the years between 1937 and 1955. One wonderful old tree, a *Cryptomeria japonica* in the centre of a sloping lawn, is ample excuse in itself for a visit. Otherwise the service area has been heightened with a Fig Garden, the original figs died in 1979, and a Scented Garden 'with visitors with sensory impairments in mind',[11] a sign of desperation and vocabulary failure. The grounds are celebrated for red rhododendrons and the Trust has created a new area since the 1960s, the Carcaddon, with more of the same. A little thatched Summerhouse, reminiscent of Alice's Seat at Trebah, gives a reason for walking out to viewpoints. As the Trust says, Trelissick is 'a real plantsman's garden',[12] one of many in the county, and not much else.

The next two gardens chronologically, Ince Castle of the 1960s and Bosvigo, begun 1969, have infinitely more character though neither could be described as Modernist or Brave New World. Ince exudes the contentment of a Conservative politician, a cabinet minister no less, in his productive retirement. The seventeenth-century brick Castle with its four-square tiled and conical-roofed corner towers is a toy, though it did withstand a brief siege in August 1646.[13] An old postcard[14] of about 1911 shows it a near wreck, strangled in ivy. Another of about 1960, the year when Patricia, Viscountess Boyd (née Guinness), and her husband, Alan Lennox-Boyd, the former Colonial Secretary, bought the Castle from Captain Bobby Somerset, shows the simple lawns on three sides with woods on the eastern kitchen side. Now it is hard to say which breathes the more whimsical charm, the meticulously restored castle or its three imaginatively detailed and contrasting gardens. The Boyds were gardeners of real ambition working in the 1960s in the spirit of the neo-Georgian.[15]

The Castle enjoys a perfect isolation on a peninsula looking across the Lynher to the woods of Antony and over the Hamoaze to Plymouth. Two rampageous lions on Corinthian bases[16] mark the end of a long, informal drive of wind-stunted beech trees and oaks. Fuchsias cluster around the high flight of steps to the first floor entrance to the Castle. Hidden away on the right is a new garden brimming with flowers and centred on a pyramidal yew enclosure sheltering a white ironwork seat whose back has a formidable cat. The Boyds had a penchant for lead statues of little boys riding on the backs of enormous snails, they are everywhere.

On the far side of the Castle, where the Antony view is everything, a wide lawn with grand sphinxes and a deep ha-ha gives the estuaries their due, but saves one corner for a tiled sitting-out area with pots for plant favourites. The principal garden, very grand though small, faces west up the Lynher. It opens from a stone terrace and a second sitting-out area below two big magnolias climbing the west wall. A lead cistern with a cherub centres this. Then comes a lawn which bursts into a Sundial Garden lavishly herbaceous and not at all Cornish (*76*). 'Make time, save time, while time lasts. All time is no time when time is past' the sundial reads. The paths are geometrical and cobbled with small pebbles; obelisks balanced on

76 *The Sundial Garden near the end of Lady Boyd's main axis at Ince Castle breathes the reverent air of 1960s' Georgian Revival*

balls are almost hidden in flowers; cherubs ride more snails; there are semi-circular seats and the whole rewardingly crowded formality ends in the cross stroke of a lily pond with black and golden carp. This should leave the fine estuary view wide open, but buddleias frustrate the aim. To one side is Lord Boyd's monument to a happy retirement: an octagonal Shell House encrusted with his shell work. This was begun in 1963 with the shells Lord Boyd had collected during the course of his colonial duties. Even its door handle is a cowrie, lovely slices of golden agate substitute for glass in its windows and swirling patterns of shells cover the walls entirely with shimmers of mother of pearl. No other garden in the county expresses quite so openly the love which its owners have lavished upon it.

Bosvigo, almost its contemporary, is another testament to the care of a gardening couple, and it is a pleasure to record so close together two gardens so detailed and thoughtful in their planting. *Bosvigo Plants* of 2004 is a model guide for anyone seriously interested in planting as it not only lists every plant, but has eighty-eight named and coloured photographs of them. A walk around Bosvigo is a genuine learning experience. The garden at Ince Castle was of 1930s inspiration, Bosvigo's is Vita Sackville-West and that celebrated series of garden rooms she planted around Sissinghurst. Wendy and Michael Perry did not, apparently, garden seriously until 1980, though they bought their 1780s solicitor's suburban house up above Truro in 1969. By 1980 Sissinghurst's gardens were much in vogue, but Bosvigo is a notably subtle and multi-coloured example of the style. A series of five enclosures gathered closely around the back and the side of the house raises, what in most such houses would be dull back yards, into places of enchantment. There is a sixth 'Hot' Garden further out by the plant nursery above the drive. This is a predictable blast of reds, oranges and purples with dahlias, crocosmias, cannas, ricinus and dark, sultry roses. It is not fair to include Bosvigo in a 'lee of the plant-spotter's' chapter without pointing to its most un-plant-spotter and very welcome bias towards summer flowers. There are choice camellias and azaleas out in its little woodland, but Bosvigo is at its best from July to September when most plant-spotter gardens have sunk into the arms of hydrangeas.

Its peculiar charm is the way it draws visitors into just those back premises and service areas of the house from which we are usually excluded (77). Black pansies and white wisteria dramatise the Kitchen Courtyard, white pink and grey gardens cluster around the visitors' toilet; and after the golden yew cones and white, four-part geometry of the Vean Garden, this most domestic of garden tours climaxes in a conservatory of rare climbers like the Purple bell vine, *Rhodochiton astrosanguineum* from Mexico. *Bosvigo Plants*, sold at the house, is a rare jewel for £1; it would be folly not to buy it. I went back a second time to browse with it.

Tregenna Castle, a John Wood the Younger house, once owned by the Bolithos, has long been a hotel. In 1996 the owners spent a fortune on a new subtropical garden within the old Walled Garden while turning the old formal front garden into a putting green. They have their necessary priorities, and the new garden to the rear of the hotel, designed by John Moreland who was advised

77 *It was the particular achievement of Wendy and Michael Perry at Bosvigo in the 1970s to have demonstrated that the Vita Sackville-West colour treatment can make even backyards and passages a floral delight*

by plantswoman, Barbara Lumsden, has resulted in a feast of colour.[17] There is a rippling box-lined serpentine border of salvias and dahlias along the southern edges of the garden and paths throughout the area wind around an obsession of circles. Virtually every prominent feature: palm, pool or striking plant, is circled emphatically in a thick round of yew, box, lavender or herb. Each garden leaves its particular memory; mine for Tregenna is one of rich, green circles.

To end this chapter with Heligan, lost and found, it is necessary to leap ahead of it chronologically to the year 2000 to the garden at Pengersick Castle which, paradoxically, claims to be very old, a revival of the garden John Milliton might have laid out around the romantic Tudor complex that stands today on fine sandy soil near the shore at Praa Sands. With the help of Nigel Matthews, the County Landscape Officer, Angela Evans has found a Tudor bowling alley, relaid the 'Medieval Herb Garden', planted the 'Nine Sacred Herbs' on the woodland walk to the probable site of an 'Oratory Chapel', located a prehistoric settlement, an early Orchard and begun to develop a Tudor 'Knott Garden'.[18] I admired Angela's enthusiasm, enjoyed my visit and relished the view from the top of the tower of all this horticultural and educational activity.

Tim Smit's Eden Project is so obviously a Modernist garden that it may seem perverse to include his nationally famous 'Lost' Gardens of Heligan at the end of a 'lee of the plant-spotter's chapter', and immediately following Angela Evans' Pengersick project. The only excuse is that both gardens are unique and fit closely together in their dates. Tim Smit began the recovery of Heligan in 1991; Angela Evans set about Pengersick's recovery on much less evidence in 2000.

I have not met Tim Smit to discuss my assumptions, but it seems that his masterful recreation of Heligan led logically to the Eden Project, which was more than masterful, more a creation of genius in garden communication. Through the benign neglect of their twentieth-century owners, Heligan's grounds had become totally overgrown, a Cornish jungle no less, and with his talent for raising enthusiasm and funds Smit carried out on television the restoration of not one, but four gardens: an early nineteenth-century Gardenesque layout, a Brownian-style carriage circuit, a Victorian fruit, flower and vegetable garden and a plant-spotter's valley like those on the Helford River. It was a remarkable achievement, but Heligan had been a major Cornish garden, one that filled several gaps in the county's garden history, and it deserved this inspired return to life.

What is of twentieth-century interest at Heligan is the archaeology of Tim Smit's garden thinking. Between his charmingly relaxed guidebook of 1993, *The Lost Gardens of Heligan: A Brief History and Guide* and his glossy 2004 *Handbook and Essential Guide to The Gardens & Wider Estate* with ten pages in colour, he has grown more ambitious, more ecologically ready to embrace bats, badgers, barn owls and Country Codes, more, one hesitates to write it, politically correct, or at least horticulturally correct. In that 1993 guide he had yet to tackle Squire John and Jack Tremayne's plant-spotter's valley, The Jungle, and was writing of restoring the lost paths. By 2004 The Jungle had become the Lost Gardens' main attraction, the first area that the coach-loads of visitors headed for; and to cope with them a wide boardwalk (*78*), not a restored nineteenth-century path, had been laid down, high, dry and isolating, from which visitors could observe and photograph a marvellous sequence of restored and enhanced exotic treescapes around the four ponds, snatches of Chinese, Californian, Australian and new Zealand woodland. The boardwalk offered all that without much danger of tripping over roots and stones, or, in fact, any real physical contact. The Jungle was not a restored plant-spotter's garden of the nineteenth century; it was a new phenomenon, a twenty-first century visitor's strip: 'See the horticultural wonders of the world without effort, without the need of travelling to them'.

That surely was when Smit conceived the logical extension of The Jungle: the biomes of the Eden project where the boardwalks would become winding galleries, a geodesic roof would cut out rain, frost and storm and, in a controlled climate, the woodlands of the world could really be recreated with spices, bananas and all the tropical trimmings. It would be educational, ecologically correct and it would put Cornwall's gardens on an international tourist circuit. Modernist architecture and enhanced plant-spotting would come together triumphantly.

78 *The contrast between the artificial security of the boardwalk in The Jungle at Heligan and the exoticism of the planting around it is not entirely pleasing. It hints at an unusually ambitious municipal park*

10

Hesitant steps towards a Modernist apotheosis

Imaginative modern gardens are not common in Cornwall, though beautiful modern gardens are two-a-penny, yet it was back in 1961 that the County Council itself, which could so easily have filled the space with a predictable assortment of camellias and azaleas, commissioned Geoffrey Jellicoe,[1] the greatest living English Modernist, to help design a garden that would relieve, yet accord with, the austere monotony of its new County Hall at Truro. Possibly dismayed by a building of concrete frame construction, similar to something designed for post-war Düsseldorf, they then 'felt the need for a work of art in the enclosed courtyard'.[2] The landscape architect was J.D.G. Benney, but it was Jellicoe, acting as consultant with F.K. Hicklin, who realised, after taking in the building which he was being asked to endow with some human appeal, that the way to respond to its remorseless repetitive rectangularity was not by cloaking it with camellias, but by making rectangles sing in a garden Mondrian of causeway bridge, stepping stones and geometric canal (*79*). There is not a curve in his shallow waters that step, rather than flow, on their way to escape the prison of that courtyard out into the open grounds. That is the essence of a Modernist garden: it responds to its parent building and context, it does not try simply to cloak them or distract from them with greenery and flowers, the outworn Cornish response. Jellicoe's Water Garden accepts the idiom of the office block and makes a game of crossings and directions out of it.

Made bold by the leap that admirable Council, 'after some consultation … decided to commission Dame Barbara Hepworth to carry out the work, "Rock Form, Porthcurno" … seen from both within and without the building, situated upon the members' terrace'.[3] In 1964 Hepworth delivered a sculpture of sinewy elegance, one which it is no condescension to describe as feminine, a lilting pierced form that rises like a curl of bronze smoke to escape upwards, as Jellicoe's canal escapes outwards.

The combination of the two works should have been a forceful lesson to a timid, horticulturally conservative and self-satisfied county, but it would

79 *Even a building as grim as Cornwall's County Hall at Truro could not quench the invention of England's greatest twentieth-century garden designer, Geoffrey Jellicoe. In 1961 he accepted the challenge of angular concrete blocks and used water surfaces, causeways and stepping-stones to make them sing*

seem that twenty years were to pass before a small, well-designed, Modernist garden was laid out in 1984 at Acton Castle up on the cliffs of Mount Bay at Rosudgeon. John Wood the Younger, a dutiful rather than an inspired architect, had designed the Castle, of classical symmetry and cursory Gothick trim, for John Stuckhouse, a keen marine biologist who specialised in seaweed. Whoever actually built Wood's design contrived to make his blocks of granite look like chunks of concrete crudely mortared. But the Castle enjoys fabulous views out south to the Mount and Newlyn, so from 1889 it was a popular hotel with apartments alongside.[4] Stuckhouse had constructed a subterranean pool for seaweed in front of his house with an underground passage down to the beach and a rock-cut bathing pool. These gave rise to the predictable, tiresome legends about the smuggling brothers, John and Harry Carter. But when a garden was being considered that would cope with the ugly Castle, that subterranean pool offered the possibilities of a sunbathing pit. As a result an amphitheatre of angular features (*80*) in a beautiful blue and grey slate now lies below the Castle terrace, more than holding its own for decisive form and persuading the visitor that harsh features can easily become seductive.

Three main flights of steps and four stepping stones of steps lead down the lawns of the arena to where a fiercely angular pool of water lilies and reeds

80 *The handsome sunbathing pit that fronts Acton Castle works perversely by avoiding the exceptionally fine views of St Michael's Mount's that it could have commanded. It was, in fact, built out of a vast seaweed storage tank*

deliberately upsets expectations of symmetry in its siting relative to the steps and in the projecting peninsulas that jut into it, three on one side, one on the other, and three fountains. There is a tempting possibility that a jump across might be successful and the eye keeps working over the contradictions of its smooth masonry. In contrast the half circle of plant containers that rims the arena's front edge is of rough yellow granite flowering with cotoneaster and succulents. Two fine stands of pampas make unexpectedly lordly statements. Beyond the amphitheatre little nooks, planters and seats of stone have been constructed for anyone who wishes to absorb the winds and that astonishing view. For less hardy souls two exactly round stone tables or seats stud the inner amphitheatre. The whole severe yet sheltering composition cries out for brown sunbathing bodies on those smooth slate flags. This is how to respond to Cornwall's sea and cliffs. There is not a rhododendron in sight.

In fairness to the National Trust it needs to be noted that, pursuant to a tenancy agreement, Lady Carew Pole began in 1983 to plant a densely floral geometry in the Summer Garden at Antony. As usual with anything that the Carew Poles touch in the garden line, whether it is a terrace, a vista, a forecourt or, in this case, a hedged enclosure, the Summer Garden is the best of its kind

81　*By a wise tenancy agreement with the National Trust the Carew Pole family have considerable freedom to continue to plan and enrich their garden at Antony. This 1997 sculpture in the Summer Garden, Hypercone by Simon Thomas, is one result of this*

in the county. Each of its riotously flowering beds is centred on a tall crab apple tree leaded with Yeatsian golden fruit. The diamonds of its Knot Garden are executed in contrasting shades of green and Simon Thomas' 1997 Hypercone (*81*) bemuses perspectives of receding circles down a vista of white fuchsia and dark yew, banishing any possibility that this aggressive battery of flowers could be classed as a conventional herbaceous border. Even more daringly, considering it stands right in the forefront of the county's grandest and greenest yew terrace, William Pye's 1996 Water Cone (*colour plate 27*), that cleverly repeats a nearby topiary cone, has been set up and made to exude a thin film of water that catches the light deceptively. Whether nude or abstract, a sculpture should demand a response; these do; the conventional new seat at the end of the terrace does not. By its function, the National Trust must often face difficult garden decisions. Here at Antony Sir Richard and Lady Carew Pole have been the driving forces,[5] the enthusiastic embracers of modern sculpture while at the same time keeping a sensitive eye on tradition.[6]

When counties like Dorset and Wiltshire ventured into Modernist gardening, expectations of what was right and possible had often been shaped by earlier oriental gardens with their revolutionary aesthetics. Sir William Chambers'

Chinese House at Amesbury Abbey and Louis Greville's exquisite Japanese Tea House set over the Avon at Heale are examples of this invigorating influence.[7] But Chambers was designing in 1772 and Greville in 1913, so Wiltshire's gentry had time to digest the possibilities. Conservative Cornwall had to wait for its Japanese Garden until Robert and Stella Hore began working and arranging in 1985, and their Japanese Garden at St Mawgan was not opened to the public until 1997. When we remember that Gloucestershire had a refined and ambitious Hindu Garden at Sezincote during the Regency,[8] it does put Cornwall's provincial isolation into perspective and goes some way to explain why those earnest late-nineteenth-century Quakers imported endless foreign shrubs with virtually no interest in foreign garden design. That reservation being made, the Hores' Japanese Garden was worth waiting for. It provides an aesthetic education in the space of one hour; more particularly it should offer insights into how abstract art, sculpture for instance, can be interpreted, whether it leaves a visitor spiritually as well as aesthetically refreshed will be up to the visitor. But to the right of the entrance is a Dust Hole. Into that selfish desires should be thrown before going any further!

The garden occupies no more than an acre, excluding the world by a willow thicket, and it immediately makes a visitor an expert in what is beautiful and what is not.[9] As I sat under one of its bamboo-roofed contemplation seats, watching the drip of rain, I began to notice that one branch of an acer was all wrong. Nature is not perfect, but it can be perfected. The danger is that one can become terribly precious, but it is worth the risk. There are no directions in the garden. Visitors wander in a maze of visual subtleties with casually perfect seats from which to absorb them. Acers, azaleas, grasses and clipped box balls play rounded outlines of green and bronze. Diagonals and sloping ascents are the dominants. Japanese trees rarely do anything as obvious as growing straight up. To express the 'In' and 'Yo' of positive male, negative female energy, dark pines, glossy camellias, prostrate conifers and elegant fastigiated yews are planted along the paths. The Tea House is too open; it should be for contemplation, not observation; the pool is the Ocean. Plank areas are for martial display. Odd numbers are preferred for asymmetry. The Zen Garden (*82*) is re-raked each day so the garden dies and is reborn. Its rocks could represent Heaven, Earth and Man. It is up to you.

On my last visit, in that drizzle, a row of potential aesthetes was solemnly seated on the covered bench facing the Zen Garden. They sat in absolute silence absorbing the area of raked gravel with its four subtly shaped rocks poking up with a significance that only subjective contemplation could define. One could do just the same in the Hepworth Garden except that there would be too many distractions. Shape awareness, interaction of water, branch and pathway: that is what the St Mawgan garden is about; or any garden for that matter, but not many visitors will emerge as unaware as when they entered.

Statuary and foreign garden aesthetics are two of the influences behind Modernist gardens. Biodiversity and sustainability are the other influences, all that Green Party, ecological awareness, vegetarianism and Gaia business. There

82 *The gravel in the Zen Garden within the Japanese Garden at St Mawgan is raked afresh each day to symbolise the garden's death and rebirth. Its rocks could, according to personal choice, represent Heaven, Earth and Mankind*

seemed to be a whiff of it in Lady Carew Pole's Summer Garden at Antony, I may be wrong. In Dorset the influence flows out from a wonderful cottage garden called Sticky Wicket,[11] where Pam and Peter Lewis grow hedges to feed the birds, strip off any soil polluted by chemical fertilisers and create miracle colour symphonies of flowers and grasses. Tim Smit's Eden project is strongly ecological. There is a quotation from Xenophon (400 BC), flying over its entrance:

> Earth is a goddess and teaches justice to those who learn, for the better she is served, the more good things she gives.

Potagers, like Prince Charles' at Highgrove, Rosemary Verey's at Barnsley House and Sue Nathan's at Bonython Manor, all tend to organic, ecological awareness. Every county needs a fountainhead like Sticky Wicket, with its presiding priestess or priest. Cornwall is fortunate in such a powerful source at Tresillian, Summercourt, near Newquay, owned by George Robinson, but presided over by its Head Gardener, lecturer and author, John Harris.[12] Sticky Wicket inclines to flowers and an earth mother, but Tresillian is masculine, with fruits and vegetables.

I found it stimulating to enter these gardens of idealistic conservatism, where apparently eccentric faiths in nature are vindicated by what grows there. In Tresillian, Cornwall's historic horticulture lives on, with eighty-six of the county's 100 native apple varieties; the fourteen still missing are being hunted down; and it grows fourteen of its native plum varieties. I tried one, a Callington Seedling plum; it was light, lemony and infinitely worth preserving. The oldest apple is a Tresillian Seedling dating back to 1504. All are under threat of extinction from the buying policies of the big chain stores. Perhaps my most succulent memories of Tresillian are of tomatoes. Its long greenhouse was radiant with their scarlet clusters and odd shapes, pointed, bulbous, miniature, profuse and impossibly tasty; every one I sampled was distinctive and characterful. They can be as characterful in their flavours as apples.

Tresillian is not just a fruit sanctuary; it is a faith; it is a Moon Garden. Lunar gardens like Tresillian are never watered, not even in droughts. They depend upon the water table rising and falling to the cycle of the moon. In the garden house off the big eighteenth-century Walled Garden a lunar calendar hangs prominently and everything happens to the waxing and waning of the moon's quarters. In the dry last quarter it is important to dig and fertilise with organic hedgerow fertilisers because the soil is most receptive when the water table is low. Planting and sowing is done in the quarters of most moisture. Young trees and bushes should go in early during the second quarter when moisture is rising and pressure induces sap flow. Pruning and felling should be carried out in the fourth quarter when the least sap will be lost. Harvesting should be done when plants are driest and when fruit stores best.

This information is all from John Harris (*83*). He is an impressive lecturer. That Walled Garden is alive with his plant lore. Beans supply the soil with nitrogen, so next year he will plant brassica where the beans grew. Most weirdly, half the vegetable rows were interplanted with deadly nightshade because that too enriches the soil. Blue spires of lupins rise for the same reason between rows of peas and beds of white carrots. Only bumble bees are keen to pollinate French beans and bumble bees are a dwindling species, so John Harris plants sweet peas next to the beans to lure foolish house bees to pollinate them by accident.

Walking Tresillian with Mr Harris was a rare treat. Groups come over from as far away as Germany for his seminars because he was trained intensively for eight years in gardens. That is DPhil level in lunar gardening. Rough woodland surrounds his garden. Squirrels eat virtually the whole crop of 1200 nut trees and the Nut Walk doubles as a Bat Walk because it is a flight path for the moths that bats feed upon. As at Melbury in Dorset, the woods are allowed to decay gently so that woodpeckers can nest, insects can flourish and twenty badgers, with untold foxes, can have their dens. There is also a deliciously scummy green pond with a fountain

83 *John Harris in the Walled Garden at Tresillian where he practises Moon Gardening. Sowing, nourishing and harvesting in this Greenest of plots is all timed to phases of the moon and their subsequent influence upon water levels*

in the middle as a refuge for small creatures threatened by local buzzards.

Is Tresillian idealism gone wild? I met John Harris with a mix of admiration and caution. He is a Cornish national treasure who deserves to be listened to, not only for his folkloric expertise, but because my mouth still waters at the memory of his tomatoes.

Between Tresillian and its undercover cousin, the Eden Project, there is only a modest scatter of Modernist ventures. The county was obviously in no hurry to commit itself to a rethinking of garden design. The Hon. Evelyn Boscawen went geometric at Tregothnan in 2000 with a vast sweep of garden designed by Robert Myers where Nesfield's complex parterres had flowered (*84*). The terrace overlooking the Fal now offers a severity of double parterres of cut grass centred with canals and surrounded by a graceful ribbing of white, gravelled paths. When you have two wooded, tidal estuaries to look at, why distract attention with flowers?

At Bonython Manor on The Lizard, Sue Nathan, a South African, has two Modernist ventures in addition to the hot flower fringes to two of her three lakes. One is a sensationally bright Potager with gorgeous red beet in box hedged enclosures and giant chives at the corners. Cabbages make centrepieces with yellow herb surrounds; white roses and wisterias arch the way to the Summer Tea House which is thatched and fig-flanked. In the biggest lake, Lake Joy, made by the Lyles who were at Bonython from 1949-89, there is a sinister island of gunnera, but the lake itself is a prodigy because at first sight it is so covered with bright green weed that it seems a lush extension to the lawn. Sue was clearing weed herself from a dinghy in her own Lake Sue, on my visit. This is a garden on the move with a sublime Quarry Lake the most recent addition; it has a lively future. Visitors are offered an honesty selection of teas and homemade cakes in the Tea House and Sue leaves her windfall apples out for visitors to sample. The National Trust should take note of that simple, natural generosity.

Bonython's most impressive Modernist garden is close up to the windows of the manor: a Water Garden with double geometric moats brimming around a square block of grey marble. The paths are yellow, the water clear; reeds and variegated grasses infill between the geometries. It breaths a refined restraint and comes close to the Water Garden at Kiftsgate in Gloucestershire.

And then at last we come to the Eden Project, the natural child of Heligan, the garden where Cornwall's two garden traditions: the lusty plant-spotter syndrome

84 *The austerely Modernist double parterre garden of cut turf and gravel at Tregothnan was designed by Robert Myers*

and the frail Modernist tendency, come together in what justifiably styles itself as an 'Eighth Architectural Wonder of the World'. How does prose do justice to the 'eighth wonder'? The answer is: with difficulty, though *Eden: the first book*, the Project's latest guide, makes a very good shot at it. Eden has never been reluctant to sell itself as part of the entertainment industry. Projected by Tim 'Demand the Impossible' Smit in 1995, at a presentation for Nicholas Grimshaw; funded by the Millennium Commission to the tune of £37.5 million in 1997; building to Grimshaw's inspired designs began in 1998. It is aimed to attract 750,000 visitors a year and be 'one of the greatest destinations on earth'.[12] The only mystery about this very open project is why Smit, a great idealist who can both communicate and organise, is not in the Lords as Baron Heligan. If anyone merited the honour he does. Perhaps his Dutch nationality prevents it, but it should certainly not prevent him from being offered an honorary knighthood.

The approach is pure theatre. In run down industrial country visitors drive to car-parks where silken banners by Angus Watts, first orange, then pale blue, fly bravely in the wind. Nothing is visible until the last moment when the earth falls away into the Bodelva Pit, so deep it could swallow a cathedral. A sabre-cut of a building, the Gateway to Eden, bars the way, but beyond it, far down below terrace after terrace, are Grimshaw's two linked Biomes (*colour plate 28*), transparent foil and steel bubbles of hexagons, triangles and the occasional pentagon, looking like homes for invading Martian colonists. On my visit a horrid thunder of drums filled the pit with insistent sound. Children were being entertained. There is always something going on in Eden. It aims to educate by entertainment. Even the food in its restaurant between the Biomes is entertainingly delicious with exotic ingredients.

Nothing is simple in Eden. One Biome is for the humid tropics, where a twenty-five metre waterfall crashes down past Africa and Indonesia into the Amazon basin; the other, which is only mildly entertaining, is the warm temperate Biome for the Mediterranean, California and South Africa. But the third or notional 'Biome' has no roof.[13] It is mild, moist Cornwall where the plant-spotter's gardens flourish as usual in the open, but it lacks a directional route. There are little pavilions and a big bumble bee lying across brilliant stripes of flowers (*85*). Along the terraces that circle the Pit motor trains carry lazy visitors down and up; active visitors use the steps or slopes.

The humid, tropic Biome is the real draw because it makes visitors sweat at the bottom as they begin to circle their way slowly up through the plant marvels, and it frightens them a little with signs for escape routes in case the humidity brings about heart attack or some physical collapse. Towards the top of the Biome, where the waterfall bursts in, the climate changes miraculously with warmer drying winds, as if there had been a change in altitude of about 5000 feet.

I was frankly entranced and enriched. There were Knobthorns growing: giraffes eat the black pods, monkeys eat the flowers, elephants eat the leaves; no wonder it grows vicious thorns. Ginger has spectacularly ugly pink flowers; Pond Apples are buoyant, but they can be made into jellies and wine; Travellers Palms point

85 *A giant bee in the Bodelva Pit at the Eden Project where popular culture is more in evidence than in the two enclosed Biomes*

east and west and preserve dirty water; African Blackwood is used to make wind instruments; Wild Coffee berries are poisonous and cause hallucinations; the pods of Pigeon Pea are used in curries; Peach Palms fruit twice a year and must be cooked in salt water; Rice, Wheat, Potatoes and, surprise, Bananas, are the world's four most important food crops; Guavas have between twice and five times the vitamin C content of oranges; the alkaloid components of a Madagascar Periwinkle are used to treat childhood leukaemia; Bamboos can be thick enough to make scaffolding for houses.

That was a long sentence, but it was a long climb; and I saw all those useful plants actually growing, together with a bay Rum bush, pepper, cinnamon, rice, tamarind, avocado and cassova; all without the pain of injections for yellow fever or having to take pills against malaria. As extras there were wickerwork baboons hanging on the cliffs, leopards looking coyly at toy flowers, a wicker man hanging, Thamani wall paintings from Peru by Francisco Shuna and Yolanda Baneo, an African hut, a Malaysian village house and a big joke area with a quiz around multiple types of bananas that were teeming with sinister ants. The attendants were all undimmed by custom and a pleasure to meet.

Tim Smit has understood and then realised practically the logical conclusion to the gardens of those Falmouth Quakers of the nineteenth century. If those imported tender exotics were not going to be organised into formal or Arcadian gardens then the obvious next step, given the Modernist marvels of applied technology, was to recreate their natural wild environment. Smit's Project invites visitors to walk into a virtual reality world of botanical riches and experience those riches at first hand. The experience is unreal in that we suffer no insect bites, take no malaria pills, and do not have to watch out for poisonous snakes or tigers. But it is as real, as sanitised, as most people want. Whether it is, as the guidebooks claim, a valuable educational experience around which conferences of experts can be held remains to be proven. Other questions can be asked. Does a Biome only work as an experience when it is a green jungle experience? Has a survey been conducted to compare the average time a visitor spends in the humid tropics and how long in the other Biome, the warm, temperate Mediterranean one (*86*), which although it has a few birds, lacks a Mediterranean light, a sea and a beach?

The German equivalent of the project is a simple Biome in Hanover. It goes full-tilt for the humid forest, adds sound tracks and lets brilliantly plumaged birds fly loose. Was that the wiser solution? Lastly, does Smit's third, unroofed 'Biome' sell Cornwall, as it is claimed, with direction, experiences and education? The projected educational Biome might solve this problem. While remaining full of admiration at what the Eden Project has done for the Duchy in image, in employment and in pleasure, I leave these questions hanging.

86 *Nicholas Grimshaw's twenty-first-century 'construction kit for giants' arching over the warm, temperate Biome at the Eden Project*

Notes

Introduction – to an off-beat Duchy

1 Notes to the Catchfrench Red Book are in the Cornwall Record Office (hereafter CRO), FS 3/1187.

2 Eagles Nest is, however, private and not open to the public.

3 C.S. Gilbert, *An Historical Survey of the County of Cornwall*, 2 volumes (Plymouth, 1817 & 1820), 2, p.586.

4 Out of hours visiting can be arranged with the guardian, Barry Litton.

Chapter 1
Chysauster and Tintagel – early gardens of utility and Romantic gesture

1 Patricia M.L. Christie, *Chysauster and Carn Euny* (English Heritage, 1997).

2 See, however, Jacqui Wood's controversial reappraisal in *Cornwall Archaeology*, vol.36 (1997), pp.95-107.

3 Jacqui Wood interprets these stones as querns for grinding corn. Ibid.

4 If Jacqui Wood's interpretation is accepted the houses would have had two storeys with a raised gallery under a high roof.

5 Richard Carew, *The Survey of Cornwall*, 1602 (Redruth, 2000), p.142.

6 Ibid., p.143.

7 For a useful account of the Arthur legend see Brian K. Davison, *Tintagel Castle, Cornwall* (English Heritage, 1999), pp.24-40.

8 See Peter Rose, 'The Medieval Garden at Tintagel Castle', *Cornwall Archaeology*, vol.33 (1994), pp.170-82.

9 Carew, *Survey*, p.142.

10 Quoted in Rose, *Cornwall Archaeology*, p.170.

11 Ibid.

12 Davison, *Tintagel Castle*, p.10.

13 See Peter Goodchild, 'John Rea's Gardens of Delight: Introduction and the Construction of the Flower Garden', *Garden History*, vol.9, part 2 (Autumn, 1981), pp.99-109. For the Kip and Knyff views see Timothy Mowl, *Gentlemen & Players: Gardeners of the English Landscape* (Stroud,

2000; paperback 2004), Chapter Five.

14 Carew, *Survey*, p.158.

15 Ibid., pp.86-7.

Chapter 2
'A place of diverified pleasings' – Tudor and Elizabethan gardens

1 The Prideaux drawings are in two leather-bound volumes in the possession of Peter and Elizabeth Prideaux-Brune at Prideaux Place, Padstow; I am most grateful to them for allowing me access to the drawings. The Prideaux drawings have been the subject of an article by John Harris in *Architectural History*, vol.7 (1964).

2 See H. Dalton Clifford, 'Tudor Houses of Cornwall', *Country Life*, 13 April 1961; and by the same author, 'A Cornish Manor Rich in Legend', *Country Life*, 13 September 1962. Dalton Clifford calls Trewane, 'Trewarne', but the present owner assures me that the house is now known as Trewane.

3 Gilbert, *Historical Survey*, 2, p.611.

4 I owe my information to Peter Herring, 'Cornish Medieval Deer Parks' in Robert Wilson-North (ed.), *The Lie of the Land* (Exeter, 2003), pp.34-50.

5 Ibid., p.42.

6 A.L. Rowse, *Tudor Cornwall*, 1969, p.45, footnote.

7 Carew, *Survey*, p.76.

8 'Map of part of the Parishes of Budock and Mylor, drawn about AD 1580 with a notice of Arwenack House,' 2 December 1887, *Journal of the Royal Institution of Cornwall*, vol.IX (1886-9), pt.2, pp.160-4.

9 Ibid.

10 This has been re-sited in front of Arwenack House on the main street in Falmouth.

11 Quoted in Pett, *Parks and Gardens*, p.128.

12 The map is in the British Museum, Cotton MS., Aug. 1, 38 and reproduced as figure 7 in John Cornforth, 'Place, Fowey, Cornwall', *Country Life*, 21 June 1962. Carew, *Survey*, describes Place as a 'fair and ancient house, castle-wise builded and sufficiently flanked, [which] overlooketh the

town and haven with a pleasant prospect' (p.160).

13 Carew, *Survey*, p.123.

14 Ibid., pp.124-5.

15 *Cothele House* (National Trust, 1991), p.30.

16 Michael Trinick, *Cotehele House* (National Trust, 1989), p.14.

17 Michael Trinick, *Trerice, Cornwall* (National Trust, 1991), p.31; see also F Holland Hall, 'Trerice', *Cornwall Garden*, 1986, pp.26-9.

18 Douglas Ellory Pett, *Parks and Gardens of Cornwall* (Penzance, 1998), pp.64-5.

19 John Schofield, *Godolphin, The Side Garden: A Brief Guide* (Helston, 2003).

20 The Debois Landscape Survey, carried out in 1994.

21 By Richard Cole, Peter Herring, Charles Johns and Ann Reynolds, September 2001. Peter Herring had earlier prepared an October 1997 ('Archaeological & Historical Assessment') report on the site.

22 CRO, RH/210.

23 Quoted in Herring, 1997, pp.60-1.

24 Ibid., pp.60-1.

25 Carew, *Survey*, p.158.

26 Ibid., p.159.

27 Ibid., p.158; p.100.

28 Lines 1-4.

29 *The Prelude*, Book 4, lines 323-27.

Chapter 3
The county in a cautious dalliance with formal garden design

1 Pett, *Parks and Gardens*, p.64.

2 Richard Haslam, 'Godolphin House', *Country Life*, 12 May 1994.

3 *Country Life*, 25 December 1915.

4 For a graphic and disdainful account on the site see Carew, *Survey*, pp.19-24.

5 For Wilton I see Timothy Mowl, *Historic Gardens of Wiltshire* (Stroud, 2004), pp.23-5.

6 For Theobalds see Roy Strong, *The Renaissance Garden in England*, 1979, pp.51-7.

7 George London worked at Longleat for twenty years costing the Thynne family £30,000. No Cornish landowner was prepared to make such a financial commitment; see Mowl, *Wiltshire*, pp.50-1.

8 CRO, RH 2936: 'Plan of Part of the Manor of Godolphin'.

9 A sycamore avenue was considered a novelty at Longford Castle, Wiltshire in 1590, but already disparaged by 1660: see *Country Life*, 12 December 1931.

10 Nikolaus Pevsner, *The Buildings of England: Cornwall*, 2nd edition, 1970, p.73.

11 The Spoure Book is in a private collection. There are copies in the Courtney Library and in CRO, FS 3/93/1 (1-43).

12 Illustrated in Pett, *Parks and Gardens*, fig.87, p.210.

13 The report, carried out in 1995, is deposited in the Cornwall Record Office (X 897/54).

14 Mentioned informally on a personal visit to the garden.

15 For *Britannia Illustrata* see John Harris, *The Artist and the Country House*, 1979, pp.88-100.

16 CRO, DDP 68/28/1.

17 CRO, 1153: Tremayne Papers; see also 1143, 1144, 1146 & 1152.

18 Ibid.

19 CRO, 1143 & 1152.

20 I am most grateful to Elisabeth and Peter Prideaux-Brune for allowing me to consult the volumes, and to Sue Goodsir for her hospitality on a day of wild weather at the Place. For illustrations of many of the drawings see John Harris, 'The Prideaux Collection of Topographical Drawings', *Architectural History* vol.7 (1964). They also feature prominently in Pett, *Parks and Gardens*.

21 Bodleian Library, Gough Maps 5, 21B. I owe this reference to Dr Pat Hughes, who had not seen this map at the time of writing (see subsequent footnote).

22 I am indebted to Dr Pat Hughes, who is conducting research for a conservation plan for Mount Edgcumbe, for her help with the dating of features in the landscape. New information is still being unearthed at the time of writing, which may alter some of the dates given for landscape features on the estate in the next chapter. Dr Hughes has already identified a rectangular garden on the site of the later Amphitheatre on a 1643 map of the fortifications of Plymouth: 'A True Map and Description of the Town of Plymouth'.

23 All the ironwork is Edwardian in date. The court was originally quite open to the south and centred on a statue now lost. A brick wall is shown closing the courtyard in an anonymous eighteenth-century view shown in the House Museum.

24 There are similarities between Antony's two storeys and the three-storey house illustrated on plate 57 in Gibbs' *Book of Architecture* of 1728 which encourage this attribution. Antony House was begun in 1718 by a Devon builder, John Moyle of Exeter, with no first rate designs to his credit.

25 See *Country Life*, 28 July 1960.

26 For illustrations see *Country Life*, 9 January 1904. Pett, *Parks and Gardens* reports (p.233) that Jekyll 'felt that the ball finials were out of proportion', but she still featured them in her *Garden Ornaments* of 1918.

27 Ibid.

28 I am indebted for much of my information on
Stowe to Michael Trinick's presidential address
to the Royal Institution of Cornwall, published
in their *Journal*, new series, vol.8, part 1 (1978),
pp.90-108 and to Rob Wilson-North's 'Stowe:
the country house and gardens of the Grenville
family', *Cornwall Archaeology*, no.32 (1993), pp.112-
27.

29 Trinick, p.92; quoted from Burnet, *A History of my
own Time*, vol.1, 1724, p.168.

30 Trinick, quoting Borlase, p.93.

31 The van Diest painting is reproduced in Trinick's
article, plate 2.

32 CRO, CF4/X/273/1.

33 CRO, D.D.E.N, 1315: King's carefully costed
proposals.

34 Ibid.

35 The total cost was £183 4s 9d.

36 CRO, X897/54.

37 CRO, D.D.E.N, 1315.

Chapter 4

The problem of Arcadian gardens in a naturally Arcadian county

1 For the European context see John Dixon Hunt,
The Picturesque Garden in Europe, 2003.

2 For Castell see Mowl, *Gentlemen & Players*, pp.111-
14.

3 John Cornforth, 'Prideaux Place, Cornwall – II',
Country Life, 8 February 1962.

4 See Pett, *Parks and Gardens*, pp.39-40 & fig.16.

5 This drive probably dates from Repton's
involvement at Pentillie, which will be discussed
in a later chapter.

6 Gilbert, *Historical Survey*, vol.1 (1817), p.441.

7 Ibid., p.438.

8 Ibid., p.439.

9 Lewis Melville, *Life and Letters of William Beckford*,
1910, p.123.

10 *Paradise Lost*, Book IV, lines 705-8.

11 Ibid., Book IV, lines 140-2.

12 Christopher Morris (ed.), *The Illustrated Journeys
of Celia Fiennes c.1682-c.1712*, 1982, p.203. In 1643
this was a rectangular garden: information from
Dr Pat Hughes.

13 The Garden House survives in the present English
Garden, between two wings added in 1820 when
it was turned into a bath house with hot and
cold water. The Badeslade view is now lost, but
Mount Edgcumbe has a copy from which the
illustration here was taken.

14 See Bodleian Library, Gough Maps 5, f.29B.

15 For Walpole's garden see Timothy Mowl, *Horace
Walpole: The Great Outsider*, 1996, chapter 12.

16 Information from Dr Pat Hughes: letter from Lord
Edgcumbe to Lord Camelford in the British
Library.

17 As recorded on an 1819 map of the gardens
from Warner's guidebook preserved at Mount
Edgcumbe; information from Dr Pat Hughes.

18 The Blockhouse originally had a two-columned
Tuscan portico on its seaward side. This is
visible in the Bampfylde view of 1755 and,
more prominently, in an undated engraved view
by J. Mason, which also shows a flagpole with
the Union Jack flying and the row of canon:
Bodleian Library, Gough Maps 5, f.28B.

19 It is to be hoped that this will be addressed when
the conservation plan, now in preparation, has
been presented.

20 J. Cartwright (ed.), *The Travels through England of Dr
Richard Pococke 1750-57*, 2 vols (Camden Society,
1888-9), 2, p.6.

21 Ibid., 1, p.134.

22 Ibid.

23 I was not allowed access to the park; a good
illustration of the Sugar Loaves is given in
Barbara Jones, *Follies & Grottoes*, 1974, p.302.

24 For adaptations of the Tomb see David Coffin,
The English Garden: Meditation and Memorial
(Princeton, NJ, 1994), p.169.

25 Cartwright, *Travels*, 1, p,134.

26 Gilbert, *Historical Survey*, vol.2 (1820), p.523.

27 See Michael Trinick, 'William Borlase – Gardener',
Journal of the Royal Institution of Cornwall, vol.2,
pr.1 (1994), pp.28-42.

28 'Plan of the Barton of Trelowarren' by Dionysius
Williams (CRO,V/P/1).

29 William Mason, *The English Garden: A Poem*,
4 vols., 1783 (Gregg International reprint,
Farnborough, 1971) 1, lines 430-5.

30 Dating for this area is problematic. The
Summerhouse is clearly shown on a plan of 1770,
but the other features are undated and do not
appear on a plan of the intended alterations at
Heligan by Thomas Gray; see Tim Smit, *A Brief
History and Guide to Heligan* (St Austell, 1993),
p.13 & p.5.

31 William Borlase, *Observations on the Antiquities
Historical and Monumental, of the County of
Cornwall* (Oxford, 1754), p.360. I am grateful to
Joe and Sam Parsons for showing me the stone
and sharing their research on it.

32 Written from Camelford by Jos. Pomeroy; vol.XV
(June, 1745), p.304.

33 Borlase, *Observations*, p.360.

34 Ibid., 2, pp.477-8.

35 For the Whiteford estate see Ronald & Juliet Plant,
'We live in garden history', *Cornwall Gardens Trust
Journal*, 1996, pp.25-8.

36 The Landmark Trust guide to the Temple suggests

Philip Stowey, architect of the Exeter Sessions House, as the author on grounds of stylistic similarities.

37 I was not allowed access to Trebartha and so have relied on Pett, *Parks and Gardens*, pp.209-10.

38 Borlase, *Natural History*, p.122.

39 Quoted in P.G. Embrey & R.F. Symes, *Minerals of Cornwall and Devon*, 1987, p.64; I owe this reference to Angela Broome.

40 Quoted by Pett, *Parks and Gardens*, p.156 from a mysterious source: 'Paris, 1824: 206', not given in the bibliography.

41 An illustration of the Grotto is given in: Pett, *Parks and Gardens*, p.156, 'from a painting by G. Boney in 1805, the present whereabouts of which are not known'.

Chapter 5
Humphry Repton in a county designed for Picturesque gardening

1 For Brown's career and his working methods see 'Lancelot Brown (1716-83) and the Landscape Park', *Garden History*, vol.29:1 (2001).

2 For the exotic planting of Chyverton, which is still under way, see Nigel Holman, 'Some new introductions at Chyverton', *Cornwall Gardens Trust Journal*, 1994, pp.14-15.

3 CRO, X897/4/1; also S. Pring's 1990-1 survey for the Cornwall Gardens Trust.

4 For Repton see Stephen Daniels, *Humphry Repton: Landscape Gardening and the Geography of Georgian England*, 1999; see also Douglas Pett, 'Humphry Repton in Cornwall', *The Cornish Garden*, no.44 (2001), pp.35-43 and Ferrers Vyvyan, 'The Picturesque Landscape in Cornwall', *Cornwall Gardens Trust Journal*, 1998, pp.5-10 & 2003, pp.5-9. For Repton and Portland see Mowl, *Gentlemen & Players*, pp.180-1.

5 Antony Red Book (facsimile edition), under 'Ornamental Gardening'.

6 Ibid., under 'Character and Situation'.

7 The Antony Red Book records that Repton made the site visit on 17 October 1792 and completed the text by December.

8 See Daniels, *Humphry Repton*, Gazetteer compiled with John Phibbs, pp.255-70. I am also indebted to André Rogger's work on Repton.

9 See Daniels, *Humphry Repton*, pp.192-205.

10 For the Peacock illustration see Daniels, *Humphry Repton*, fig.180 on p.184.

11 The Corytons, who commissioned Repton, still live at Pentillie, but guard their privacy.

12 Antony Red Book, under 'Water Approach'. There is an eighteenth-century Bath House near the site of Repton's proposed lodge.

13 Ibid., under 'The Terrace'.

14 Ibid., under 'View: Explanation continued'.

15 Ibid., under 'Plantations'.

16 This and subsequent references in this paragraph are taken from the Antony Red Book, under 'Explanation continued'.

17 Ibid.

18 Extensive notes on the Catchfrench Red Book are in CRO, FS 3/1187; subsequent quotations are taken from this source.

19 Ibid. The gentry drive to pass through a plantation 'without any suspicion of its parallel twin'.

20 CRO, DDG/1957.

21 Ibid., under 'Conveniences'.

22 Ibid., annotations on the Map.

23 For Tehidy see Pett, *Parks and Gardens*, pp.80-2.

24 The Red Book is still at Port Eliot. I am most grateful to Peregrine, 10th Earl St Germans, for allowing me access to it and for his advice and warm hospitality. All subsequent quotations are taken from this source.

25 Ibid., under 'Plantations'.

26 Ibid., under 'Of Unity'.

27 Ibid., under 'Plantations continued'.

28 Pett accepts Repton's claim and has a useful discussion on it in his article on Repton in *The Cornish Garden*, 44, p.43.

29 Port Eliot Red Book, under 'The Craggs'.

30 Burke's seminal thesis on the Sublime and the Beautiful was first published in 1757. For Burke and the Savage Picturesque see Mowl, *Gentlemen & Players*, Chapter 13.

31 Gilbert, *Historical Survey*, 3, p.866.

32 The Cornwall Gardens Trust survey (CRO, X 987/44/1) has a photograph of the Gardener Survey Map of 1784 and records that 'a classical style 4 pillared temple on the south side of the quarry would have given views over the river. On the river bank below Craggs Wood was a contemporary style folly, a simple "Tent" placed over an elaborate octagonal cobbled floor. A flagpole was near by'. I could not locate the map in the Record Office.

33 Gilbert, *Historical Survey*, 3, p.866.

34 Ibid. The Memorial Urn was dated 1795.

35 For an architectural history of Port Eliot and Soane's work there see *Country Life*, 15, 22 & 29 October 1948.

36 Port Eliot Red Book, under 'Of Unity'.

37 Ibid., under 'Of Gothic'.

38 Shown on CRO, EL/21/415: P Cadman, 'Plan of the Borough Town of St Germin in Cornwall', 1790.

39 To be accurate the church has not been a cathedral since 1050 and before that it was a more modest Saxon structure.

40 Elihu Burritt, *A Walk from London to Lands End and*

Back, 1868, p.272, quoted in CRO, X 897/44/3.

41 The Red Book is still at Tregothnan. I am most grateful to the Hon. Evelyn Boscawen for allowing me access to the Red Book and for his advice and hospitality at Tregothnan. Subsequent quotations are taken from this source. This quotation is under 'Character and Situation'.

42 Ibid., under 'Introduction'.

43 Ibid., under 'The Drives'.

Chapter 6
Nineteenth-century gardens outside the magic circle of the plant-spotter dynasties

1 See Brent Elliott, *Victorian Gardens*, 1986, pp.32-6.

2 See Sandra Morris, 'Legacy of a Bishop: The trees and shrubs of Fulham Palace Gardens introduced 1675-1713', *Garden History*, vol.19:1 (Spring, 1991) & vol.21:1 (Summer, 1993); see also Nigel Mathews, 'Plant introductions to Cornwall', *Cornwall Gardens Trust Journal*, 1999, pp.5-11.

3 For Mason see Mark Laird, *The Flowering of the Landscape: English Pleasure Grounds 1720-1800* (Philadelphia, 1999), Chapter 9.

4 Port Eliot Red Book, under 'View from the House'; also Mason, *English Garden*, 1, lines 243-8.

5 Mason, *English Garden*, I, lines 336-9.

6 Ibid., 4, lines 223-9.

7 Ibid., 4, lines 79-101.

8 Ibid., 4, lines 200-213.

9 Ibid., 4, lines 217-21.

10 Burritt, *A Walk*, p.272.

11 The first Minute Book of the Royal Cornish Horticultural Society (not actually Royal at this date) is in the Courtney Library, Royal Institution of Cornwall.

12 Carew, *Survey*, p.75.

13 For Tullimaar see Pett, *Parks and Gardens*, fig.51, p.130.

14 Another Italianate garden of the same period survives partially at Porthgwidden in Feock. Here there is a whitewashed, balconied Italianate house with a formal terrace overlooking the Carrick Roads. It was built in 1829 for Edmund Turner, MP for Truro. Edward Twycross, *Mansions of England and Wales: County of Cornwall*, 1846, p.87 illustrates it with flowerbeds, central fountain, elegant couples strolling and a pair of peacocks: see Pett, *Parks and Gardens*, fig.40, p.96. The terrace is now laid to lawn and the house is divided into flats.

15 This was built with Gothic stonework brought here in 1819 after the fire at Nanswhyden and built in 1832 as the family's private garden, a gesture of seeming no-confidence in the rest of the layout.

16 Quoted in Pett, *Parks and Gardens*, p.71.

17 CRO, X/897.

18 Noted by the *Gardeners' Chronicle* of 1842; quoted by Pett, *Parks and Gardens*, p.192.

19 Noted by Twycross, p.27; Twycross's plate is in Pett, *Parks and Gardens*, fig.79, p.192.

20 Illustrated in Pett, *Parks and Gardens*, p.193, fig.80.

21 The painting of Sir William is by Alfred Edward Chalon. The bill of sale for the dog's collar is preserved at Pencarrow and dated 1845. Information from James Reynolds.

22 Conifers, pines, beech, birch and chestnuts underplanted with laurel and holly in September 1804 have almost hidden the Obelisk. This planting was recorded in a 'Diary of Works' (British Library, Add, MS. 69176, f.77). Information from Cynthia Troup, 'Lady Anne Grenville: an unsung heroine in garden history?' MA Dissertation, University of Bristol, November 2004.

23 Pam Dodds & Joy Wilson, 'Recording Boconnoc Garden', *The Journal of the Cornwall Gardens Trust*, 2004, pp.5-14; p.5.

24 An estimate for the Cold Bath in the Cornwall Record Office lists 'Boconnoc Quarry Stone' for the 'Margin' and 'Moorstone Paving at least 4 inches thick' for the floor. I am most grateful to Cynthia Troup for alerting me to this estimate. It may have been designed by John Mulholland, a pupil of James Wyatt: Dodds & Wilson, 'Recording Boconnoc', p.9.

25 Ibid., fig.40.

26 Twycross, *Mansions*, 1846, p.56.

27 According to Pett, *Parks and Gardens* (p.163), Nesfield's plan is dated 1843, but the pamphlet for the garden gives 1845.

28 Nesfield's plan is illustrated in Pett, *Parks and Gardens*, fig.66, p.163. I am grateful to Tom Hudson for sharing his knowledge of Tregrehan with me on my visit there.

29 Quoted in Pett, *Parks and Gardens*, pp.163-4.

30 Information from Shirley Evans who has access to the Nesfield Archives.

31 Edward Luckhurst writing in the *Journal of Horticulture*, quoted by Pett, *Parks and Gardens*, p.99.

32 See the last chapter of this book.

33 This area originally had a simple formal layout of enclosures around the house including a Flower Garden and a Bowling Green; there a Wilderness further out in the park. This is shown on Joel Gascoyne's Lanhydrock Atlas of 1698, which is preserved at the house. It is illustrated in the National Trust guidebook to Lanhydrock (1995), p.39. Information from Paul Holden.

34 I am most grateful to Paul Holden for sharing his

discovery with me. His article on Truefitt and
Lanhydrock will be published in *Apollo* in late
2005. The Truefitt design is in the Lanhydrock
archives.

35 Information from Paul Holden.

36 Ibid.

37 Ibid., p.35.

38 For The Downes see Daphne Lowry, 'A very
private garden', *Cornwall Gardens Trust Journal*,
1996, pp.19-22.

39 J.D. Sedding, *Garden-Craft Old and New* (2nd
edition, 1892), p.135.

40 Ibid.

41 Ibid.

42 Pett, *Parks and Gardens*, p.63

Chapter 7
The Edens of the Quaker plant-spotters

1 Alfred Tennyson, *The Morte d'Arthur*.

2 For Chusans see Tim Miles & David Rowe, *The
New Cornish Garden* (Truro, 2003), p.82.

3 Information from the Cornwall Gardens Trust's
excellent survey of Rosehill: CRO, X897/34;
see also Stella Harvey, 'An Informal Look at Fox
Rosehill Gardens', *Cornwall Gardens Trust Journal*,
1997, pp.22-5.

4 For a family tree of the Foxes see Charles Fox,
*Glendurgan: A Personal Memoir of a Garden in
Cornwall* (Penzance, 2004), p.118.

5 Quoted in Pett, *Parks and Gardens*, p.122.

6 Ibid., p.121.

7 Fox, *Glendurgan*, p.17.

8 This figure is taken from a well-supported article
by Dougals Pett in *Cornwall Garden Society
Journal*, no.39 (1996), pp.30-7. The Williams
family alone gardened fifteen sites and allied
with the Daveys of Bochym, Philpotts of
Porthgwidden and Carus Wilsons of Penmount,
also with the Bolithos and the Vyvyans.

9 The Minute Book (not paginated) is available
for reference in the Courtney Library at Truro
Museum; subsequent quotations are taken from it
without page references.

10 Booth wrote the text for Alfred Chandler's
Illustrations and Descriptions of the Camilliae, 1831.

11 For the Veitch dynasty see Sue Shephard, *Seeds of
Fortune: A Gardening Dynasty*, 2003.

12 There is a full account of the Lobb brothers' plant
hunting in Toby Musgrave, Chris Gardner & Will
Musgrave, *The Plant Hunters: Two Hundred Years
of Adventure and Discovery Around the World*, 1999,
pp.131-53.

13 Fox, *Glendurgan*, p.54.

14 For this and other tender exotics see W. Arnold-
Forster, *Shrubs for the Milder Counties*, 1948
(Penzance, 2000 edition).

15 I am grateful to Alison Clough, head gardener at
Trewidden, for making my visit possible when
the garden was closed.

16 Fourteen years is nothing; one magnolia at
Caerhays waited thirty years before flowering and
then flowered with small, drab petals.

17 My thanks go to Penelope Hobhouse for guidance
through the plant jungle in her section on
Trewithen in *Private Gardens of England*, 1986,
pp.12-17. I owe this reference to Trish Gibson.

18 The ponds were laid out in the shape of an eagle,
the Hawkins family emblem: Pett, *Parks and
Gardens*, p.148.

19 I am grateful to Mr F.J. Williams for allowing me
to consult the Garden Book, which is preserved
at the Castle.

20 See Musgrave, Gardner & Musgrave, *Plant Hunters*,
pp.177-97.

21 See Richard Haslam's two excellent articles on
Tresco in *Country Life*, 10 & 17 April 1980.

22 They include *Primus*, an iron barque built at
Sunderland in 1869 and *Friar Tuck*, built at
Aberdeen in 1856, wrecked in St Mary's Pool in
1863.

Chapter 8
The great gap in Cornish Garden History

1 See David Ottewill, *The Edwardian Garden*, 1989.

2 See Jane Abdy and Charlotte Gere, *The Souls*, 1984.

3 See Mowl, *Wiltshire*, pp.138-42.

4 Pett, *Parks and Gardens*, p.161, citing Geoffrey
Beard's slim 1976 monograph on Mawson, states
that the architect was asked for advice. As yet, no
documentary evidence has emerged to prove that
Mawson actually carried out the design; Pett says
no commission was given.

5 See Mowl, *Dorset*, pp.131-4.

6 Ibid., pp.154-6.

7 I am grateful to Sarah Treffry who showed me
original photographs of the formal layout on my
visit to Place. There is no precise dating for the
layout, but it does not appear on the Ordnance
Survey Map for 1906 and so must be later.

8 Thomas Mawson, *The Art & Craft of Garden Making*
2nd edition, 1901, p.70: 'it will generally be found
to be much the wisest and most economical in
the long run to have the structures in stone or
brick, or, where wood has to be used, in oak'.

9 Ibid., p.68.

10 Ibid., figures 58, 69 & 70.

11 Ibid., fig.62 of woodland walks at Mount Stuart,
Isle of Bute.

12 Ibid., p.75.

13 For Lutyens see Lawrence Weaver, *Houses
and Gardens by E.L. Lutyens*, 1913 (Antique
Collectors' Club reprint of 1981).

14 The two best accounts of the gardens are: Diana
    Colville, 'Penheale: the rebirth of a House', *JRIC*,
    vol.x, pt.3 (1989), pp.267-82 and Hobhouse,
    Private Gardens, 1986, pp.30-5. The house
    featured in *Country Life* on 28 March 1925, just
    after Lutyens had completed his alterations and
    restoration.

15 From Blomfield's *The Formal Garden in England*,
    1892, quoted in Richard A Fellows, *Sir Reginald
    Blomfield: An Edwardian Architect*, 1985, pp.38-9.

16 I am indebted for guidance here to Penelope
    Hobhouse's descriptions of the flora at Penheale
    in her *Private Gardens*.

17 The 'Map or Plan of Penheale' was drawn by
    William Hole for Charles Phillipps, Mrs
    Elizabeth Long and Margaret Davie. I am most
    grateful to James Colville for showing me this
    map, preserved at the house.

18 See CRO, X 897/44/4 & 4A.

Chapter 9
In the lee of the plant-spotter storm – twentieth-century gardens

1 See Arthur Hellyer, 'The Making of a Gardener:
   Maj-Gen. E.G.W. Harrison at Tremeer,
   Cornwall', *Country Life*, 30 October 1980.

2 See Douglas Ellory Pett, *The Cornwall gardens guide*
   (Penzance, 2003), entry no.64.

3 *Country Life*, 9 November 1924. The Garden Guide
   at the Mount gives 1780 as a likely date.

4 I am most grateful to the Heron Estate for
   allowing me access to this private garden and to
   Chunky Penhaul for guiding me around it so
   expertly.

5 She died of a heart attack after spending a night in
   a local cottage. This, and other local information,
   is taken from Alison Symons, *Tremedda Days, A
   View of Zennor*, 1992; p.41. I owe this reference
   to Shirley Evans of the Cornwall Gardens Trust
   who first alerted me to Eagles Nest garden.

6 Woolf's diary for 13 July 1920: 'Ka has taken the
   Eagles Nest...I wish it were mine'. Quoted in
   Michael McNay, *Patrick Heron*, 2002, p.35.

7 Arnold-Forster gives a full account of *Embothrium
   coccineum* in his *Shrubs for the Milder Counties*,
   pp.119-20.

8 Quoted in McNay, *Patrick Heron*, p.35. Frieda was
   in trouble, being an enemy alien in wartime.

9 McNay, *Patrick Heron*, p.63.

10 Pett, *Parks and Gardens*, p.87.

11 *Trelissick Garden* (National Trust, 1997), p.9.

12 Ibid., p.3.

13 Gilbert, *Historical Survey*, 3, p.434 believes it was
    built by the Nosworthys after 1660, but surely
    on an existing earlier building. There is a
    1653 reference to a 'new-builte bricke house';

information from Viscount Boyd of Merton who
has been a model of helpfulness.

14 The postcards were kindly given to me by Viscount
    Boyd.

15 Lady Boyd, who died in 2001, was a Vice-President
    of the Cornwall Garden Society.

16 These were carved to go on the Admiralty Arch
    at the end of The Mall in London. The present
    Lord Boyd brought them here.

17 See John Moreland, 'Making a Garden at Tregenna
    Castle' in *Cornwall Gardens Trust Journal*, 1997,
    pp.19-21, which has a plan of the layout.

18 See Angela Evans, *The Cornish Garden*, no.44
    (March, 2001), pp.20-3. The catalyst for the
    recreation at Pengersick was the discovery in the
    British Library of 'either a licence for, or a plan
    of, a thirteenth century physic and apothecary
    garden' (p.20). The Cornwall Archaeological Unit
    failed to find evidence of the existence of such a
    document, but Angela pressed on regardless.

Chapter 10
Hesitant steps towards a Modernist apotheosis

1 See Sheila Harvey (ed.), *Geoffrey Jellicoe* (Landscape
   Design Trust, Reigate, 1998) and Michael Spens,
   Gardens of the Mind: The Genius of Geoffrey Jellicoe
   (Antique Collectors' Club, Woodbridge, 1992).

2 Council brochure, CRO, CC/AG.1.

3 Ibid.

4 It is now all divided up into apartments. I have
   not been able to track down the name of the
   designer.

5 See Sir Richard's interview in *Cornwall Gardens
   Trust Journal*, 2003, pp.13.

6 Ptolemy Dean has recently designed an eyecatcher
   Arch for Tomboy Hill on the estate based on
   the cloister end pavilions and Repton's abortive
   terrace pavilions. See Ptolemy Dean, 'Ptolemy's
   Arch, Tomboy Hill, Antony, Cornwall', *The Follies
   Journal* no.4 (Winter, 2004), pp.1-10.

7 See Mowl, *Wiltshire*, pp.96-8 & pp.146-8.

8 See Timothy Mowl, *Historic Gardens of
   Gloucestershire* (Stroud, 2002), pp.117-21.

9 I am indebted for much of my interpretation to
   the Stella Hore's article, 'Creating a Japanese
   Garden' in *The Cornish Garden*, no.40 (1997),
   pp.36-40.

10 See Mowl, *Dorset*, pp.166-9.

11 R.J. Harris, *Moon Gardening* (Shrewsbury, 2002).

12 Martin Jackson, *Eden: the first book* (St Ives, 2000),
    p.19.

13 A third Biome is now being constructed (Spring,
    2005) for educational purposes.

Gazetteer

The following is a list of gardens of significant historic importance, which are covered in this book and are open to the public.

Abbreviations

NT	National Trust
EH	English Heritage
P	Privately owned, but regularly open
NGS	Privately owned but open occasionally as part of the National Gardens Scheme
H	Hotel
LA	Local Authority
C/TS	Conference Centre and Time Share
HV	Holiday Village

Antony (NT)
Boconnoc (P)
Bonython Manor Estate Gardens (P)
Bosvigo, Truro (P)
Caerhays Castle (P)
Carclew (NGS)
Carwinion (NT)
Chymorvah, Marazion (H)
Chysauster (EH)
Clowance, Crowan (C/TS)
Cotehele (NT)
The Downes, Hayle (NGS)
Enys, Gluvias (NGS)
Eden Project (P)
Glendurgan (NT)
Godolphin House (P)
Headland, Polruan (NGS)
Heligan (P)
Hepworth Sculpture Garden, St Ives (P)
Ince Castle, Saltash (NGS)
Japanese Garden, St Mawgan (P)
Kenegie, Mount's Bay (HV)
Lanhydrock (NT)
Long Cross Victorian Garden (P)

Mount Edgcumbe (LA)
Pencarrow (P)
Pengersick Castle (P)
Penjerrick (P)
Prideaux Place, Padstow (P)
St Michael's Mount (NT)
St Nectan's Glen (P)
Slaughterbridge (P)
Stowe, Kilkhampton (NT)
Tintagel Castle (EH)
Trebah (P)
Tregenna Castle, St Ives (H)
Tregrehan, St Blazey Gate (P)
Tehidy Park, Illogan (LA)
Trelissick (NT)
Trelowarren (P)
Trengwainton (P)
Trerice (NT)
Tresco Abbey (P)
Tresillian (P)
Trevarno Estate Gardens, Crowntown (P)
Trewidden (NT)
Trewithen (P)

Index

Page numbers in bold refer to illustrations and captions